W9-BWN-418

Theology and Society

Gregory Baum

Paulist Press
New York/Mahwah

Copyright © 1987 by Gregory Baum

All rights reserved. No part of this book may be reproduced or transmitted in any form or by any means, electronic or mechanical, including photocopying, recording or by any information storage and retrieval system without permission in writing from the Publisher.

Library of Congress Cataloging-in-Publication Data

Baum, Gregory, 1923–
     Theology and society.

         1. Sociology, Christian (Catholic)   2. Theology.
3. Catholic Church—Doctrines.   I. Title.
BX1753.B365   1987   261   87–25786
ISBN 0-8091-2931-0 (pbk.)

Published by Paulist Press
997 Macarthur Boulevard
Mahwah, New Jersey 07430

Printed and bound in the
United States of America

Contents

Foreword

Over the last decade or so, I have been greatly impressed by the evolution of Catholic social teaching. The official ecclesiastical documents from Latin America, from the Vatican and from the Canadian and American bishops have presented us with a critical social theory, grounded in evangelical values, that transcends traditional Church teaching and stands out as a remarkable witness to radical social change in an age given over to conservative ideologies. Inspired by this new movement in the Church, I have tried to explore, in my research and teaching, the relation of Catholic theology to society and the struggle for social justice. The same perspective has guided the dialogue I have entertained over the years with critical social theory in order to examine and evaluate contemporary culture and its intellectual trends.

Because these issues remain at the center of the debate in Church and society, I am grateful to Paulist Press for publishing this volume. It is a collection of lectures and articles previously published in various reviews, including *The Ecumenist,* of which I am the editor, *Concilium, Cross Currents* and *Theological Studies.* The first article of this collection was published in *Vatican II: Open Questions and New Horizons,* edited by Gerald Fagin.

The volume is divided into three parts. The first part deals with the remarkable evolution of Catholic social teaching, the second with theology and the questions raised by the modern quest for emancipation, and the third with the application of critical social theory to a number of issues in Church and society, including the nature of social science itself.

Some of the articles were written as papers with carefully prepared footnotes, while others were lectures given to various audiences that were later printed without accompanying notes. Since these lectures occasionally contain summaries of material treated at length in other publications of mine, I felt that it was not necessary to add notes in this context.

I am grateful to the readers of *The Ecumenist* who have given me great encouragement over the years to continue my research in the area of critical thought where theology and sociology intersect. I am also grateful to the encouragement I received from the Social Affairs Commission of the Canadian Catholic Conference of Bishops in Ottawa to pursue my study of the radical implications contained in recent Catholic social teaching.

I
The Church's Evolving Social Teaching

1.
Faith and Liberation: Development Since Vatican II

Vatican Council II has been a turning point in the life of the Catholic Church. It is easy to make a long list of the changes initiated by the Council. The Council recognized other Christians as Christians and other Churches as fulfilling a function in the divine plan of salvation; it relativized the self-understanding of the Catholic Church which no longer sees itself as simply identical with the Church of Christ; the Council recognized the presence of the Holy Spirit in the ecumenical movement; it acknowledged an echo of God's Word in the religions of the world and accepted humanity's religious pluralism; it came to a new appreciation of Jewish religion and freed the Church's teaching from the inherited anti-Jewish rhetoric; the Council tried to replace the monarchical by the collegial model for understanding the social organization of the Catholic Church; it recognized the priesthood of all the baptized and affirmed the participation of all Christians in the essential functions of the Church, implicitly raising a question mark behind the monarchical style of contemporary church government; the Council moved the Church from a static to a more dynamic self-understanding; the Council recognized God present in history as Voice and Empowerment touching the entire human family; it endorsed the "new humanism," in which human beings are defined above all by their joint responsibility for history and for one another; the Council affirmed the ideals of modern, pluralistic society and defended people's civil rights, in particular their religious liberty; the Council arrived at a new understanding of the Church's mission, one which takes into account the total range of promised salvation, including people's deliverance from oppression; the Council's emphasis on liturgy promoted a new spirituality beyond individualism, where worship becomes the joint surrender of the people with and in Jesus Christ to God's ever gracious design.

This list could, I think, be extended. The Vatican Council was a marvellous event, a *kairos,* an historical moment of grace and renewal. Yet what I want to examine in this paper is the emergence of a new orientation in the Church since Vatican II, an orientation that builds on the Council but that also significantly transcends it. I shall tentatively call this new orientation "liberationist."

Religious Experience and Biblical Warrant

The new orientation is grounded first of all in new religious experience.[1] Christians living under special historical conditions have experienced the divine Summons in their lives in a new way. One way of describing the new Christian experience is to say that it has joined faith and justice in an indissoluble way. The encounter with God in Jesus Christ makes people recognize that this God is on the side of society's victims. God is revealed as the God of love, but in a society marked by oppression love manifests itself in justice. That faith had a love-dimension has always been recognized. Theologians spoke of *fides charitate formata.* Today the religious experience of many Christians caught in structures of oppression reveals that charity includes justice and that faith, fully formed faith, carries with it a justice dimension, *fides justitia formata.* This new religious experience differs from pietist experience which embodies the soul's encounter with God, the alone with the Alone, and hence excludes other people. The new experience enlarges the self and creates a new consciousness of solidarity, in which the others, especially society's victims, are present. The new religious experience is also different from the encounter with the sacred as the *tremendum et fascinosum,* de-

scribed by Rudolf Otto. For in the new experience the sacred is
the holy One who turns right-side-up the world turned upside-
down by human sin. Faith and justice are here joined in a lived
experience.

In faith people receive the Gospel, accept God's judgement
on a sinful world, acquire a new orientation toward society, and
receive a vision of what social life is meant to be. Faith makes
people critics of the present order. People suffering under grave
oppression and struggling against it find in the Gospel message
confirmation and hope. While the sinful world negates them, Jesus Christ affirms them. People who do not suffer under grave
injustices but are in solidarity with society's victims hear in the
Gospel God's judgement on social sin and God's promise of new,
emancipated life. Conversion to Jesus Christ here means not only
repentence of personal sins: it also means recognition and repudiation of the social sins pertaining to the society with which one
is identified. Conversion resituates people in relation to their society and generates in them social involvement. The encounter
with God in faith communicates direction and empowerment.

Who are the people who have had and who still have this
new religious experience? They are, first, people born into subjugation now struggling for emancipation. They are, secondly,
people who recognize this struggle for freedom and self-determination as the significant "sign of the times" and believe they
cannot grasp the Christian message apart from this. Thus in Pope
John XXIII's *Pacem in terris* (nn 39-43), the significant "sign of
the times" to be understood in the light of the Gospel, are the
freedom struggles of colonized peoples, of disenfranchized workers, and of women caught as they are in structures of subjugation.
In his *Laborem exercens* (n. 1) Pope John Paul II also regards as
an historical turning point the emergence on the political scene
of groups, classes and peoples, formerly excluded from self-determination, who now struggle to free themselves. The Pope considers their struggles as the dynamic element of modern society.
His encyclical promotes the solidarity *of* the workers (and the
poor) in a joint struggle as well as the solidarity *with* workers
(and the poor) on the part of those who love justice (n. 8). According to the encyclical, the Church itself, in fidelity to Jesus

Christ, must be in solidarity with the oppressed struggling for justice. The Christians involved in emancipatory movements, then, are the ones who have had the new religious experience.

New religious experiences have a future in the church only if they stand up under the test of the Scriptures. Catholics tend to be reticent in regard to their own spiritual experiences. They realize how easy it is to be fooled by emotions. The Christians committed to emancipation found that their religious experience was confirmed by the Scriptures. God revealed Godself as on their side, in solidarity with them, giving them strength and direction. They did not look in the Bible for a few proof texts. They regarded the Scriptures as a spiritual criterion, a test that sorts out the human heart, a divine norm available not only to biblical scholars but more especially to the ordinary faithful.[2] The themes of the Bible that became very important to them were the Exodus as paradigm of salvation, classical Hebrew prophecy, Israel's poetry of the good life, the messianic promises made in the Old Testament, the disturbing memory of Jesus as troublemaker and critic, friend of the outcasts of society, and preacher of the approaching kingdom, the logic of his persecution and crucifixion, the proleptic vindication of the faithful in Christ's resurrection, the eschatological promises, the apocalyptical images, and the persecution of the apostolic church by the Roman empire. These Christians speak of the dangerous memory of Jesus Christ.[3]

In much of Christian preaching and teaching, including the theological tradition, the Bible has been tamed. The subversive memories are left in the margin; and the passages that occupy the centre of attention are those that stabilize the present, integrate society, and summon people individually to greater love and holiness. Christians committed to an emancipatory struggle read the Scriptures from the viewpoint of the people at the bottom. They hear in the Bible a message that remains hidden from Christians identified with the successful classes, nations or races. In one of their pastoral letters, the Canadian bishops ask the faithful to reread the Scriptures to hear in it the divine summons to social justice.[4] Many familiar passages take on a new meaning once we read them from the new perspective. I read the Magnificat for many years; but it was only after my encounter with liberation theology that I heard its radical message: "God has put down the mighty from their thrones and exalted those of low degree; he has filled the hungry with good things and the rich he has sent away empty." The approaching kingdom rectifies society's sins.

The Christians touched by the new religious experience and confirmed by the reading of Scripture were in need of dialogue with theology. They looked for a critical clarification of their concepts. In fact, there were theologians committed to emancipation who shared the new religious experience of faith-and-justice. They tried to clarify the meaning of the Gospel in the light of this new experience. They produced a critique of traditional theology and developed a new approach to theological reflection. Latin American liberation theology has become famous. Yet similar and parallel theological efforts have been made in other parts of the world, including the United States. What characterizes these liberationist theologies, and distinguishes them from traditional theologies, is their theory of knowledge. According to liberationist theology, action precedes the entry into truth, practice precedes theory,—or, more concretely, solidarity with the poor is the presupposition for the authentic grasp of the Gospel.[5]

Traditional theologies tended to be mainly concerned with people's personal lives. Sin meant personal transgression, conversion meant personal repentance, and grace referred to the transformation of persons. Liberationist theologies, on the other hand, reading the biblical message from the viewpoint of society's victims, recovered the *social* dimension of sin, conversion and grace.[6] Sin includes the structures of oppression, conversion includes the raising of consciousness in regard to these oppressive conditions, and divine grace includes the Spirit-guided and Spirit-empowered struggle for a more just social order. Liberation be it economic, political or social, is then not simply a secular process: it is like all transitions from sin to justice 'supernatural.' Liberation is a movement produced by struggling people, sparked and sustained by divine grace. Liberation does not exhaust the meaning of salvation; at the same time salvation cannot be defined without reference to people's liberation from oppression.

It is not my intention in this article to examine the extensive theological literature produced by this new orientation. What I

Back banter /

wish to present instead is the extraordinary impact which this new orientation has had on the Catholic Church's official teaching. The new religious experience of faith-and-justice tested by Scripture, has led to a new life style in the Church and produced new theological reflections. At first church authorities were cautious: some episcopal voices even disapproved of the new orientation. Warnings were uttered against the politicization of the Christian faith. Yet there was also acceptance and approval. I wish to show that the impact of the new orientation on the Magisterium has been considerable. The new orientation *in* the Church is at a point of becoming a new orientation *of* the Church.

The Medellin Conference

Let me begin with the Latin American Bishops Conference held at Medellin, Colombia, in 1968, which was influenced, in part at least, by the new social justice orientation. In the Medellin Conclusions we find side by side, largely unreconciled, two distinct orientations to the problems of Latin America, one defined by the teaching of Vatican II, the other by Latin American liberation theology. It is useful for our purposes to analyse the difference between the two. Since the word 'liberation' has assumed such importance in Latin America, since it is biblically rooted and in keeping with Christian aspirations, the Latin American bishops have decided to adopt the word. They gladly speak of the liberation which Jesus brings. Christ is liberator. His truth shall make us free and introduce us to life in abundance. Yet the Medellin Conclusions contain two distinct meanings of the word 'liberation.' One of these I wish to call 'soft': it corresponds to a liberal, reformist understanding of social change and agrees with the perspective of Vatican II. The other could be called 'hard': it names the concrete conditions of oppression and implies a certain rupture or discontinuity with the prevailing order.

The soft meaning of liberation, found especially in the chapter, "On Justice,"[7] refers to the transformation produced by divine grace in the lives of people: people expand in love, they are led into greater holiness, they are united more closely to God, they are more ready to make sacrifices, and as a result of these changes, they will build a more just society. Faith, hope and love issue forth into social justice. We are told that "authentic liberation" is "a profound conversion" to the way of God's reign. "The origin of the disdain of all mankind, of all injustices, should be sought in the internal imbalance of human liberty, which will always need to be rectified in history." We are told that "in the economy of salvation the divine work is an action of integral human development and liberation, which has love for its sole motive." Later we read that "we have faith that our love for Christ and our brethren will not only be the great force liberating us from injustice and oppression, but also the inspiration for social justice, understood as a whole life and as an impulse toward the integral growth of our countries." This is a reformist perspective in keeping with Vatican II. This understanding of liberation does not name the plague from which people suffer; it does not offend anyone because it does not specify the cause of injustice; it presupposes that the societies in question are capable of evolving toward greater justice.

This 'soft' notion of liberation would not have given much consolation to the people of Israel under the rule of Pharaoh. The Israelites did not think that Egypt could be reformed; they wanted to be freed from the system of tyranny. Nor would this notion of liberation have given much consolation to the people of Israel during the Babylonian exile: the Israelites yearned for a radical change at the top so that they might be allowed to return to Jerusalem.

In the chapter, "On Peace," of the same Medellin Conclusions[8] we find the 'hard' notion of liberation. Here we are told that injustices have created "a sinful situation" in Latin America. We move beyond the consideration of personal sins. There is structural sin, and unless we analyse and name it, we cannot see clearly, be converted to God, and wrestle against evil. The chapter mentions the twofold colonialism that oppresses the peoples of Latin America, first "the external colonialism" caused by the location of Latin America in the margin of the world capitalist system, and secondly "the internal colonialism" created by the extreme inequality between social classes, especially in countries marked by "a bi-classism," i.e. a small group of rich facing the marginalization of groups and peoples. According to the text, the internal colonialism in Latin America is derived from external colonialism: the class division is created by the dependency on outside powers, generated by the economic system and upheld by cultural and political forces. The text denounces imperialism as the enemy of human life in Latin America.

This 'hard' notion of liberation, drawn from Christians engaged in the struggle for liberation, analyses the concrete conditions of oppression, names the systemic cause of human misery, and signifies a certain rupture with the present order. The 'hard' notion of liberation inevitably offends some people, especially among the rich and powerful, and creates enemies for the Church. The 'soft' notion of liberation supposes that oppression in society is produced by sin, which in one way or another we all share, and hence must be overcome by the conversion of people from sin to grace, while the 'hard' notion of liberation considers reflections on sin in general or the sin in the hearts of people as an inappropriate analysis. It is necessary to focus on social sin, in the Latin American case on imperialism, colonialism and the structures of marginalization. These shall not be overcome by the entry of individuals into greater holiness, but if at all, only as the oppressed in solidarity wrestling together to overcome the evil system.

The difference between the two notions of liberation is considerable. Both have validity: which of the two is more relevant depends in part on the ethico-political judgement whether gradual reform is appropriate or whether people should struggle for more radical social change. The two notions also differ in the place they assign political commitment in people's lives. The soft notion of liberation presents the human person as growing in virtue and grace until at a certain point concern for society as a whole emerges: then political commitment is added to the wider quest for holiness. The hard notion of liberation presents human persons as caught in repressive structures beyond their personal choice, structures that affect every aspect of their being; thus personal growth becomes available to them only as they, in solidarity, struggle for emancipation. Here the political commitment is a basic dimension of the new being Christ offers them: it liberates all the other aspects of their personal lives.

Both notions of liberation have their validity; but they cannot both be applied simultaneously to people in the same situation. A choice is necessary. Often the people at the top come to different judgements than the people at the bottom. The ethico-political decision involved in this choice is in part derived from social scientific reasoning. Sociological analysis is indeed necessary to understand the structural inferiorization of groups and peoples. But the ethico-political decision does not depend on purely scientific insights. Social analysts using different sociological conceptual tools come to different sociological conclusions: hence the choice among different sociological approaches is crucial, and this choice is not a purely scientific one, but includes an ethico-political element.

The Canadian government, relying on the wisdom of their scientific advisers, has asked the Native Peoples to be patient, trust the government agency, and await the gradual transformation of their condition. If the Canadian government had hired theologians they would have proposed the soft notion of liberation to the Native Peoples. Politics is not everything, they would have said. Strive for personal growth and holiness; and then the time will come when you will even escape your present painful predicament. Yet the Native Peoples of Canada have lost their trust in the government; they have been deceived too many times. Since the structural marginalization inflicted on them affects every aspect of their lives, including the very formation of their consciousness from childhood on, their leaders have now opted for a more radical policy. They have made land claims which disrupt the legal system and the social peace of Canada. They struggle for radical social change. The Canadian Churches have decided to stand with the Native Peoples and support their claims. The theologians associated with the Churches present an interpretation of the Gospel based on the hard notion of liberation.[9]

The Latin American bishops gathered at Medellin in 1968, and at Puebla in 1979, were not united in their judgement about which of the two notions of liberation would be more appropriate for the populations of their continent. That is why they inserted both notions in an unreconciled manner. Only subsequent history will decide which of these two notions will define the thrust of the Catholic Church on that continent. At the moment the Church is still divided.

Looking Back at Vatican II

Before continuing our examination of ecclesiastical documents, let us cast a glance at the teaching of Vatican II. The Council did not use the word "liberation." Still, the conciliar document, *Gaudium et spes,* significantly modified the Church's traditional stance toward society. *Gaudium et spes* affirmed modern society, albeit in a critical way. It affirmed the modern, industrial, technical, developmental society as the instrument through which justice could come to all people. "For the first time in human history, all people are convinced that the benefits of culture ought to be extended and actually can be extended to every one" (n. 9). Without weakening the primacy of the spiritual, *Gaudium et spes* affirmed the growth orientation of modern society, its global outreach, its quest for ever further development, even in remote areas which are as yet undeveloped. Vatican II asked Christians to engage themselves in social action. It criticized a purely individualistic ethics (n. 9). The holiness demanded at the present time includes concern for social justice and active participation in society. The Council recognized the emergence of "a new humanism" where human beings were defined primarily by their joint responsibility for history (n. 55). *Gaudium et spes* admitted that modern society was threatened by sin in many ways. It was tempted in particular to make its goods and achievements available only to a limited group of people and exclude others, especially the poor from the wealth produced (n. 29, 66). Here Christians, joined by others who love justice, should engage in the political arena and promote greater social justice. *Gaudium et spes* summons Catholics to universal solidarity. At the Council, the entire Church declared itself in solidarity with the human family. This shift was new and exciting.

Vatican II presented an optimistic view of modern society.

It looked upon the modern world through the eyes of the reform-minded Christians of the developed, capitalist countries of the West. Influential in shaping the new teaching and progressive outlook of the Council were bishops and theologians from the successful European countries, Holland, Belgium, France, Germany, and Switzerland, supported on the whole by the bishops of the United States and Canada. These bishops and theologians, open, critical and reform-minded as they were, participated in the cultural optimism of the early Sixties. This optimism was grounded in the extraordinary economic progress that had been made in the West since World War II and supported by the expectation, confirmed by then current scientific theories, that this economic development could be exported to the less developed countries, the poor nations, until they would produce their own wealth. *Gaudium et spes* conveyed the impression that despite the selfishness of people, especially among the rich and powerful, there now existed networks of industrial, economic and political institutions that promised to lift the world beyond poverty and protect the freedom of persons.

The first draft of *Gaudium et spes* submitted to the Council said very little of human sin. In the conciliar debate many bishops demanded that the Church's teaching on sin and the devil be introduced into the document. This was done. A special paragraph on sin was added (n. 13), which acknowledged the dividedness of the human heart, the human inclination to do evil, the abuse of freedom and the surrender of people to the lure of the Evil One. We find here not a single word about social sin! There is no reference to the structures of oppression in which people find themselves, which must be analysed, named, fought and eventually overcome. Vatican II affirmed the best of liberal society. Men of conscience should be able to steer the present, liberal, capitalist society away from exploitation and oppression so that it may become an instrument of justice and peace in the universe. While the word 'liberation' was not used, Vatican II actually endorses the idea of what we have called soft liberation.

In this context I recall a conversation I had during the Council with Paolo Ricca, an Italian Protestant, a Waldensian to be precise, who was a graduate student of New Testament, then act-

ing as a journalist at the Council. (In the meantime he has become
professor of historical theology at the Waldensian theological
faculty in Rome.) We had become good friends. As I expressed
my excitement with the conciliar draft of *Gaudium et spes,* he
replied that for him the document was too much an endorsement
of liberalism and liberal values. At the time, not being conversant
with political science, I did not understand what he meant. I readily admitted that the Council promoted liberal values, especially
the growth, unfolding, and self-determination of human persons
under the impact of divine grace. This was to me a progressive
step over against the former, more collectivist and authoritarian
Catholicism, in which individuals were easily subordinated to the
common good and the authorities that claimed to protect it.
What I failed to see at the time, because my education had not
acquainted me with the appropriate classical texts, was that this
liberal notion of the self-development of persons corresponded
to the aspirations of the Western middle classes, but did not shed
light on the emancipatory struggles of people, including the
working class, who were structurally oppressed.

Turning Point 1971

The new liberationist perspective, partially acknowledged at
Medellin, was recognized in the declaration of the 1971 Synod
of Bishops, entitled *Justice in the World.* Over the years the influence of third world Christian communities on the administra-
tive centres of the Christian Churches had been growing. This
was true for the World Council of Churches, for the various
world-wide denominational fellowships, and for the Vatican, the
centre of the Roman Catholic Church. The Roman Catholic
Church, more than any other, is still firmly planted among the
poor and dispossessed of the third world and among the working
classes in many first and second world countries. In 1971, which
I regard as a turning point, two Roman documents, *Justice in the
World,* composed by the third Synod of Bishops, and *Octogesima adveniens,* written by Pope Paul VI, adopted the new liberationist perspective.

In the introduction to *Justice in the World,* the Synod recognizes that there is being "built up around the world a network of domination, oppression and abuses, which stifle freedom and which keep the greater part of humanity from sharing in the building up and enjoyment of a more just world" (n. 3). The Synod acknowledges that over against this system of domination has emerged among people "a new awareness that shakes them out of fatalistic resignation and spurs them on to liberate themselves and be responsible for their own destiny" (n. 4). Where does the Church stand in regard to this social conflict? "Listening to the cry of those who suffer violence and are oppressed by unjust systems and structures, and hearing the appeal of a world that by its perversity contradicts the plan of the Creator," the Synod affirms "the Church's vocation to be present in the world to proclaim the Good News to the poor, freedom to the oppressed, and joy to the afflicted" (n. 5).

The system of domination of which the Synod speaks is undoubtedly imperialism and colonialism in its various forms, capitalist or communist, which inflicts oppression on sectors of populations. Over against these, the Synod sees liberation movements aiming at self-determination and self-reliant development. In this situation, if I understand the above text correctly, the Church takes the side of the poor and announces to them the Good News of their liberation. This is 'hard' liberation: for the synodal text analyses the conditions of oppression, names the system of domination, takes sides in the conflict, and implies a discontinuity with the present order.

In the next paragraph the synodal document declares that the redemption Jesus Christ has brought includes "the liberation of people from every oppressive condition." Action on behalf of justice, we are told, is therefore "a constitutive dimension of the Church's proclamation of the Gospel" (n. 6). The paragraph acknowledges the new religious experience of faith-and-justice and the liberationist perspective that has emerged from it. The grace which Jesus Christ offers the world includes the empowerment that renders people capable of struggling for their emancipation. For this reason the proclamation of the Gospel is not confined to words; it includes as "an integral part" witness and action on behalf of justice. The synodal teaching represents a significant development of doctrine.

This new teaching is not yet found in *Gaudium et spes*. The conciliar document recorded a doctrinal development that was the stepping stone for the new, more radical position. *Gaudium et spes* clearly affirmed that the grace of Christ was operative in the whole human family, that wherever people were, in whatever religion or even without religion, they lived a conflictual existence defined by the pull of evil on the one hand and the divine summons toward a new, more human life on the other. "Since Christ died for all men, and since the ultimate vocation of man is in fact one and divine, we ought to believe that the Holy Spirit in a manner known only to God offers every man the possibility of being associated with the Paschal Mystery" (n. 22). What was not said in the conciliar document was that this divine grace, this association with the Paschal Mystery, was concretely offered to people in their struggle for justice and peace. This is affirmed for the first time in *Justice in the World:* the redemption which Christ has brought includes the liberation of people from their oppression.

In the same year 1971, Pope Paul VI sent the letter, *Octogesima adveniens,* to Cardinal Roy, Archbishop of Quebec, President of the Commission on Justice and Peace. The letter represented a considerable shift to the left on the part of the Church's official teaching. I wish to mention three points made in the letter, the acknowledgement of socialism as an option for Catholics, a new, more nuanced approach to the phenomenon of Marxism, and the appreciation of the critical function of "utopia," an idea derived from the revisionist Marxist philosopher, Ernst Bloch.

In previous papal teaching socialism had been condemned without qualification. In *Quadragesimo anno,* published in 1931 during the great depression, this condemnation extended to the revolutionary socialism of the Communist Party as well as to the democratic socialism of the European social democratic parties. Socialism was simply out of bounds for Catholics. There were hints in the encyclicals of John XXIII and the social teaching of

Vatican II that these condemnations were dated and had lost their meaning in the present. But *Octogesima adveniens* was the first papal document that faced the new situation squarely. The letter acknowledges that many Catholics have in fact become socialists: they have done this, we are told, not merely on the basis of pragmatic considerations but as a political step inspired by their Christian faith (cf. n. 31). They see in the turn to socialism the forward movement of history. In this context, Paul VI writes, it is important to distinguish between various kinds of socialism (cf. n. 31). Some socialisms are irreconcilable with Christian faith, for they are wedded to a total philosophy or world view that excludes Jesus Christ. But socialisms that remain ideologically pluralistic are acceptable. With this letter, Paul VI opened the door for Christians in third world countries to join the building up of their own African and Asian socialism. Socialism was no longer taboo.

While papal teaching in the past rejected Marxism as a single, monolythic phenomenon, *Octogesima adveniens* takes a more nuanced approach (cf. nn. 32-42). It distinguishes between Marxism as a philosophy of history, as a political movement, and as a form of social analysis. As a conceptual system of world interpretation, as we have seen, Marxism must be rejected: as political movement Marxism is identified with dictatorship and domination and hence must be rejected by Christians. The papal letter here refers to Leninism, the official Marxism of the Soviet bloc; it does not deal with the democratic origins of organized Marxism prior to World War One, nor with the return to this origin in the emerging Euro-Communism and other revisionist Marxist movements. As a form of social analysis, the letter tells us, Marxism has its usefulness. Many Christians, we learn, regard a Marxist analysis of society as a scientific method helpful for understanding the revolutionary potential of society. While Paul VI does not dispute this, he tells Christians that this method must be applied with the greatest care. Since there is a certain inner unity between these various aspects of Marxism, an uncritical confidence in Marxist social analysis easily leads Christians to where they do not want to go.

This more nuanced approach to Marxism is new in the

Church's official teaching. After 1971 several national hierarchies have published pastoral letters dealing with Marxism in which they follow the approach of *Octogesima adveniens*. In a pastoral statement on Marxism, the French bishops added a fourth dimension to the three mentioned by Paul VI: they spoke of "cultural Marxism."[10] By this they refer to the impact of Marxism on philosophy, social science, literary criticism and the cultural self-understanding of people who on the whole do not regard themselves as Marxists at all. Cultural Marxism is a widespread phenomenon in France. Dialogue with Marxism, the bishops tell us, has affected Catholic theology itself. They offer an example of this influence. They claim Marx's discovery that labor, i.e. the organization of production, has a great impact on the formation of consciousness and has been taken seriously by modern philosophy and theology. Human consciousness is no longer regarded as floating above the material conditions of life; consciousness always remains, however free and creative it may be, grounded in particular socio-economic conditions and hence reflects people's concrete historical circumstances. If we are to believe the French bishops, this insight has also affected Catholic theology.

Finally, *Octogesima adveniens* borrows from Ernst Bloch the radical notion of "utopia" and recognizes its usefulness for the presentation of Christian social teaching (n. 37). Paul VI realized of course that for most people the word "utopia" referred to an impossible dream that inhibits action. "The appeal to utopia is often a convenient excuse for those who wish to escape concrete tasks in order to take refuge in an imaginary world. To live in a hypothetical future is a facile alibi for rejecting immediate responsibilities." But "utopia" may have a different meaning altogether. Paul VI here introduced Ernst Bloch's notion: utopia is the vision of an alternative world which generates "the kind of criticism of existing societies that provoke the forward-looking imagination both to perceive in the present the disregarded possibilities hidden within it, and to direct itself toward a fresh future." We read that "utopia sustains the social dynamics by the confidence it gives to the inventive powers of the human mind and heart." If utopia refuses no overture, Pope Paul

VI continued, then it can also meet the Christian appeal. Utopia breaks down horizons, it leads beyond the present system and every ideology. Utopia, according to Paul VI, fits well into the Christian understanding of the world's future. While not every dream of an alternative society exercises a utopian function, there are impossible dreams that are extremely practical: utopias initiate a realistic, scientifically verifiable critique of the existing order, they uncover the as yet hidden potentialities of the present and of past tradition, and they generate ever new imaginative patterns of reconstructing life in accordance with greater justice.

By integrating the Blochian notion of utopia into the Church's teaching, Pope Paul VI has made room for radicalism in Catholic social thought. While it is necessary to entertain reformist plans for the society to which we belong, i.e. the U.S.A. or Canada, it is equally important and possibly even more urgent to entertain the vision of an alternative society and to think, speak and act out a commitment to an America that shares its wealth and is organized in a participatory manner.

The Canadian Catholic Bishops

The shift to the left that has taken place in the Roman documents in 1971 has profoundly affected the social teaching of the national hierarchies in many parts of the world. This can be verified by the evolution of the social teaching offered by the American bishops. It is not my intention to do this in this paper. Instead I wish to document very briefly the shift to the left in the social teaching of the Canadian bishops. After 1971, the Canadian bishops joined with the other Christian Churches in the promotion of social ministry in Canada. Several inter-church committees were founded whose task it was to examine various sectors of social life from a social justice point of view, including Canada's relation to the third world. The reports written by these inter-church committees were received by the Churches and strongly influenced the stance which the Churches adopted vis-à-vis the Canadian government and the social problems of Canadian society. The Canadian bishops made use of the material supplied by the inter-church committees to prepare their Labor

Day Statements and pastoral letters on social justice addressed to
Canadian Catholics. While a detailed analysis of the bishops'
teaching would be worthwhile, especially on such issues as world
hunger, unemployment, regional disparity, Quebec's right to
self-determination, and the rights of the Native Peoples in the
North, I shall confine myself to a commentary on a single document, the bishops' Labour Day Statement of 1976, *From Words
to Action*.[11]

From Words to Action suggests that the present economic
system no longer serves the best interests of the majority of people. Why? Because capitalism widens the distance between the
rich and the poor, especially between the rich and poor countries,
and secondly because capitalism allows the control of resources
and production to pass into the hands of an ever shrinking elite.
The bishops ask for "a new economic order." The terminology,
we note, is taken from debate at the United Nations. Why is the
Church concerned about these issues? Christian faith in our own
day, we are told, has come to include commitment to social justice.

How can the Christian community be faithful to this commitment? *From Words to Action* outlines several practical steps
that Christians should take. The first one is of a religious nature.
The Canadian bishops ask Catholics to reread the Scriptures to
hear in them God's call to social justice. Sacred texts with which
we are familiar may well reveal new meaning and power when
we read them from a new perspective. Today the Church has
learnt to discern in the Bible God's partiality for the poor and
oppressed. Secondly, the bishops ask Catholics to listen to the
voice of society's victims. The marginalized are able to tell us
something important about our society which we could not discover if we only talked to our friends. If we confine our conversation to the middle classes, to people who belong to the cultural
mainstream, we shall not arrive at a critical and truthful self-understanding. The cultural mainstream tends to disguise from people social sin and exploitation operative in society. The Native
Peoples, the poor, the unemployed, women and the underdeveloped regions, the non-white groups—they all have a message revealing the truth about Canadian society. (In this context I want

to mention that in 1967 the Canadian bishops said that French Canadians were a people and argued that no peace would come to Canada until their peoplehood was recognized and institutionally protected.)

As a third step, *From Words to Action* asks Catholics to analyse the historical causes of oppression in society. In one way or another, the various forms of marginalization are linked to the present economic system that excludes certain sectors of the population from the wealth of society. (In another Labour Day Statement, that of 1977, the bishops claim that to understand the causes of injustice in society "a Marxist analysis," if utilized in nuanced fashion, can be very useful.) Finally, *From Words to Action* urges Catholics to become politically active to help overcome the causes of oppression in society.

At the same time, the bishops recognize that only a minority of Catholics follow this new way of the Gospel, a minority called "significant" because it summons the whole Church to greater fidelity. The bishops admit that this minority is often criticized within the Catholic community, especially "by the more powerful and affluent sector." This remark suggests that class conflict produces tensions even within the Church. The bishops regard it as their duty to defend and encourage this minority in the Church. The perspective of *From Words to Action*, supported by several other Canadian episcopal statements, is an instance of the liberationist perspective described in this paper. Here we have a minority emerging in the Church, a minority deeply marked by new religious experience, Christians for whom faith and justice are inextricably intertwined, who read scripture and ecclesiastical doctrine in a new light, who discover in them the transformative power of Jesus Christ, and who for this reason find themselves in solidarity with the poor and marginalized, see their own society from a new perspective, entertain the vision of an alternative social order and commit themselves to social reconstruction.

Pope John Paul II

This new orientation has been fully endorsed by the teaching of Pope John Paul II. Because of the Pope's conservative approach to a number of strictly ecclesiastical issues, the mass media have tried to convince us that he is a conservative, protecting the status quo and assigning a low priority to justice issues. The facts are different. In his social teaching, Pope John Paul II not only affirms the turn to the left of the Church's official teaching but carries it further to a significant degree. In this paper we shall cast a brief glance at two of his encyclicals, *Redemptor hominis* (1979), and *Laborem exercens* (1981).

In his first encyclical, *Redemptor hominis* Pope John Paul II introduced three ideas that confirm and promote the new radical orientation. The first has to do with the Church's mission. We are told that Jesus Christ in his redemptive incarnation has united himself in some way to every human being and that therefore the dignity of people is grounded in Christ's presence to them (nn. 8, 13). What follows from this is that the Church's protection and promotion of human rights is a service rendered to Jesus Christ (nn. 10, 11). The Church's social ministry has a christological foundation. In the past it was customary to distinguish between the "supernatural" or evangelical mission to preach the Gospel so that the world may believe and the "natural" or secular mission, secondary and subordinate to the first, to promote human justice on earth. Today the papal encyclical affirms, on the basis of recent doctrinal development, that the Church has a single mission, grounded in Jesus Christ, which includes at one and the same time the proclamation of the Gospel and the engagement on behalf of social justice. The two belong together. They have become as inextricably intertwined as faith-and-justice. The redemption promised by Jesus Christ includes the emancipation of the oppressed; and the proclamation of the Good News must be accompanied by action for social justice.

While Vatican II put considerable stress on the Church's social ministry, on the service the Church is called upon to render to the world, the conciliar texts still allowed a conservative reading which distinguished between the primary mission to preach the Gospel and a secondary mission, subordinate to the first, to serve the world. *Redemptor hominis* no longer allows this dualistic reading. The Church's mission is one and indivisible: proclamation and witness to justice.

Pope John Paul II has repeatedly demanded that priests not assume leadership positions in political organizations. Again, the mass media have interpreted this as if he wanted priests to be silent on political issues and restrict their preaching to strictly religious matters. This is a grave misinterpretation. For Pope John Paul II, the preaching of the Gospel includes demands for justice and witness to solidarity. He himself has acted accordingly, not only in regard to Poland but also in supporting national hierarchies, such as the Brazilian bishops, in their emphasis on the inseparable unity of faith and justice. While priests should not normally assume high office in political organizations, they are to be mediators of Christian faith and social teaching with its inevitably political thrust.

Secondly, *Redemptor hominis* developed the concept of "concrete man" (n. 13). There is no "man in general" neither is there a humanity in the abstract sense. There are only people existing in concrete historical conditions without which their suffering, their struggles, their aims and purposes cannot be defined. It is impossible to understand humans abstracted from these conditions. Man is always concrete. For this reason, the encyclical argues, God's gift of the Spirit offers people not grace in general nor new life as such, but new life in the precise conditions defined by their historical reality. Divine grace is therefore also concrete. When the encyclical proclaims the primacy of the spiritual in people's struggle for a truly human existence, including social justice, it does not designate the spiritual life as the first step to be followed by a second, namely active engagement; what the encyclical affirms is, rather, that the spiritual life is the interior dimension of people's efforts to live humanly in the world. Spirit is always concrete. Spirit is always incarnate, always empowerment to act in the world, always oriented toward the humanization of life. The encyclical's stress on the primacy of the spiritual is the repudiation of the reductionist understanding of a world-building process that leaves out the Spirit and interiority, whether this be in Western, technologically-defined capitalist projects of world development or in Eastern European, technologically-defined communist projects of constructing a new society. Unless the primacy of the spiritual be protected, world-building endeavors will only lead to human alienation. Concrete spirit defines the true nature of praxis. The Pope engages here in dialogue with liberation theology.

Redemptor hominis introduced into the Church's official teaching another idea, closely related to the new perspective. We are told that today more than ever "man is under threat from what he produces, that is to say from the result of the work of his hands, and even more so, of the work of his intellect and will. All too soon, and often in an unforeseen way, what this manifold activity of man yields is not only subject to alienation, in the sense that it is simply taken away from the person who produces it, but rather that it turned against man himself" (n. 15). We have here a reference to the classical Marxist analysis of the historical dialectics. The product of human labor stands over against the producer, not only, as Marx and John Paul II argue, because workers no longer own the work of their hands, but more deeply because the product acts according to a logic of its own, no longer in accordance with the intentions of the producer. The human task, therefore, is to reappropriate the product of human labor, i.e., to reassimilate and become subject to the industries and technologies they have produced. Marx argued that capitalism prevents people from reappropriating the works of their hands; Pope John Paul adds to this that the same is true of communism. Yet the Pope acknowledges that it is indeed the human task and vocation to become the subject of human history.

The most radical expression of what I have called the new orientation is Pope John Paul II's encyclical *Laborem exercens*. This is not the place for offering an analysis of the papal document. I have done this elsewhere.[12] In the following pages I shall simply single out four points, made in the encyclical, which reveal the radical orientation of Pope John Paul II's social teaching.

According to the encyclical, the source of oppression and injustice in the world and the threat to the peaceful coexistence of nations is the unresolved conflict between capital and labor. Because humans constitute themselves by laboring, the domination built into the economic system is the principal cause of human degradation (n. 3). The rightful order, the encyclical argues, is the priority of labor over capital (n. 7). The arguments with which John Paul II demonstrates this fundamental principle are drawn from rational analysis and historical experience (n. 12). Presently the priority of labor is violated in the capitalist countries of the West where capital is for the most part in the hands of giant corporations, and it is violated in communist countries of Eastern Europe where the state-owned industries are managed by a bureaucracy that seeks to enhance the political power of the communist state. The priority of labor over capital means, according to the encyclical, that capital must be made to serve labor, that is serve first the workers employed in the particular industry, serve secondly the improvement of the industrial machinery and finally serve the entire laboring society. Justice in today's society is defined by labor's priority over capital.

How can this justice come about? According to the encyclical, the agent of social change in our societies is the workers' struggle for justice (n. 8). This struggle, based on the solidarity of workers, must be supported by the solidarity of all who love justice, including the Church itself. The workers' struggle for justice is the dynamic element of contemporary society. This struggle, we note, is not in the first place against the ruling class, the ruling class is not the enemy—the Pope distinguishes his ideas from Marxism—; the struggle of the workers is for justice, for the priority of labor over capital, and only when those in power are unwilling to recognize the norms of justice does the struggle turn against them. We have here a Catholic version of "class conflict."

What would a just society, in which the priority of labor is observed, look like? The nationalization of the industries, however necessary at times, in and by itself does not guarantee the priority of labor. What is important about capital is not ownership but use. To assure the priority of labor, what will be necessary in the first place is the co-ownership of the industries by the workers who labor in them (n. 14). Eventually workers themselves must become co-responsible for industrial policy. Secondly, what is required is a planned economy to meet the material and employment needs of the entire population (n. 17). This planning should be done by an agency, not part of the government, made up by representatives of the classes, regions and industries of the country, in conjunction with government. Pope John Paul's socialism is characterized by a principle of de-centralization, the workers' ownership of the industries, and a principle of centralization, the planned economy: the tension between these two principles is seen as protecting personal freedom and pluralism.

Finally, in a brief paragraph, Pope John Paul II extends his radical theory to the third world. He argues that even in the underdeveloped countries where the masses are excluded from production and hence are workers only potentially, the dynamic element of society is the struggle of the poor for social justice. The Church must therefore preach the solidarity *of* the poor and *with* the poor (n. 8). The encyclical endorses and extends what the Latin American bishops mean by the Church's "preferential option for the poor." Pope John Paul II gives the phrase a more obviously political meaning. The Church itself, we are told, because of its fidelity to Jesus Christ, must be in solidarity with the poor struggling to remake society.

This concludes our survey of recent ecclesiastical documents. We conclude that there exists in the Church a new movement or orientation, sparked by the new religious experience of faith-and-justice, tested by Scripture, explored and guided by an appropriate liberation theology, and approved by a doctrinal development within the ecclesiastical Magisterium. While this new orientation was encouraged by the social teaching of Vatican II, it also significantly transcends it. It is even possible to contrast the liberal perspective of Vatican II with the more radical or liberationist perspective of the new movement.

The Future of the Faith-and-Justice Movement

The openness of Vatican II to the modern world raised the question in the minds of some Christians whether the biblical faith was not in danger of being assimilated to contemporary culture.

These Christians felt that Vatican II did not define sufficiently the distance between Gospel and world. The new, more radical orientation in the Church puts greater emphasis on the gap that separates Christianity from the cultural mainstream. The new religious experience of faith-and-justice makes Christians be at odds with society. Here Christians regain a strong sense of what the Bible calls "the sinful world." They attain to a greater awareness of their own Christian identity over against the self-definition of modern society. All they have to do is to pick up a newspaper to know that they are Christians. They find themselves swimming against the stream, critical of "the wisdom of the flesh" taught at schools and universities, critical of the culture of injustice produced by contemporary society, at odds with the dominant ideology designed to legitimate an unjust and oppressive world.

What is the future of the liberationist orientation in the Church? What do these faith-and-justice Christians do? How do they involve themselves in society? This paper is not the place to examine this important question in detail. Allow me to make two brief remarks, both of which deserve longer and more systematic treatment.

The first remark is that the ethico-political thrust of the Gospel has two distinct though interrelated dimensions, the cultural and the political. If the cultural dimension is neglected, people become activists. Since activism does not question the dominant presuppositions, it tends to remain on the surface. The ethico-political thrust of the Gospel affects first of all people's consciousness and their cultural self-understanding. Since the present unjust society is legitimated by cultural symbols and cultural values (often even in the name of Christianity) and held in place by the taken-for-granted common sense mediated by the cultural mainstream, the new social justice Christians engage first of all in a cultural mission, which is then joined to involvement in political action. The struggle for justice has a cultural, intellectual, spiritual dimension. While Christians want to be active in political issues in their countries, not least among them opposition to the contemporary nuclear madness, they may also regard the raising of consciousness, the intellectual, educational, and spiritual apostolate, as their primary concern. Supported by the Church's social teaching, they will help people to decode the message of society, to resist the lies that pass for common sense in a sinful world, and to look upon their own country from the alternative vision of society, more in keeping with the divine promises.

The second remark I wish to make has to do with the minority character of the new movement in the North American Church. The Canadian bishops, we recall, reminded us that these Christians constitute only "a minority," albeit "a significant minority." Since Canada and the United States are on the whole closely identified with an economic system in which the important decisions are made in terms of maximizing profit and power, it is not likely that the majority of North Americans, be they Christian or not, will assume a critical social-justice stance. The neo-conservative spirit which is presently penetrating into many levels of society, including the ecclesiastical, is generated by the true insight that commitment to social justice will demand a high price from North Americans. Many people who know what should be done in North America to create conditions of greater justice in the world, believe that the price will be too high. It would be a strategic mistake, therefore, to engage in an effort to transform entire institutions, i.e., to change the parish, the diocese, the Catholic college, the theological faculty, or the teachers' association. To engage in such endeavors at this time would only produce failure, bitterness and despair. We would become depressed and endlessly lament over pastors, bishops, presidents and chairpersons. Even bishops who share the new religious experience of faith-and-justice are unable to transform their diocese and their parishes.

What is of great importance, therefore, is to find an appropriate minority strategy. Relying on a theory of social change, derived from Max Weber, I have suggested that social change takes place through the promotion of countervailing currents.[13] The ruling structures are too firmly implanted to be modified: they are held down by society's own common sense. But the people who experience the existing system as oppressive are often willing to follow countervailing trends. These trends are sparked by new ideas and a new imagination that account for people's suffering and offer solutions to present problems.

Some of these countervailing currents may be irrational and blind, some may even be dangerous; others, on the other hand, may be based on a sound analysis, attract people, threaten the dominant structures and then be crushed by those holding power. Under certain historical circumstances, which are difficult to foresee, countervailing currents may converge, gain a certain power, and at a particular moment in time succeed in transforming the dominant structures. This theory of social change certainly sheds light on what happened to the Catholic Church at Vatican II: here several countervailing trends in the Church, the liturgical movement, the biblical movement, the ecumenical movement, and the lay movement, which had existed for several decades partly underground and often under the frowns of the hierarchy, were allowed by Pope John XXIII to come to the surface and influence policy-making at the top. The same theory can also be applied to understand social change in secular society.

What I propose, therefore, is that the liberationist orientation, well grounded as it is in religious experience, biblical assurance, theological reflection and ecclesiastical approval, promote countervailing trends in Church and society. While it would be futile to try to change entire institutions, it is effective to find a few people, a minority, dedicated to social justice within these institutions, organize them in small groups and centres, create networks between them and establish sets of communication with similar church groups and sympathetic secular organizations. While the various groups may be engaged in different tasks, some more educational, others more political, others again issue-oriented, the common network binds them together and gives them a sense that they are part of a new movement in the Church, possibly a new movement *of* the Church. Imagine for a moment that in a city there were five justice Christians in every parish, involved in local projects and joined in a lively network, what impact would such an active minority have on the Church and on the city! The advantage of this minority strategy is that it does not depend on the cooperation of those in charge of the institutions, even though their cooperation is of great consequence. Thanks to such a minority strategy, moreover, there is always something we can do. We are never caught in total impotence. We can always find others with whom to promote a counter-vailing current of social justice, knowing that this is not a waste of time, but a contribution that in the long run prepares significant social change.

Because the powers of injustice are growing at this time, I believe that the justice movement in the Churches will assume ever greater proportions. To counter the destructive forces unleashed by the two world systems and their clash, religion may be the only available resource. I foresee the rebirth of the old world religions, but especially the emergence of a radical Catholicism renewed by the faith in Jesus Christ as the compassionate protector of humans on this earth.

Notes

1. There is considerable literature on the new religious experience. For Latin America see the work of Segundo Galilea, "Spiritual Awakening and Movements of Liberation in Latin America," *Concilium* 89, pp. 129–38, "Liberation as Encounter with Politics and Contemplation," *Concilium* 96, pp. 19–33, and his Spanish publications, especially his *Espiritualidad de la liberación,* Santiago, 1973. His work is introduced in English in A. T. Hennelly, *Theologies in Conflict,* Orbis Books, 1979, pp. 30–31. For the new religious experience in the USA see the work of Michael Crosby, *Thy Will be Done: Praying the Our Father as Subversive Activity,* Orbis Books, 1977, and *Spirituality of the Beatitudes,* Orbis Books, 1981.
2. Many contemporary books treat the Bible in its totality as the record of God's call to justice: J. S. Croatto, *Exodus: A Hermeneutics of Freedom,* Orbis, 1981, J. D. Smart, *The Cultural Subversion of the Biblical Faith,* Westminster, Philadelphia, 1977, L. J. Topel, *The Way of Peace: Liberation Through the Bible,* Orbis, 1979.
3. The dangerous memory of Jesus Christ is a theme examined by J. B. Metz, *Faith in History and Society,* Seabury, New York, 1980, pp. 88–99, 200–204.
4. The 1976 Labour Day Statement of the Canadian bishops,

From Words to Action, cf. G. Baum, D. Cameron, *Ethics and Economics,* Lorimer, Toronto, 1984, pp. 162–169.

5. A brilliant introduction in the new theological approach is Matthew Lamb, *Solidarity With Victims,* Crossroads, New York, 1982.

6. Cf. G. Baum, *Religion and Alienation,* Paulist Press, New York, 1975, pp. 179–208.

7. "Justice," Medellin Conclusions, in *The Gospel of Peace and Justice: Catholic Social Teaching Since Pope John,* edit. by J. Gremillion, Orbis Books, 1976, pp. 445–454. The subsequent quotations are taken from these pages.

8. "Peace," Medellin Conclusions, in *op. cit.,* pp. 455–463.

9. For an analysis of the Native People's land claims and the involvement of the Canadian Churches, see Hugh and Karmel McCullum, *This Land is not For Sale,* Anglican Book Centre, Toronto, 1975.

10. For analysis of the French bishops' statement, see G. Baum, *The Social Imperative,* Paulist Press, New York, pp. 184–201.

11. For a detailed analysis of the Canadian bishops' teaching see G. Baum, "Toward a Canadian Social Theory," in this volume, pp. 66–87. For *From Words to Action,* see note 4.

12. See G. Baum, *The Priority of Labor: A Commentary on Laborem Exercens,* Paulist Press, New York, 1982.

13. For a brief statement of Weber's theory of social change, see G. Baum, *Religion and Alienation,* pp. 170–174.

2.
Class Struggle And Magisterium: A New Note

Catholic social teaching from Leo XIII has always repudiated class struggle. It offered several reasons for this. Class struggle was rejected because (1) it sought the victory of one class over another instead of a new mode of co-operation; (2) it was nourished by resentment against the powerful instead of Christian love of neighbor; (3) it easily led to violence and new forms of domination; and (4) it was often associated with an ideology that made class struggle the dynamic principle of history moving society toward the overcoming of its contradictions.

This repudiation of class struggle was in keeping with the organic understanding of society upheld in Catholic social teaching from Leo XIII until the late sixties. Here society was seen as a social body, organically united, based on class levels and co-operation, in constant need of reform through the spiritual submission of all members to the norms of justice. It was the task of government to stand above the conflict of the classes, promote the common good, foster co-operation, and protect the poor from exploitation by the rich. While this teaching had strong reformist impulses, its main emphasis was on shared values and respect for authority. Political action for justice, including the struggle of workers, had to take place within this social context. Class struggle did not fit into this.

Vatican Council II still upheld this teaching, even though its vision of society was more democratic and pluralistic. It perceived society in co-operative terms, now expanded to the global scale. Ultimately the distance between the rich and the poor nations, scandalous in its proportions, was to be overcome by a new sense of humanity and an outburst of generosity that would make the rich nations, on ethical grounds, find ways of sharing wealth and power and allow the poor nations to escape from their misery.

New Emphasis at Medellín

In 1968 the Latin American Bishops Conference at Medellín introduced a new note in Catholic social teaching, one that was soon to be accepted in Vatican teaching, by several national hierarchies, and eventually by Pope John Paul II. Medellín introduced a conflictual understanding of society. The section of the Medellín documents entitled "Peace" recognized that the Latin American societies were caught in the clutches of an economic system, world-wide in extension, that impoverished them.[1] The decisions affecting the economic well-being of Latin Americans were made by transnational corporations with head offices in the North, by men whose aim was to increase corporate profit and power. Even development projects sponsored by agencies of the North tended to increase the dependency of Latin America and often led to greater misery. A small class of Latin Americans, linked to the transnational corporations, greatly increased their standard of living. They often became the political actors protecting the existing order, despite the grave injustices. Medellín spoke of Latin America caught in the sway of "external" and "internal colonialism." In this context it would have been absurd to speak of societies in organic terms. Societies were conflictual realities.

Related to this new note is a second point made by Medellín: the need for institutional change. The call for greater virtue is wholly inadequate unless it is accompanied by an equal emphasis on structural changes.[2] What has to change in Latin America is both structure and consciousness. The organic perception of society encouraged the view, often defended by church people, that what was needed for the reform of society was the conversion to greater virtue on the part of all people, on all levels of society. Medellín went beyond this. What was needed was structural change and entry into a new consciousness. The call for greater love and generosity in societies as gravely unjust as the Latin American ones, unaccompanied by the demand for the reform of institutions, only disguised the sinful structures that inflicted suffering on the majority of people. Medellín called the double aim of structural change and new consciousness "liberation." The bishops here followed a perspective worked out previously by Christian grassroots communities in Latin America, often supported and aided by theologians.

Thirdly, Medellín recognized that the struggle for justice was an essential element of the faithful Christian life. While previous Catholic social teaching understood the dedication to social justice as based on the natural virtue of justice, a new ecclesiastic trend emerged at Medellín, again reflecting the Christian experience of grassroots communities, which saw the dedication to justice as a contemporary form of Christian discipleship. Faith, hope, and love, the theological virtues, summoned forth involvement in the struggle for justice.[3]

Fourthly, Medellín put new emphasis on the raising of consciousness among the masses of ordinary people.[4] It was the task of the Church, according to Medellín, to make people aware of the obstacles that prevented them from exercising responsibility for their own lives. Part of the Christian message was that people were called by God to be the subject of their own history. In the past, Catholic social teaching, even while recognizing the harm done to people by unjust structures, addressed its demand for social reconstruction to the powerful, to the leaders, to the government. They were seen as the agents of reform in society. With its emphasis on the raising of consciousness, Medellín was understood as addressing the people, the victims, the poor and oppressed, as the agents of social transformation. Justice would come about only as the result of liberation struggle by the people themselves.

Four new points, then, were made at Medellín: the conflictual view of society, the double need of structural change and personal conversion, the social struggle as a form of Christian discipleship, and the oppressed as agents of social transformation. Yet Medellín made these points in a tentative way. It did not endorse the new perspective with full consistency. It was therefore important to see how subsequent episcopal conferences and especially the Vatican would react to this. Since 1968 the new approach has been fully endorsed by the Catholic magisterium. In the following pages I shall refer to this development in the briefest manner.

Reception by Magisterium

The conflictual understanding of modern society was endorsed in the declaration *Justitia in mundo* made by the 1971 Synod of Bishops held in Rome. How does modern society appear to the Synod? "We recognize the serious injustices that are building around the world of men a network of domination, oppression, and abuses which stifle freedom and which keep the greater part of humanity from sharing in the building up and enjoyment of a more just and more fraternal world."[5] At the same time, the Synod sees "the arising of a new awareness which shakes people out of any fatalistic resignation and which spurs them on to liberate themselves and be responsible for their own destiny."[6] It is with these struggling people that the Synod declares itself in solidarity. Why? Because it believes that the Church's mission is the preaching of Christ's redemption, and this includes liberation "from every oppressive situation."[7]

The conflictual view of modern society was later strongly affirmed by the Latin American Bishops Conference at Puebla (1979), when it called the whole of the Church to "the preferential option for the poor."[8] This option had two dimensions, one perspectival, the other activist. The option for the poor implied looking at society from the viewpoint of the oppressed and, secondly, giving public witness of solidarity with them. Society is here seen not as a well-functioning social body in need of a few reforms (the organic view), but rather as a set of dominant structures that hurt a wide sector of the population and therefore demand reconstruction. What is needed is new awareness accompanied by the struggle for structural change.

The conflictual view of modern society, as we shall see further on, was fully endorsed by Pope John Paul II in his *Laborem exercens* (1981).

The second point, the demand for structural change and conversion of consciousness, was not new in ecclesiastical teaching. During the Great Depression, Pius XI had already called for this double task: "Two things are necessary for the reconstruction of the social order: the reform of institutions and the conversion of morals."[9] After Medellín, ecclesiastical documents returned to this double demand, very often using the term "liberation." Occasionally ecclesiastical voices warned us of a one-sided interpretation of "liberation," one that focused only on the structural aspect and omitted attention to the conversion of mind and heart. But if liberation from oppression was understood as a double task, it was fully endorsed by Catholic social teaching.[10]

Once this point has been admitted, it is no longer possible to preach the conversion to greater love and generosity as the answer to the injustices of the present day. "We cannot take refuge in the position that, as Christians, our duty is simply to worship God and give alms to the poor. To do this alone in our present situation would be to incur the wrath of Christ."[11] Preaching of greater selflessness, unaccompanied by the demand for institutional change, obscures the sinful situation in which we live and hence exercises an ideological function. Moralizing always helps the *status quo*. Moral demands must be joined to demands for just institutions.

The third point, the supernatural origin of the Christian's commitment to justice, has also been confirmed by the magisterium. This was done in *Justitia in mundo*, the important document already mentioned. The redemption which Jesus Christ has brought, we are told, includes the liberation of people from every oppression.[12] Action on behalf of social justice is a constitutive part of Christian witness and Christian proclamation.

The strongest support for this new point of view is found in Pope John Paul II's first encyclical, *Redemptor hominis*. He laid a Christological foundation for the Church's social ministry. The encyclical argued that Jesus Christ had identified himself in some sense with all human beings in their historical groupings.[13] What follows from this is that the Church in its defense of human rights and its demand for social justice is not simply involved in a humanitarian, purely this-wordly activity, but is, properly speaking, serving Christ present in people and hence exercising its essential, supernatural mission. The mission of the Church to proclaim the gospel and serve God's approaching reign remains incomplete and unfinished if it does not express itself in public witness to social justice and human rights.[14]

Pope John Paul's Christological foundation of the Church's social ministry was a new development in the ecclesiastical magisterium. It certainly moved beyond Vatican II and the Medellín Conference. According to the new teaching, the Church's proper and essential mission has a clearly defined sociopolitical thrust. Because John Paul does not want priests to assume leadership positions in political organizations, the secular press and the public media have often created the impression that he does not want priests and bishops to speak out on social justice and human rights. The contrary is true. Unless the Christian message be accompanied by the demand for justice, it lacks its own proper integrity. In this task the Church's contribution is not a scientific but an ethical one. In the name of the values and the vision revealed in the gospel, the Church must speak out on the rights and dignity of workers and the poor in general and "condemn those situations in which that dignity and those rights are violated."[15] More than that, the Church must help "guide the social changes so as to ensure authentic progress by man and society."[16]

The Christological base for the Church's social involvement is startling. Many churchmen, brought up on the more traditional teaching, are still uncomfortable with it. They fear that the Christological basis thrusts the Church inevitably into political debates and demands that it take sides in certain social conflicts.

The Poor as Historical Agents

What of the fourth point tentatively made at Medellín? Have subsequent ecclesiastical documents accepted the position that the people, especially the poor and oppressed, are to be the historical agents of social change? In his first encyclical, *Redemptor hominis*, John Paul offered a radical analysis of the conditions of oppression and misery in the world and called for bold changes in the economic and political order, in a manner critical of communism and capitalism at the same time. Yet this exhortation seemed to be addressed to the men who held power and were capable of making decisions on the highest level. It was up to the power elite to modify the inherited order.

On his trip through Brazil, John Paul moved beyond this position.[17] In his address at Vigidal, after recognizing the structures of oppression and expressing his solidarity with the poor, he still appealed to the powerful in the country to introduce institutional change. "Do all you can, especially you who have decision-making power, you on whom the situation of the world depends, do everything to make the life of every person in your country more human, more worthy of human persons."[18] After longer acquaintance with the Brazilian situation, the Pope shifted the emphasis. In his address at Favela dos Alagados, near Salvador de Bahia, he told the masses that they themselves were the agents of social change, that they should be actively involved in shaping their future. And all who love justice must be in solidarity with them in this struggle. "God grant that there may be many of us to offer you unselfish cooperation in order that you may free yourselves from everything that enslaves you, with full respect for what you are and for your right to be the prime author of your human advancement." The Pope continued: "You must struggle for life, do everything to improve the condition of poverty, disease, unhealthy housing, that is contrary in many ways to your dignity as human persons."[19] The prime mover of radical social change must be the victims themselves. And the Church must be in solidarity with them.

This position was developed in a formal manner in John Paul's encyclical *Laborem exercens*. In this document the Pope argued that the dynamic element of modern society was the labor movement. Workers were the principal agents of the struggle for justice. Justice in modern society was defined by the encyclical as "the priority of labor over capital." Those who did not belong to the working class but loved justice should be in solidarity with their struggle. The Church itself, John Paul insisted, must be in solidarity with the workers' struggle for justice.[20] The Pope formulated this basic principle as "the solidarity *of* workers and *with* workers."[21] In the same paragraph, alluding to the conditions of the Third World, the Pope called for "the solidarity *of* and *with* the poor."[22] Again, the agents of social reconstruction were the victims of society, united in a joint struggle for justice, supported by all citizens committed to justice. I wish to call this principle "preferential or partial solidarity." Universal solidarity remains the goal. Universal solidarity stays alive in the human heart as a constant hope. But in a situation of grave injustice, solidarity begins with the disadvantaged and oppressed in the hope of creating historical conditions that permit universal solidarity. In a sinful world, then, solidarity is preferential or partial, starting with the least of the brothers and sisters.[23]

We conclude from this brief examination of ecclesiastical texts that the four points tentatively made at Medellín were subsequently accepted by the Church's magisterium. The reader will have noticed that I have only looked at ecclesiastical documents; I have not examined whether and to what extent the ecclesiastical authorities have acted in accordance with the more recent teaching.

The question that poses itself at this point is whether John Paul's theory of partial solidarity is just another name for class struggle. Some Catholics have argued this. The Canadian bishops, who have followed *Laborem exercens* very closely, have been accused by several Catholic members of Parliament of propagating a Marxist approach in their *Ethical Reflections on the Economic Crisis*. The following two sentences composed by the Canadian bishops provoked a great deal of comment and opposition: "The needs of the poor have priority over the wants of the rich; the rights of workers are more important than the maximization of profits; the participation of marginalized groups has precedence over a system which excludes them." And, "As long as technology and capital are not harnessed by society to serve basic human needs, they are likely to become an enemy rather than an ally in the developments of people."[24] Some Canadian

commentators, including Catholic critics, have decried this conflictual perception of Canadian society, where the rich and powerful appear on one side and the poor and powerless on the other.
They have also taken exception to the suggestion that under certain conditions the decision-making elite deserves to be called the
"enemy" of the majority of the people. This, the critics said, was
a call to class struggle derived from Marxist theory, which has
always been condemned by the Church.

Is John Paul's "solidarity *of* the workers and *with* the workers" and Puebla's "preferential option for the poor" a Catholic
formulation of class struggle? If not, how does the theory of partial solidarity differ from theories of class struggle? In his excellent study of the Church's social teaching, Donal Dorr recognizes
that "the word 'solidarity' seems to play, in the thinking of John
Paul, a role analogous to 'class struggle' in Marxist writings."
Then he asks the question, "How different is the Pope's position
from Marxism?"[25] He deals with this question in the final chapter of his book. In my own commentary on *Laborem exercens,* I
concluded that the Pope proposed "an imaginative rethinking of
class conflict."[26] In this article I wish to argue, admittedly very
briefly, that even after the evolution of the Church's social teaching and the theory of partial solidarity, the traditional Catholic
objections to class struggle (summed up in four points at the beginning of this article) still hold. Class struggle was rejected, I
proposed, because (1) it sought the victory of one class over another instead of a new mode of co-operation; (2) it was nourished
by resentment against the powerful instead of Christian love of
neighbor; (3) it easily led to violence and new forms of domination; and (4) it was often associated with an ideology that
made class struggle the dynamic principle of history moving society toward the overcoming of its contradictions.

Partial Solidarity versus Class Struggle

I wish to show that the theory of partial solidarity is different
from theories of class struggle. Despite the doctrinal development that has taken place, the magisterium continues to repudiate class-conflict theories for the same reason it did in the past.

Assumed in this article is that Marxist theories of class struggle are appropriately described by the four characteristics raised against them in ecclesiastical literature. In itself this point would require detailed examination. What I shall do is simply show that the Catholic theory of partial solidarity does not share the four characteristics of which class-conflict theories have been accused.

1) Solidarity does not aim at the victory of one class over another. In the first place, solidarity is not defined in terms of the material self-interest of an economic class. Solidarity is an ethical achievement. People stand together in the struggle for justice, impelled by several motives, including ethical ones. As victims of society, they seek to escape their bondage: this is the element of collective self-interest. But they are also guided by alternative values and the vision of a just society: these are the ethical elements. For many religious people, especially Christians, this solidarity is strengthened by faith in God's promises. This struggle for justice, moreover, is joined by people from other social strata who share the same alternative values and vision.

The solidarity movement, I repeat, is an ethical achievement. It is not generated by historical necessity through the collective self-interest of an economic class, but produced through the dedication and generosity of people with high ideals who desire to escape their oppression. The solidarity movement, as described in ecclesiastical texts, is made up of various sectors of the population. The Canadian bishops, in particular, emphasize that the solidarity movement is made up of various groups, unionized workers, nonunionized workers, the unemployed, the native peoples, people living in depressed regions, recent immigrants, and so forth, so that each group must modify its aim somewhat in order to build and protect solidarity. Each group must sacrifice certain elements of its immediate self-interest in order to create a movement of solidarity that can reach out to the majority of the population and thus exercise influence on society. Here again solidarity appears as an ethical achievement.

Partial solidarity, we note, does not aim at the destruction of another class. What it aims at is a more participatory society. The struggle for social justice is therefore not opposed to negotiations, nor to new proposals of those in power to share their wealth and allow workers to participate in decision-making. The history of the labor movement reveals the readiness of workers to consent to new forms of co-operation, even though the same history also shows that these compromises were often used by those in power to derive the greater benefit. While there may be different views among those struggling for justice as to what concessions should be regarded as adequate, partial solidarity aims at a new mode of co-operation. Non–co-operation is more characteristic of the powerful who refuse to let go of their power.

2) Partial solidarity is nourished not by resentment and vengeance but by the yearning for justice and liberation. It does not regard the rich and powerful as the enemies of the poor; enemies, rather, are the institutions that oppress and damage the people. Solidarity desires the transformation of these institutions. Following traditional teaching, Catholics hate the sin but try to love the sinner. They desire the conversion of the sinner to a new consciousness and material restitution.

How is this preferential solidarity related to Christian charity, which reaches out to the whole of the human family? Liberation theology has shown that in situations of grave injustice and oppression, charity transforms itself into a yearning for justice that would remove the burden from the poor. The preferential option for the poor, or partial solidarity, has a built-in impatience: it produces a longing for the liberation of the oppressed so that it becomes possible to embrace all members of society, working together for the common good, with the same good will. Universal solidarity remains the final goal.

Liberation theology, which has explored and defended the new orientation of the magisterium, has been well aware that the great temptation of the oppressed is to envy the oppressor, desire to replace him, and thus become oppressor after him. Against this temptation, the Catholic theory of partial solidarity articulates that the aim of the struggle for justice is the qualitative transformation of society. What is required is structural change accompanied by conversion of mind and heart. Liberation theology has been aware that oppressive structures damage not only the humanity of the oppressed; they also damage, though in a different way, the humanity of the powerful who defend the un-just institutions. Cutting themselves off from justice and mercy and justifying this in their own minds by a false sense of life's meaning, they caricature themselves, draw their own distorted self-portrait. Partial solidarity, therefore, strives not only for the liberation of the oppressed; it also promises to liberate the power elite from the self-imposed distortions of their humanity. Again, the partial solidarity is nourished by universal charity.

3) What is the relation of the solidarity movement to vio-lence? Usually this movement becomes the object of persecution, sometimes even violent persecution. Those who yearn for justice and hope in the kingdom are often regarded as enemies and sometimes gunned down by the protectors of the existing order. The contemporary Church has its crown of martyrs. Archbishop Oscar Romero was assassinated because he was in solidarity with the poor.

The solidarity movement does not aim at introducing struc-tural change in a violent manner. People trust that if their move-ment is supported by the great majority of the population, those who hold power will be forced to resign or negotiate. In societies with a democratic tradition this poses no difficulty.

A solidarity movement that becomes a ground swell will be able to use democratic institutions to gain political power and reconstruct economic institutions. Even in countries lacking democratic institutions, nonviolent ground swells have some-times led to significant institutional change. What about coun-tries in which an unjust order is upheld by violent means? This is the difficult St. Joan of Arc question. Even in the face of insti-tutionalized violence, contemporary Church teaching counsels a nonviolent struggle, though the magisterium has never commit-ted itself to a pacifist position. In their pastoral letter *The Chal-lenge of Peace* of May 1983, the American bishops recall both the just-war and the just-revolution theories of the Catholic tra-dition.[27] For U.S. Catholics, this theory has a certain importance, since their country was created by the violent overthrow of a co-lonial regime.

Of greater importance is that the solidarity movement does not aim at domination. What inspires the more recent Catholic social teaching is the vision of a participatory society. People are called to become the subjects of their own history. This vision excludes not only totalitarian forms of government; it also excludes authoritarian political parties. It excludes, for instance, the style of the communist party, which sees itself as a vanguard party, guided by scientific principles, centralized in its decision-making, intent on imposing its analysis upon the workers without paying attention to the workers' own aspirations.

The preferential option for the poor, moreover, has revealed itself as a transcendent ethical principle; for it is operative before, during, and after radical social change. As new historical conditions allow the emergence of new power groups, society will again suffer from contradictions and oppress sectors of its own population. The preferential option for the poor makes Christians loyal supporters of justice struggles as well as critics within the limits of solidarity.

4) The theory of partial solidarity in no way corresponds to a deterministic understanding of history. *Laborem exercens* calls the workers' struggle for justice the dynamic element of contemporary society. There is no mention here of universal history. Partial solidarity is not linked to a particular philosophy of the historical process. Secondly, as mentioned above, the driving force of the struggle is not necessity, not generated by purely economic forces, nor therefore predictable by scientific analysis. The struggle for justice is freely chosen, an ethical achievement, yet a fragile project that could turn sour at any point and lead to harmful results. It is a movement that remains in need of ongoing guidance through ethical reflection and commitment. Finally, the theory of solidarity is not linked to the expectation of a future classless society, in which man's domination by man will be wholly overcome and people move from the realm of necessity into the realm of freedom. According to Catholic teaching, sin and brokenness define the character of earthly existence. While a society more just, more participatory, and less cruel than the present one is an altogether realistic goal, even this improved society, delivered from some of its gravely unjust features, will remain subject to sin, generate new structures of injustice, and be

in need of an ongoing critique by the preferential option for the poor.

We conclude from these brief remarks that while the theory of partial solidarity has a certain resemblance to Marxist ideas of class struggle, it is significantly different. Without any contradiction, therefore, the magisterium continues to reject theories of class struggle. Liberation theology, which is a theological elaboration of the preferential option for the poor, has never forgotten the gospel call to love of neighbor and hence, despite certain terminological similarities, has always stood apart from Marxist theories of class struggle. This is true especially of the writings of Gustavo Gutiérrez, who more than any other theologian has been concerned with the doctrinal basis of liberation, namely, God's gracious presence in history as the power of the poor. One gets the impression that many Catholics, including Catholics in high places, disagree with the theory of partial solidarity presented by the magisterium, but are unwilling to say this publicly; instead they choose to attack Catholic theologians who defend, clarify, and explore contemporary Church teaching.

As a final remark, allow me to repeat an observation made elsewhere[28] that the more recent Catholic social teaching has been produced by an extended dialogue of the older Catholic social teaching with the religious experience of the oppressed struggling for justice, with the prophetic tradition of the Scriptures, and with Marxist social theory. The final result, in my opinion, is an original Catholic contribution to social theory, one that has much to offer a troubled world at this time. At this moment, when Western Marxism is in a state of crisis, when many Marxists begin to recognize the one-sided emphasis on the economic factor and the neglect of cultural and spiritual factors in their intellectual traditions, when socialist thinkers in all parts of the world begin to appreciate community values and pay attention to the ethical factors involved in the creation of solidarity, friendship, and fidelity, all issues neglected in their traditions, the emerging Catholic social theory has a very important contribution to make.

Notes

1. Medellín Documents, "Peace," nos. 1—13, in *The Gospel of Justice and Peace,* ed. J. Gremillion (Maryknoll, N.Y.: Orbis, 1976) 455—58.
2. Ibid., "Justice," no. 3 (*Gospel* 446).
3. Ibid., "Justice," nos. 4 and 5 (*Gospel* 447).
4. Ibid., "Justice," nos. 17 and 20 (*Gospel* 452–53).
5. *Justitia in mundo,* no. 3 (*Gospel* 514).
6. Ibid., no. 4 (*Gospel* 514).
7. Ibid., no. 6 (*Gospel* 514).
8. Puebla, Final Document, no. 1134, in *Puebla and Beyond,* ed. J. Eagleson and P. Scharper (Maryknoll, N.Y.: Orbis, 1979) 264.
9. *Quadragesimo anno,* no. 77, in *Great Encyclicals,* ed. W. J. Gibbons (New York: Paulist, 1963) 147.
10. Puebla, Final Document, nos. 189, 281, 475, 480, 482, 1026 (*Puebla and Beyond* 147, 161, 189, 190, 252).
11. Canadian Bishops, *From Words to Action* (1976) no. 10; see G. Baum and D. Cameron, *Ethics and Economics: Canada's Catholic Bishops on the Economic Crisis* (Toronto: Lorimer, 1984) 168.
12. *Justitia in mundo,* nos. 5 and 6 (*Gospel* 514).
13. *Redemptor hominis,* no. 8 (*Origins* 8 [1979] 631).
14. Ibid., no. 17 (*Origins* 637).
15. *Laborem exercens,* no. 1 (G. Baum, *The Priority of Labor* [New York: Paulist, 1982] 96).
16. Ibid.
17. Here I follow Donal Dorr, *Option for the Poor* (Maryknoll, N. Y.: Orbis, 1983) 223—32.
18. Ibid. 228.
19. Ibid. 229—30.
20. For a detailed analysis of the social theory of *Laborem exercens,* see Baum, *The Priority of Labor* (n. 15 above).
21. *Laborem exercens,* no. 8 (*The Priority of Labor* 110).
22. Ibid. (*Priority* 110).
23. Cf. D. Mieth, "Solidarity and the Right to Work," in *Unemployment and the Right to Work,* ed. J. Pohier and D. Mieth (Concilium 160; New York: Seabury, 1982) 58–65.
24. Canadian Bishops, *Ethical Reflections on the Economic Crisis,*

nos. 1 and 3; see Baum and Cameron, *Ethics and Economics* 6, 10.
25. Dorr, *Option for the Poor* 266.
26. Baum, *The Priority of Labor* 29.
27. National Conference of Catholic Bishops, *The Challenge of Peace*, in *Origins* 13 (1983) 10.
28. Baum and Cameron, *Ethics and Economics* 51.

3.
The Impact of Marxism
on the Thought of John Paul II

To study the impact of Marxism on the thought of Pope John Paul II is a major task, one that must be undertaken by a scholar with a knowledge of Polish, who can read the writings of Karol Wojtyla published in his own country. According to Professor John Hellman, the Archbishop of Krakow was associated with a group of Polish Catholic intellectuals, followers of Emmanual Mounier's personalism, which engaged in critical dialogue with Marxism.[1] Their purpose was not to refute Marxism but to open up its categories, reveal the ongoing human interaction behind its reified concepts, and arrive at a humanist perspective that took seriously Marx's "materialist" approach, i.e., the recognition that the human struggle to transform nature and create the conditions for human survival laid the foundation for human culture and consciousness.

The purpose of the present article is quite limited. I wish to study the impact of Marxism on John Paul II's encyclical, *Laborem exercens*. I shall also refer to some of the speeches given by the Pope in Canada and the United States. Since some of the new ideas introduced by John Paul II into Catholic social teaching are not fully explicated and since the perspective of *Laborem exercens* is not consistently pursued in the other encyclicals, the conclusions of this article are bound to be tentative. Still, *Laborem exercens* is such an original document and introduces such

a new methodology into Catholic social thought that the encyclical will remain for a long time a document read and studied by theologians and an inspiration for the social teaching put
forth by episcopal conferences. The influence of *Laborem exercens* on the Canadian bishops, especially their statement
"Ethical Reflections on the Economic Crisis" (1983), has been
considerable.

The impact of Marxism on the thought of John Paul II can
be analyzed in three stages where each stage relies on the validity
of the preceding one. The third stage, as we shall see, raises questions that demand further reflection and clarification.

The Worker as Subject

John Paul II is the first Pope to introduce into Catholic social theory the notion of the alienation of labor. While the Pope does not
use the word, he laments not only the exploitation of workers,
but also "the radical separation of work from ownership" which
excludes workers from sharing in the decision regarding the use
of the goods they produce and the organization of production.[2]

Previous Catholic teaching praised labor as a participation
in God's creative work, as a service offered to the community,
and as the activity that enabled workers to sustain themselves
and their families. Previous Catholic teaching laments the exploitation of labor through inadequate and hence unjust wages,
through harsh and dangerous conditions of work, and through
lack of security at times of illness, accident and old age. But this
social teaching did not analyze the alienation of labor, the separation of work from ownership, though there were occasional
references to "co-determination" to which workers were entitled.[3]

In *Laborem exercens*, Pope John Paul II explores the natural
link between work and ownership (n. 14).[4] Workers live under
conditions of injustice whenever they are excluded (separated, alienated) from the ownership of their products. Workers are entitled to work for themselves; they are entitled to be co-owners
of the giant workbench at which they labor. In practical terms
this means that thanks to the value and dignity of labor, workers

have the right to participate in the decisions affecting the use of the capital they produce and the manner in which production itself is organized. In the existing systems, capitalist and communist, workers are treated unjustly, alienated from their human powers, even if they should be paid adequate wages and enjoy relative security in their work.

Another way of explicating the value and dignity of labor is to say, with *Laborem exercens,* that the worker is "the subject of production." In the one-sidedly materialistic civilization to which we belong, John Paul II writes, workers tend to be regarded as "instruments of production" (n. 7). Along with raw materials and the machinery, they are the factors of production controlled by the owners or managers of the industries. *Laborem exercens* argues that workers must be treated as "subjects of work and its true maker and creator" (n. 7). They have the right to assume responsibility for the organization of labor and the use of their products. Systems on which the true order is reversed John Paul II calls "capitalism" (n. 7), and he adds that this term applies even to systems that present themselves under a different name. What he undoubtedly suggests is that in the existing socialism in Poland and other Soviet bloc countries, workers are looked upon as instruments rather than subjects of production and that for this reason the system deserves to be called state capitalism.

In his attempt to clarify the alienation of labor, John Paul II argues that work has often been understood as "merchandise" (n. 7), that the worker—especially the industrial worker—sells to the employer who is the possessor of all capital, i.e., of all working tools and means that make production possible. This manner of looking at work is offensive and degrading. Work is human activity of great dignity. It may not be looked upon as commodity. It is the activity through which people transform nature into a home for themselves and in the process realize their own humanity. As we shall see, work has an objective dimension, the product, and a subjective dimension, the process of self-realization that takes place through work (n. 6). To think of work as a commodity to be sold overlooks its subjective dimension, its spiritual, personalist meaning. According to *Laborem exercens,* the subjective dimension of work holds "pre-eminence" (n. 6) over the objective one. The dignity of labor resides in the human self-actualization involving the body, the intelligence, the moral virtues and all human talents. Work has an ethical, spiritual value. This is so, the Pope argues, because "the one who carries it out is a person, conscious, and free subject, that is to say a subject who decides about himself" (n. 6).

John Paul II not only laments the commodification of work: he also recognizes the cultural impact of commodification. In his speeches given in the United States and Canada, he repeatedly warns his listeners of the all-pervasive consumer mentality.[5] We are constantly tempted to define ourselves and evaluate other people in terms of what we and they possess and consume. Implicit in an economy ruled exclusively by the market is an understanding of the human as utility-maximizer. Thus we tend to become individualists and utilitarians, even when our professed ideals are spiritual. The exchange values tend to replace other values in society. The Pope's speeches delivered on his Canadian tour gave the impression that from his perspective third world countries suffer from economic oppression, second world countries from political oppression, and first world countries, such as Canada, from cultural oppression. Capitalist societies are wealthier than others, and they enjoy democratic freedoms, but individualism and utilitarianism, generated by the pre-eminence given to the market, undermine the sense of community and people's political will to act as a nation, thus making them unable to solve their relatively small economic problems such as unemployment and to tackle the much larger problem of the imbalance in the world economy. Commodity fetishism (the Pope does not use this word) prevents nations such as Canada from assuming collective responsibility for their society and becoming truly subjects of their history.

The concept of the human being as subject of society is new in Catholic social teaching. The notion is obviously derived from the Enlightenment as expressed in the liberal and the socialist tradition. Liberals thought of people as responsible agents in the nation's *political* life while socialists held that people were to exercise responsible agency in the nation's *economic* life. Catholicism, in line with the conservative tradition, rejected this concept. Society was largely perceived as a given, as preceding the individual, as an organic reality that could be enhanced or even reformed, but whose organic, interdependent hierarchical character had to be respected. It was not the people's task to create their own society. Catholics, moreover, tended to distinguish between *maiores* and *minores,* where the *maiores,* the distinguished and powerful, exercised political responsibility in society and the *minores,* the great majority, served through their obedience. Hence the shift in Catholic social teaching that recognizes people as the subject of work and the subject of their society is considerable.

The U.S. bishops followed this new teaching in their recent pastoral on economic justice. They specifically tried to wed two Enlightenment traditions, liberal and socialist: they speak of the need for a new American experiment that will complement the civil or political rights inherited from the democratic revolution, with new economic rights, foreign to the liberal tradition but demanded by strict justice.[6] The time has come, the bishops say, to extend democracy to the economic system. In line with this thinking the U.S. bishops define injustice and justice in an innovative manner, new at least in the Catholic tradition. Injustice equals marginalization: people find themselves excluded from access to needed resources, from recognition and responsibility. Justice from this perspective is defined as the struggle to overcome marginalization by ever extended participation.[7] In other words, people are meant to be subjects of their society.

This new teaching creates a certain restlessness in the Catholic Church. Catholics now recognize that they are meant to be subjects of the Church while the present self-organization of the Catholic Church does not permit this. To be faithful to its own teaching the Catholic Church will have to create structures through which all its members, in one way or another, can participate in the important decisions that affect their lives.

How do the positions briefly summarized here differ from Marxism? First, *Laborem exercens* defines work in a much wider manner than does Marx. It does not distinguish between productive and unproductive labor. Since work is for humans, work includes the production of goods and their distribution. Work includes trade. And a deeper analysis of the economy's dependence on society, especially under contemporary conditions, persuades the Pope that almost all activity in society contributes in some way to production. Work is done not just by the industrial worker and the farmer; it is also done by the white collar worker, the employees in service industries, engineers, teachers, and managers, women (and men) engaged in housework, and persons involved in government. Because of this interdependence *Laborem exercens* argues that, in the last analysis, the subject of production is society as a whole (n. 17). Society as a whole is responsible for the economy. Still, because factory, office and service workers, wage earners all, constitute the great majority, it is of them that John Paul II thinks when he develops his theory of labor solidarity.

Second, *Laborem exercens* argues against Marx that alienation and liberation have to do not so much with ownership as with the *use* of capital. The historical experience of Soviet bloc communism persuades John Paul II that the collectivization or nationalization of the industries is no guarantee that they will respect what the encyclical calls "the priority of labor over capital." Capital respects the priority of labor when it serves the well-being of the workers, renews the productive machinery, and contributes to the common good of the whole laboring society. In line with traditional Catholic teaching against Marx, *Laborem exercens* defends private property as licit and useful. Public ownership is also licit and useful. Yet all titles to ownership, either private or public, are conditional; they depend on the respect for the priority of labor over capital (n. 12). It is the right *use* that legitimates ownership. This is a radical position that is both critical of capitalism and communism. The Pope argues that the greatest guarantee that the priority of labor over capital will be respected is when the workers themselves become "the owners of the giant workbench at which they labor." While he resigns himself to variously mixed economies at this time, he supports the movements in society that seek to extend worker ownership and other forms of worker participation in decision-making (n. 14).

At the same time, *Laborem exercens* does not regard the industrial workers as the only ones who have a title to the ownership of the goods that they produce. For one, as we saw above, work is also done by engineers, office staff and management: they too have a title to ownership. But more profoundly, John Paul II argues that industrial production draws upon two heritages, the heritage of nature which is given to the whole of humanity, and the heritage of what others have already developed on the basis of these resources, primarily technological tools (n. 12). Because the workers in the factory enter upon the labors of others, they cannot lay claim to the ownership of their products. No ownership, not even that of workers, may be regarded as an absolute. Ownership must always be justified ethically by its *use*.

"Isolating the means of production as a separate property in order to set it up in the form of 'capital' in opposition to 'labor'— and even to practice exploitation of labor—is contrary to the very nature of these means and their possession. They cannot be possessed against labor, they cannot even be possessed for possession's sake, because the only legitimate title to their possession—whether in the form of private ownership or in the form of public ownership—is that they should serve labor and thus by serving labor that they should make possible . . . the universal destination of goods and the right to common use of them" (n. 14).

The Pope agrees with Marx that industrial machinery is stored up or congealed labor. But the Pope does not want to look upon this machinery simply as a thing. The personalist principle allows him to recover in the machinery the workers who made it, their efforts, their sweat, their sacrifices, and their honor. The Pope's reflections on technology allow him to experience the daily contact with buildings, streets, cars and machinery of any kind as a conscious communion with the workers who have produced them by the sweat of their brow.

Finally *Laborem exercens* differs from Marxism in its theory of the pre-eminence of the subjective. While the products of labor are essential for the survival of humankind, the self-realization of the working person is even more important. Work not only transforms nature, it also transforms the workers. Because of the alienation of labor, workers are vulnerable to dehumanization.

Yet what labor is meant to do is to constitute people as intelligent, creative, responsible, faithful, cooperative, and patient human beings. The subjective dimension of labor constitutes an ethical principle that must be observed in the organization of production. For *Laborem exercens* work in its subjective sense is part of culture, possibly the principal part of culture. Since work is the daily necessity to reproduce the world, its impact on the personal and moral development of persons is enormous. John Paul II argues that labor shapes human consciousness. The work we do will largely determine whether we become generous or selfish, faithful or scheming, cooperative or hostile, responsible or arbitrary. This is why the Pope makes the remarkable statement that human dignity is derived from work (n. 1). Because humans are the subject of work, they are bearers of unparalleled honor.

Worker Solidarity

In the nineteenth century, we read in *Laborem exercens,* "the issue of work was posed on the basis of the great conflict between 'capital' and 'labor,' that is to say, between the small but highly influential entrepreneurs, owners and holders of the means of production, and the broader multitude of people who lacked these means and shared in the process of production solely by their labor" (n. 11). The conflict originated in the fact that the owners had to put the powers at the disposal of the entrepreneurs, and these, "following the principle of maximum profit," tried to establish the lowest possible wages for the work done by the employees. The great error of capitalism was that the industrialists organized their capital against labor (n. 13). John Paul appears to contrast this with the feudal order in which, despite great inequalities, the gentry regarded themselves as responsible for the serfs and peasants living on their land.

This error of capitalism has been passed on in the history of the West and is repeated today many times in capitalist and communist countries. The true order, we are told, is the priority of labor over capital (n. 12). In other words, capital is meant to serve the people laboring, to renew the machinery and keep the industry viable, and to contribute to the well-being of the entire laboring society.

Capital and labor, according to their true nature, are closely united: they are ultimately one and the same (n. 13). For capital is nothing but labor stored up, labor upon labor. Capital and labor are united in the same subject—the workers (n. 13). There is nothing intrinsic to the productive process that creates opposition between capital and labor. The present arrangements must be overcome so that the unity of labor and capital may take on concrete form. Since production is social, so should the use of the goods produced. What counts is not who owns the machinery—there is more than one legitimate economic arrangement; what counts is the *use* of the goods, the availability of the goods for the people who produced them.

Because of the contradiction in the economy introduced by capitalism, there exists a concrete, historical conflict between capital and labor. *Laborem exercens* argues that this concrete conflict has been transformed into an ideology by some people (n. 11). The reference is undoubtedly to Marxists. Class struggle has been raised into a universal principle, operative in all societies, modern as well as pre-capitalist, as the motor force driving history forward to the construction of a society where the means of production are owned collectively, i.e., a society of freedom, beyond man's exploitation of man. People living in Soviet bloc countries have good reason to be angry with this theory. *Laborem exercens* argues that this ideology in fact disguises the real, concrete conflict between capital and labor (n. 11). Instead of analyzing concretely how the domination of capital over labor can be overcome or at least be mitigated in a particular country, without excluding from the struggle negotiations, compromises, and cooperation, the ideologues simply aim at replacing private by public ownership without investigating how, in fact, the industries could be run so that they serve labor and the laboring society.

Those who defended the priority of capital also produced an ideology, the liberal ideology. They raised the freedom of the market into a universal principle. The dialogue now prevents them from correctly understanding the conflict between capital and labor and from being open to solutions that promote cooperation and benefit the common good of society.

While *Laborem exercens* repudiates these two ideologies, it recognizes the existing conflict, "the antinomy" between capital and labor, and regards the labor movement as the dynamic element of modern society, as the social agent destined to promote social justice, i.e., the priority of labor (n. 8). The Pope speaks of the historical mission of labor unions (n. 20): their task is not only to improve the conditions of their own members but also to work toward the transformation of society in accordance with the priority of labor over capital. In this context, he writes: "In order to achieve social justice in the various parts of the world . . . there is the need for ever new movements of *solidarity of the workers and with the workers*. This solidarity must be present whenever it is called for by the social degrading of the subject of work, by exploitation of the workers and by growing areas of poverty and hunger. The Church is firmly committed to this cause, for it considers it to be its mission, its service, a proof of its fidelity to Christ, so that it can be truly 'the Church of the poor' " (n. 8, italics added).

Laborem exercens was written in 1981 when it seemed that the union movement, Solidarity, was about to transform Polish society. What the encyclical recommends for all societies, communist and capitalist, is the struggle of workers against those who control the means of production against them. Yet this struggle is to be guided by a realistic analysis of the situation and realistic aims, making use of the power of the workers to initiate negotiations and strive for new cooperative structures. The encyclical implicitly rejects revolution in first world countries and second world countries. The Pope sees the labor movement, supported by all citizens who love justice, as the historical agent of social change capable of bringing about the gradual transformation of society.

There is no doubt that *Laborem exercens* has left behind the "organic" view of society, characteristic of traditional Catholic social teaching and even the "pluralistic" view of society that emerged in *Gaudium et spes* of Vatican Council II. Like the Latin American bishops conferences of Medellín and Puebla, John Paul

II—at least in this encyclical—offers a conflictual understanding of society. The existing domination of capital over labor (in capitalism and in communism) creates a disadvantaged class, the workers, the majority and the backbone of society destined to become the agent of social reconstruction. Those who do not suffer directly from capital's domination of labor must make a choice: if they love justice, they must extend their solidarity to the workers' movement. The same demand for partiality is expressed in the ecclesiastical formula of the Puebla Conference, "the preferential option for the poor."[8] Ultimately, solidarity must be universal, embracing all members of society; but in concrete situations, solidarity must first be partial or preferential in order to create the conditions of justice that allow solidarity to become truly universal. The Canadian bishops have applied this conflictual perspective to the understanding of Canadian society.[9] Here is one formulation: "As Christians we are called to follow Jesus by identifying with the victims of injustice, by analyzing the dominant attitudes and structures that cause human suffering, and by actively supporting the poor and oppressed in their struggle to transform society."[10]

How does this "preferential solidarity" differ from the Marxist "class struggle" that has always been condemned by the Church? We have already noted some of the differences. Class struggle for the Marxists is a universal principle, operative in the whole of history, moving societies forward toward a messianic future, freed from man's domination of man. In this perspective, class struggle is easily perceived as a necessary process, generated not so much by human effort and human ingenuity as by the contradiction implicit in the economic infrastructure, and hence necessarily taking place in society, possibly even behind the backs of the people involved. John Paul II rejects any form of determinism. For him the solidarity movement is an ethical achievement. Class struggle as an ideology blinds workers to the possibility of gradual transformation. Second, the principle of class struggle easily persuades workers to strive for a political solution, such as the expropriation of capital by the state, instead of striving for innovative alternative models of economic development that al-

low workers greater participation in the planning and the benefits of the industries, independently of the ownership question.

Finally the Marxist theory of class struggle presents itself as
a theory of evolution. History is oriented toward certain fulfillment. This poses difficulties for Christians. Evolutionary theories
always provide ideological tools to legitimate the bracketing or
by-passing of certain groups of people supposedly caught in the
an earlier phase. They are then easily brushed into "the dustbin
of history." Since the Church identifies itself with the marginal,
it cannot accept social theories that recognize certain groups to
be at the crest of the historical development while others are left
to die in the dark. In North America, Christians have begun to
understand what evolutionary theories of history have done and
are still doing to the native peoples.

Still, it seems to me that the passage of Catholic social teaching from the "organic" and "pluralistic" to the "conflictual"
view of society, and to the endorsement of the labor struggle as
the historical agent for reconstructing modern society, has been
derived from an extended dialogue with Marxism. This dialogue
has been a critical one. What is of special interest here is that
while secular critics of Marxism, with its messianic orientation,
tend to reduce Marxism to a purely scientific theory, a sociology
of oppression for capitalist society, Christian critics are able to
transcend Marxism from within by replacing the false and dangerous messianism by a more modest hope, passionately embraced, grounded in the biblical promises that God is graciously
at work in history delivering us from conditions of oppression.

The Human Being as Worker

Laborem exercens enters even more deeply into critical dialogue
with Marxist thought. It would be logically possible, I think, to
accept the first two steps of this dialogue and find the third one,
more radical than the preceding, hard to accept. John Paul II decided to define the human being as worker. Humans differ from
the animals because humans alone, through their labor, create
the historical conditions for their survival, growth and develop-

ment. And in creating the world by labor, humans also achieve
their own self-realization. They create the world, and in doing so
they also constitute themselves in history.

This theory of self-creation is here obviously understood
within a theological context. In this it differs from Marxism. According to the encyclical, God has created humans as subjects:
they are subjects because they are created in the *imago Dei*.
Moreover, God has created the earth, nature, with which human
beings are to be reconciled by their labor. Finally God is graciously present in history, empowering people to assume responsibility for their world and truly become the subjects of their
society. But within this theological context, humans create the
world by labor and in doing so also accomplish their own self-
realization. We read: "This process is universal: it embraces all
human beings, every generation, every phase of economic and
cultural development, and at the same time it is a process that
takes place within each human being, in each conscious human
subject. Each and every individual is at the same time embraced
by it" (n. 4). And again, "Man's life is built up every day by
work; from work it derives its specific dignity" (n. 1).

That human dignity is derived from labor is a startling position. John Paul II repeated this bold thesis in a speech given to
the International Labor Conference at Geneva in 1982.[11] Catholic teaching usually recognized first human dignity on metaphysical grounds and then only defended the dignity of labor.
Because people have such high dignity, their labor, even if of a
lowly kind, has also great dignity. *Laborem exercens* seems to
reverse the traditional perspective. John Paul II sees the *imago
Dei* in human beings precisely inasmuch as they are subjects, responsible, laboring agents, called to produce their human world
and actualize themselves; he can therefore say without contradiction that the dignity of humans is derived from their labor.
Does this definition of the human being neglect the spiritual dimension?

We saw that *Laborem exercens* put greater emphasis on the
subjective pole, i.e., on personal self-realization through labor,
than does Marxism. John Paul II speaks of "the pre-eminence of
the subject." More important than the goods produced is the

spiritual personal formation of people through their work. If culture is defined as the set of values, customs and institutions that mediate the relations between people and express the ethos of their society—this is how the Pope uses "culture" in his speeches—then it is correct to say that the subjective dimension of work is part of culture, and according to *Laborem exercens* the principal part. Since the objective dimension of work constantly recreates the foundation for man's continued existence on earth, the subjective dimension of this process, more than any other cultural force, shapes human consciousness and human character. If I read *Laborem exercens* correctly, labor includes more than growing food and making things; it embraces the development of practical intelligence, the orientation toward cooperation, the generation of language and the projection of symbols—these are all needed for the organization of labor. To produce and reproduce the condition of human survival involves all of these activities.

Laborem exercens even argues that the sphere of values embodied in the family, the nation and the Christian religion serve human labor, serve the world-building process through which people achieve their self-realization. We are told that on the one hand labor makes the family possible, and on the other that the family is a school of labor preparing children for the great human task (n. 10). The family produces the culture that enables young people to become responsible subjects. We are told that the nation is the great repository of the labor of generations, and that in turn the solidarity that the nation generates inspires people to become more dedicated and more inventive in their labor (n. 10). And, finally, we read that even religion is part of culture, albeit the sacred part, that nourishes human beings in the laboring task (n. 25). Religion is the worship of God, Father, Son, and Spirit. God created us in the divine image: God appeared in Jesus as simple laborer; and the Spirit empowers us to be active in the world. While family, nation and religion have their own sphere of values, they are seen in *Laborem exercens* as serving the process of production and man's self-realization through labor.

A certain ambiguity remains about what precisely human labor entails. In particular, does it include action? Does it include the organization of the labor struggle? Does it include political action on the level of government and through political parties? If labor is understood as the process of society-building, then, it seems to me, it must embrace political action. *Laborem exercens* appreciates the role of power in the making of society. It refers to labor struggles, political parties and governments that have succeeded in significantly transforming entrepreneurial capitalism into a somewhat more benign economic system (n. 20). But should not "action" be specifically mentioned? Hannah Arendt's critique of Marxism has a certain relevance here. By defining man as laborer, she argues, Marx overlooked the specific place of action in the world-building process.[12] When we collapse action into labor, we easily omit reflection on action and leave undeveloped, in theory and in practice, the place of political power. Humans are indeed subjects of their society, but the question is whether they exercise their responsibility through labor or through labor and action? This question raised by *Laborem exercens* demands clarification.

Another difficulty raised by *Laborem exercens*, a difficulty present in Marxism as well, has to do with human dignity. Should human dignity be understood as derivative of labor? Or should one argue that human dignity is a spiritual element, independent of labor, rooted in the metaphysical status of the human being? If we follow the second proposal, it would be better to say that people create their world through labor and recognition. The condition of human survival includes material things and honor, "bread and roses," as it says in the celebrated song. Development projects in third world countries often produce few results because they are based on a scientific theory taking for granted that people's needs are essentially material while in many cases it is respect and identity that are equally or even more important to people. But if we admit this, are we still in the "materialist" perspective of the encyclical? The author of the encyclical might argue that the recognition of human dignity is implicit in the laboring process. For if dignity is not respected, an economic system cannot draw upon the cooperation of people and hence remains intrinsically unstable and defective.

The great advantage of the social theory proposed in *La-*

borem exercens is that work in its subjective reality is understood as culture. Work is the process through which people become intelligent, learn to cooperate, have their character formed and their virtues developed. Work shapes human consciousness. Such a theory offers a profound critique of the present organization of labor which socializes people into competition, fear, excessive ambition and other vices. These attitudes translate themselves into the political order as national rivalries and struggles between empires that threaten the survival of humankind. If *Laborem exercens* is correct, this dangerous situation cannot be overcome by appealing to people's moral sense, by preaching to them or by other idealistic proposals. The only power that can change this perilous situation is a change of the infrastructure, a change in the organization of labor, a restructuring of the productive process on a cooperative basis. Only the transformation of the economy will generate the ethical culture that enables people to live in harmony on the earth.

From this all too brief discussion we conclude that *Laborem exercens* has engaged in an extended, critical dialogue with Marxism. We noticed that the ideas taken from Marxism have in one way or another been transformed by the author. The notion of labor has been enriched by concentrating on its subjective meaning. The personalist approach taken by John Paul II allowed him to unfold the notion of work, all too easily reified, and bring to light its ethical and spiritual meaning. The notion of the worker as subject of production and subject of society has been significantly limited by theological considerations. People are subject because God has created them in the *imago Dei*. People are meant to be subjects of their collective histories. But the subject of history, in the universal sense, is God alone because only God has power over the dead. Furthermore *Laborem exercens* has de-ideologized the notion of class struggle. Instead of regarding the conflict between economic classes as a universal principle operative in world history, the encyclical uses this conflict as what Max Weber called an "ideal type," a heuristic device to guide observation, suggest analytical categories and detect historical causes. Even notions such as alienation and consumerism are used in the encyclical as "ideal types." They do not offer a scientific description of the present reality as it is; they point rather to powerful trends in society which become manifest with more or less intensity.

However we found that the encyclical's definition of human beings as workers raised certain difficulties. Has the author sufficiently transformed this concept? *Laborem exercens* insists that this is not the only definition of the human being. It offers a reason for choosing this definition in the present context. Since the key to the social turmoil of modern society is the issue of labor (n. 3), i.e., contradictions in the economic arrangements, the encyclical looks upon the human being as worker in the hope of coming to insights and conclusions that will be transformative, i.e., promote a practice favoring the overcoming of present injustices and imbalances.

This brief article has shown that the idea, sometimes even entertained by churchmen in high places, that dialogue with Marxism and the adoption of Marxist notions inevitably entail the swallowing of the whole Marxist system, if indeed there is such a thing, is incorrect. It certainly does not apply to John Paul II's dialogue with Marxism in his famous encyclical.

Notes

1. John Hellman, "John Paul II and the Personalist Movement," *Cross Currents*, 30 (Winter 1980-81), pp. 409–419.
2. John Paul II, Address to the UN Assembly, *Origins*, 9 (October 11, 1979) pp. 257–266, 264.
3. Cf. Pius XI, *Quadragesimo anno*, n. 65, *Seven Great Encyclicals*, Paulist Press, New York, 1963, p. 144.
4. References to *Laborem exercens* in this article give the number of the paragraph in question. For a presentation of the text and a more detailed commentary, see G. Baum, *The Priority of Labor*, Paulist Press, New York, 1982.
5. See G. Baum, "Labor Pope in Canada," in this volume, pp. 99–101.
6. "Economic Justice for All: Catholic Social Teaching and the

U.S. Economy," *Origins,* 16 (Nov. 27, 1986), nn. 79–80, p. 420.
7. Ibid, n. 71, p. 419.
8. Puebla Document, nn. 1134–1154, *Puebla and Beyond,* ed. J. Eagleson, Orbis Books, Maryknoll, N.Y., 1979, pp. 264–266.
9. Cf. G. Baum, D. Cameron, *Ethics and Economics,* Lorimer, Toronto, 1984, pp. 21–39.
10. "Ethical Reflections on the Economic Crisis," n. 1, G. Baum, D. Cameron, *op. cit.,* p. 4.
11. Cf. *Origins,* 12 (July 1, 1982), pp. 111–112.
12. Hannah Arendt, *The Human Condition,* Doubleday, New York, 1959.

4.
Toward a Canadian
Catholic Social Theory

This essay presents an analysis of the emerging social theory produced by the Canadian Catholic bishops and expressed by them in pastoral documents published over the years. The bishops have generated this theory in dialogue with church groups and centers in Canada. We shall examine principally six documents, "Sharing Daily Bread," 1974, (D1), "Northern Development: At What Cost," 1975, (D2), "From Words to Action," 1976, (D3), "A Society to be Transformed," 1976, (D4), "Unemployment: The Human Cost," 1980, (D5), and "Ethical Reflections on the Economic Crisis," 1983, (D6).[1] In addition to them we shall look at the handbook, *Witness to Justice,* prepared by the Social Affairs Committee of the Canadian Catholic Conference of Bishops as a teaching instrument for parishes and schools. This Canadian Catholic development has moved in a direction that has recently been confirmed by the pivotal papal encyclical, Pope John Paul II's *Laborem exercens* (1981). I have analyzed the social theory of this encyclical elsewhere.[2] Here I shall refer to it only occasionally as clarification and confirmation.

Solidarity with Society's Victims

In the Documents to be examined Canadian society appears fraught with conflicts and contradictions. "Many people agree that there is something wrong with the present social and economic order" (D3, n.3). "The maximization of consumption, profit and power has become the operative principle of this society" (D2, n.21). When looking at Canadian society the bishops focus their attention on the victims. In the corporatist imagination of past Catholic teaching, society appeared as an organic reality, the reform of which demanded the enhancement of this organicity through extended cooperation, the return to virtue and the recognition of the necessary hierarchies. In contrast with this, the newer Catholic teaching, influenced by the Latin American experience, has produced a conflictual imagination which makes people see in society first of all the victims, the structures of victimization, and the corresponding distortion of the totality.

To understand society we must stand in solidarity with its victims. The Documents deal with world hunger (D1), with Native Peoples (D2), with the unemployed (D5), and with the other victims of Canadian society. We are told that one of the first steps in the direction of social justice is "to listen to the victims of society" (D3, n.9). If we only talk to our friends, members of our own class, if we only follow the mass media, if we only read the articles by scholars who identify with their class, we cannot come to a valid collective self-understanding. It is the victims who reveal to us aspects of our own society that are hidden by mainstream culture.

This principle is given special attention in the bishops' statement on the economic crisis. Here we look at society from the viewpoint of the unemployed, the marginal, the powerless, the workers whose jobs have become insecure and whose wages decline in effective value. The statement uses a technical term derived from Latin American Church documents—the option for the poor (D6, s.1).[3] In the Document of the Puebla Bishops Conference (1979), this expression acquired a clearly defined sociopolitical meaning.[4] It means solidarity with the oppressed and the willingness to look at the whole of society from their point of view. The preferential option includes action and entry into a new consciousness. In the language of contemporary Catholic theology, the option is "a praxis": it begins with commitment, which in turn affects how reality is perceived, which in turn leads to further action, and so forth, the entire interaction aiming at the liberation of people from oppression.

This principle was confirmed in Pope John Paul II's encyclical *Laborem exercens* in a language chosen by himself. He wrote that the Church must call for "the solidarity *of* workers and *with* workers" (s.8). The Pope argues that "the dynamic element" of modern society is the struggle for social justice on the part of workers and the underprivileged, joined by all who love justice, which includes, or at least should include, the entire Christian Church.

In their statement on the economic crisis, the Canadian bishops call "the option for the poor" the first principle of their critical reflections. They look upon Canada through the eyes of the people at the base and in the margin, i.e., through the eyes of all those who suffer injustice. The bishops reject the economic policies that define Canadian society at this time because they place the burden of the present decline on the shoulders of the workers and unemployed, the low-income people, the powerless in society. The principle of solidarity which the bishops invoke demands preferential loyalty to the underprivileged and exploited, with a view to creating a society in which solidarity achieves truly universal dimensions:

> This option calls for economic policies which realize that the needs of the poor have priority over the wants of the rich; that the rights of the workers are more important than the maximization of profit; that the participation of the marginalized groups has precedence over the preservation of a system which excludes them (D6, s1).

This sentence reveals very clearly the shift from a corporatist to a conflictual social imagination.[5]

Who are the victims in Canadian society? In my own terminology they are the people at the base and in the margin. They are the workers, employed and unemployed; they are people on welfare, Native Peoples, immigrant groups, refugees, the handicapped, the neglected old, and so forth. We note that because among all these categories the percentage of women is very high, the greater burden is often placed on women. Among these classes, groups and peoples solidarity is not spontaneous. It is a peculiar note of Catholic social teaching that solidarity has to be created, and that this is largely a moral task. Solidarity is here motivated by a joining of collective self-interest and a commitment to social justice.

Why do workers belong among the victims of society, even if they are organized in unions, enjoy relative security and are paid reasonably well? To explain this we must turn to the second principle mentioned in the bishops' statement on the economic crisis—"the value and dignity of labor" (D6, s.1). The principle means that workers, because of the value and dignity of their labor, have the right to share in the decisions affecting the work process and the use of the product of their work. In previous Catholic social teaching this was sometimes referred to as "the workers' right to co-determination."[6] More recently, especially in John Paul II's *Laborem exercens,* it has been called "the priority of labor over capital." This means that workers, because of the value and dignity of labor, are co-responsible for the management of the industries and for the use to which capital and surplus value are put. Ultimately, workers are meant to be co-owners of the industries. Only as workers assume such responsibility will capital and profit be made "to serve labor," i.e., serve the laborers in the industry, the technical development of the industry, and eventually the laboring society as a whole.

The Canadian bishops invoke this principle several times in their statement on the economic crisis. Here we are interested in it simply as an explanation why, in the emerging Catholic social theory, workers are regarded as unjustly treated even when they are organized, reasonably secure and quite well paid. In capitalist (and communist) societies workers are excluded from co-determination. The anti-democratic nature of the capitalist (and communist) organization of production violates the value and dignity of labor. Workers are prevented from being co-responsible for production and the use of capital.

Since some Canadian critics, including several Liberal MPs, have accused the bishops' statement of being "Marxist," it is perhaps important to distinguish the Catholic position from that of classical Marxism (without examining the question whether there are not revisionist Marxist theories that resemble the newer Catholic social teaching). For Marx, the origin of exploitation resided in private ownership: the owner of the industry was able to appropriate the products produced by the workers. For Marx this was theft. According to the Catholic theory, it is not the ownership question that is central. Ownership may be private (even the newer Catholic social theory defends the right to private property) or it may be, in various ways, social and public. What counts in all these cases is the *use* of capital. How is profit employed? State ownership offers no guarantee that capital will be used to serve labor. Catholic social theory fears powerful state ownership as much as powerful private ownership. What counts is the co-responsibility of the workers and the community in determining the use of capital and profits. In the long run, according to John Paul II, the only guarantee society has that capital will be used in the service of labor is the eventual transition of private and state ownership into ownership by the workers.

Of primary importance, according to the emerging Catholic social theory, is the creation of solidarity *among* and *with* the various classes and groups at the base and in the margin of society. This solidarity is not generated by some inner necessity: it is not produced by the unfolding of a dialectic intrinsic to human history. Solidarity, we noted above, is always a moral creation. One dimension of this solidarity is the collective self-interest of the victimized classes and groups; at the same time the required solidarity also transcends their respective collective self-interest. Each group must make room for the aspirations of the others, even if the struggle of these others demands some sacrifices. For instance, in terms of collective self-interest, at least on a material basis, workers derive very little benefit from the justice struggle of the Native peoples. Their struggle may even become a burden to workers. The solidarity *of* and *with* victims, advocated in Catholic social theory, demands that collective self-interest be accompanied by a commitment to social justice. Middle-class people who join in solidarity with the groups at the base and in the margin are motivated by a similar combination of collective self-interest and moral commitment to justice. Since in the long run society will be destabilized and distorted if it represses the demands for justice on the part of the exploited, the collective self-interest of middle-class Canadians, even when they are in privileged positions, calls for solidarity with the groups at the base and in the margin. This commitment is aided and strengthened by moral conviction.

Before we continue to examine the moral dimension of solidarity, we note that according to the Documents the workers, and in fact labor unions, retain their place at the center of the justice struggle in society. We recall that Catholic social teaching has defended the workers' right to organize for almost a hundred years, beginning with Leo XIII's *Rerum novarum* (1891). The statement on the economic crisis has this to say about unions.

> Labor unions should be asked to play a more decisive and responsible role in developing strategies for economic recovery and employment. This requires the restoration of collective bargaining rights where they have been suspended, collaboration between unions and the unemployed and unorganized workers, and assurances that labor unions will have an effective role in developing economic policies (D6, s.1).

At the same time the bishops "are also aware of the limited perspectives and excessive demands of some labor unions." Labor unions are in a position of power because the workers thus organized are the producers of wealth. The bishops ask labor unions to recognize more clearly their role in the transformation of society, to reach out to the unemployed and unorganized, possibly helping them to organize, and to manifest their solidarity with the powerless and marginal groups in Canada and in the Third World. The bishops appeal here to the great moral tradition of the labor movement. If the sole purpose of unions is to enhance the terms of their own contracts, they deviate from the historical role of the labor movement as an agent for the transformation of society and solidarity with all the victims of the capitalist order.

Since the moral or spiritual dimension of solidarity is so important in the emerging Catholic social theory, we shall have to examine it more carefully. We note that this moral element may be supplied in a variety of ways. Religious people, be they Christian, Jewish, or members of other world faiths, will seek in their own traditions those elements that call for justice and solidarity. Many secular people derive this moral sense from a humanist or socialist tradition which they honor and with which they identify themselves. For others the moral dimension is drawn from the requirement of practical reason, that is, from the acknowledgement of reason as the faculty of humanity's self-liberation. Others leave their moral commitment almost totally inarticulate. Marxists in particular assume that socialist society is morally superior to capitalism and often allow this moral judgment to find expression in the indignation of their prose, but they rarely formalize the ethics implicit in their judgment and even more rarely use ethical reflection in their own reasoning. Marxists have paid a high price for their lack of ethical self-clarification.

We have noted above that the principle "the option for the poor" or "solidarity *of* and *with* the workers" has epistemological implications. Society can be correctly understood only if we study it from the perspective of its victims. To understand society in terms derived from the dominant culture entangles us hopelessly in ideology. More than that, social science itself is a reliable instrument of knowledge only if it is guided by a commitment to emancipation. In particular, there is the insistence that ethical reflection on economic theories and policies is indispensable. Many Canadians, including some economists, criticized the bishops' statement on the economic crisis (D6) because the bishops were not economists themselves. However, according to the bishops' statement, economic science always operates out of a set of values, and for this reason ethical reflection on economic policies is imperative. The dominant economics, the theories out of which the government tailors its economic policies, has implicit in it a concept of human nature, in fact a truncated concept of human nature, one which leads to policies that damage people on all levels of society. What is required, the statement insists, is an economic science and economic policies that operate out of a more appropriate concept of human nature. The commitment to emancipation, then, is not only a principle of action, it is also a principle of social and economic science.

This emphasis on the moral or spiritual dimension (in the emancipatory sense described above), implicit in the building of society and its own scientific self-understanding, is characteristic of emerging Catholic social theory. In this it differs strikingly from all that is summed up under the word "necessity" in Marxism. The solidarity of the people at the base and in the margin, grounded in people's respective collective self-interests, is at the same time a moral or spiritual achievement. We have here a stress on voluntarism that brings Catholic social theory, at this point, closer to Weber than to Marx. For Christians, I am prepared to argue, human history remains open: despite the strong trends built into economic systems and political institutions, society remains open to the new, the unexpected—for good and for evil. Thus society remains open to the influence of gifted persons who create solidarity among the people and initiate qualitative social transformation—and it remains open to wicked people capable of persuading others to engage in projects of domination. Christians believe, if I may use theological language, that history remains forever open to God's grace and human sin.

The option for the poor, or solidarity of workers and with workers, is at one and the same time an expression of material self-interest and a commitment to emancipatory values. Again it is Weber rather than Marx who sheds more light on the motivation out of which people, workers in particular, struggle for social transformation. Weber suggests that a movement for social change is more effective if it is nourished by a motivation that embraces several dimensions: *zweckrational* or pragmatic self-interest, *wertrational* or commitment to value, and some form of emotion, including religious sentiment. The call to solidarity made by Catholic social teaching is, therefore, not an idealistic strategy, idealistic here being used in the Marxist sense; it is on the contrary a political policy based on people's collective self-interest to better the conditions of their lives, joined to, and often carried by, a deeper passion, the commitment to emancipatory values—which for Christians are summed up in the crucified and risen Jesus.

Lest the above remarks be misunderstood, it is important to add immediately that the Documents which emphasize the moral dimension of solidarity, also communicate a good deal of suspicion in regard to traditional morality, including Christian values. The "option for the poor" calls for a conversion, a raising of consciousness, a de-coding of the values belonging to mainstream culture and middle-class Christianity. In one pastoral letter, the Canadian bishops ask Catholics to re-read the Scriptures to hear in them God's call to justice (D3, n.9). The Documents foster the suspicion that the cultural symbols and mainstream wisdom that have put their stamp on Canadian society disguise society's victims and make the present condition appear normal, appropriate, respectable, and if not perfect, at least thoroughly decent. In their statement on the economic crisis in particular, the bishops insist that there is nothing "normal" or "natural" in the present state of unemployment (D.6, s.5), that it is in fact a situation that must be called "sinful," a "moral disorder." The reason why so many Canadians do not realize the seriousness of the social and economic crisis is that they live in a culture of injustice.

It is for this reason that the bishops introduce the vision of an alternative society. They recommend alternative models of economic development (D6, s.5,6). They make use here of what Pope Paul VI called the power of utopia.[7] Because the inherited culture imprisons us in the here-and-now and simply makes us prolong this unjust present into the future, it is important to find an imaginative moral and scientific discourse, in a certain discontinuity with the present, that projects an alternative vision of society, one close enough to the as yet unrealized and unexplored possibilities of the present to generate political action.

From what we have seen so far, it is possible to conclude, I think, that the emerging Canadian Catholic social theory is not a theory in the classical sense at all: it is rather a critical theory, a method for engaging struggling workers and struggling groups of people in reflection and analysis so that they may define the strategy for a joint movement of emancipation and social reconstruction. With this emphasis on the lived experience of ordinary people, especially the marginal, the social theory might be understood by some as a form of populism. This would be a mistake.

Popular experience is of worth only if it has been mediated by the concept of justice. Experience and analysis are inseparable. The Documents presuppose throughout that human experience is never naked or immediate: it is always mediated through forms of the imagination and paradigms derived from theory. It is the yearning for justice, even if vaguely defined, with its thrust toward universality, that provides the medium for the experience of oppression and marginalization. The populist element in the Canadian bishops' social theory is the emphasis that ordinary people, initiated into concepts of justice, are able to come to a critical understanding of their own situation, move toward an analysis of the forces that make them suffer, and make a significant contribution to the movement that seeks to liberate them.

Crisis of Capitalism

Experience calls for analysis. The Documents insist that Christians must examine the structures of injustice and search for their historical causes (D3, n.9, D5, n.7). Only if we know these causes will we be able to engage ourselves in overcoming them. The Documents suggest, moreover, that in making this analysis people begin with the injustices they experience locally, in their own community (D5, n.15, D6, s.16). What are the structures of inferiorization at the place where we live? The analysis of these ills will inevitably lead to the identification of oppressive forces operative throughout the province, the nation, throughout the world. But only if we begin this analysis locally will we get a sense that the major forces of oppression, existing in stark and terrible visibility in some parts, also affect us where we live.

How can ordinary people engage in social analysis? Since they may not have the training to do this, the Documents provide Catholics with the essential elements for such an analysis. The Documents adopt the position that the social ills in Canadian society have to do with the changes going on in international capitalism.

> The present recession appears to be symptomatic of a much larger structural crisis in the international system of

capitalism. Observers point out that profound changes are
taking place in the structure of both capital and technology which are bound to have serious social impact on labor (D6, s.2).

Some of the pastoral documents describe this crisis in greater
detail. In the statements on unemployment and on the economic
crisis (D5, D6), the bishops look for the causes of unemployment
in Canada. They argue that it is important that we identify these
causes, for otherwise we are tempted to blame innocent people
for present unemployment, for instance immigrants, women, or
the workers themselves (D5, n.8). Unemployment is very largely
due to the changing structure of capital in Canada (D5, n.9, D6,
s.2,3). And how is capital being transformed? The two documents reply to this by listing a series of factors.

First there is the concentration of capital in ever larger corporations which allows the decisions regarding production and
resources to slip into the hands of an ever-shrinking elite. Then
there is the centralization of capital in the metropolitan area of
Canada, which produces regional disparity and areas of unemployment. We have Third World pockets right in Canada. Then
there is the internationalization of capital. This refers to the
growing ability of the large corporations to shift capital, machinery and units of production to other parts of the globe where
labor is cheap, workers are unorganized, and where, in many
instances, military governments prevent these workers from organizing. This new trend has led to the phenomenon of
de-industrialization in Canada and the United States. The documents then mention the high degree of foreign ownership of Canadian industries. The decisions regarding production are in
these instances made by boards outside the country, by people
who have no reason to be concerned about Canadian workers.
Another cause of unemployment mentioned in the documents is
one that has characterized the Canadian economy from the beginning, its almost exclusive reliance on export of natural resources rather than the manufacturing of finished products. This
trend, well documented in Canadian history, has received new
strength through the various mega-projects supported by the

government, aimed at the export of raw materials, which provide few jobs for Canadians and leave the country in a more dependent and less developed state. Finally, there is the important factor of the new technology. Under its impact the industries and their offices, including banks, are becoming increasingly capital-intensive, with devastating influence on unemployment.

Many of these factors are operative on the world scale. The Documents (D5, D6) argue that international capitalism is undergoing a qualitative change. The decisions affecting resources and production are increasingly made to protect and promote capital, even when this trend damages the well-being of the great majority. While under New Deal capitalism since World War II capitalists were willing to cooperate with government to foster the welfare state, at least to a certain degree, the new phase of capitalism introduces a new brutality. Governments become obliged to follow the lead of international capital and abandon the effort to protect their people. The consequences of this change, the bishops argue, "are likely to be permanent structural unemployment and increasing marginalization for a large segment of the population in Canada and other countries" (D6, s.2). The bishops maintain

> that through these structural changes, "capital" is re-asserted as the dominant organizing principle of economic life. This orientation directly contradicts the ethical principle that labor, not capital, must be given priority in the development of an economy based on justice (D6, s.2).

The new phase of capitalism ushers in a moral crisis of major proportions. "As long as technology and capital are not harnessed by society to serve basic human needs, they are likely to become the enemy rather than an ally in the development of peoples" (D6, s.3).

A similar analysis of the coming phase of capitalism is found in Pope John Paul II's *Laborem exercens*. The encyclical thinks of capitalism in three phases.[8] The first one, the entrepreneurial phase, based on privately owned companies and guided by a free enterprise ideology, created modern, industrial society. Here capital had been largely organized against labor. It was a period of great suffering for working people and the poor. The second phase of capitalism was based on corporate ownership and the cooperation of society (with its schools, its systems of transport and communication), guided by a New Deal ideology. Thanks to the pressure of the workers' movement and legislation by progressive governments, capitalism in this phase reconciled itself with the welfare state. The encyclical called this "neo-liberalism." Here capital was made to serve labor to a considerable degree, even though the workers themselves had as yet no direct responsibility for the industries in which they worked. The third phase of capitalism, which began with the expansion of the transnational corporations, threatens to dismantle the restraints which the previous phase had put on the rule of capital.

Beginning with Paul VI's *Populorum progressio* (1968), papal social teaching has focused on the danger of the new international, economic imperialism.[9] John Paul II underlined this line of thought. The transnationals have become so powerful that small nation-states can no longer defend the interests of their peoples; their power is such that they can even force the powerful nation-state, out of which they operate, to use political pressure and military threats to make the world safe for their business. *Laborem exercens* (n.8) foresees that the suffering, the burden of injustice, produced in this third phase will be more extensive than that caused by nineteenth-century capitalism. Yet as nineteenth-century economic oppression produced "a burst of solidarity" (n.8) that resulted in the labor movement, the Pope thinks that the new, more extensive form of economic oppression, will in turn produce "a burst of solidarity" and create a new movement to remake the world order.

The Canadian Paradox

The economic crisis in Canada is linked to the new trend of world capitalism. At the same time, the Documents also speak of the specifically Canadian elements of the economic decline. The handbook *Witness to Justice* refers to "the double paradox" of Canadian society.[10] The first paradox is that Canada is an industrial society with a technological development and standard of living comparable to the great industrial nations, while it is at the same time a country that contains extended regions of underdevelopment reflecting Third World conditions. The second Canadian paradox is that while Canadians like to think of themselves as junior partners in the economic empire (in fact, Canadian-based corporations operate in Third World countries, and the Canadian national psychology tends to identify with American interests), the Canadian economy itself has many features of Third World dependency.

The Documents repeatedly mention the high degree of foreign ownership and hence the dependent character of Canadian industrial development. More often the Documents apply the theory of dependency to analyze the structures of injustice in this country. Capitalism is seen as an economic system that creates metropolitan centers and corresponding hinterlands, where the centers enrich themselves at the expense of the outlying regions. According to the Documents the economic conditions that produce underdevelopment in Third World countries are also at work in the creation of underdevelopment in Canada. This is clearly stated in the pastoral, "On Northern Development" (D2, n.12). In a pastoral statement of the Catholic bishops in the Atlantic Provinces, entitled "To Establish a Kingdom of Justice" (1979),[11] the same theory of dependency is applied to explain the poverty of the Maritime provinces as well as certain cultural and psychological trends that have gained power over people's lives. Dependency has political consequences since it places great power in the hands of a small elite that mediates the connection to the metropolitan center; and it has a great influence on people's collective consciousness since it destroys their sense of self-reliance and trust in their own creativity. The "double paradox" is really a double pattern of dependency, a massive, many-levelled phenomenon that is largely disguised by mainstream culture. Commitment to social justice calls for a raising of consciousness in this regard.

In their statement of the economic crisis, the bishops draw a picture of the present economy, which in their judgement leads to moral disaster. The present policy, they say, puts emphasis on mega-projects aimed at exporting raw materials, even though this increases the national debt and creates only few jobs. The present trend is toward unrestricted conversion to high technology and hence toward ever more capital-intensive industries. The present policy favors foreign investment. Governments offer favorable conditions to new investors and existing industries to enhance their profit in the hope that the private sector will become the engine for Canada's economic recovery. The bishops think that this hope is illusory. "Even if companies recover and increase their profit margins, the additional revenues are likely to be reinvested in labor-saving technology, exported to other countries, or spent on market speculation or luxury goods" (D6, s.4).

According to the bishops' statement, the present economic policy leads to growing permanent unemployment: it threatens an increasing segment of the population with the loss of human dignity. What is needed, therefore, is an alternative approach, flowing from a new perspective that has not only a scientific but also a moral dimension. "An alternative approach calls for a new ordering of values and priorities in our economic life" (D6, s.5). Or again, to find alternative ways of looking at our industrial future and organizing our economy, we need "a fundamental reordering of the basic values and priorities of economic development" (D6, s.6). The alternative is formulated primarily in an ethical discourse, although it is not idealistic. The Documents do not advocate an ethical or utopian socialism that was mocked by Marx and Engels.[12] The bishops' call is not an ethical appeal to the nation, to rich and poor alike, to be converted to the principles of justice. It is, on the contrary, a moral discourse derived from the commitment to emancipation, and it is addressed to the sector of the population constituted by the solidarity of workers and with workers. The ethical reflections are intended to help generate a social movement that could become the agent of social reconstruction.

What is the alternative direction recommended by the bishops? Instead of mega-projects and increasing reliance on staple exports, the manufacturing sector of the economy should be developed, producing goods for use by Canadians. Instead of increasing foreign ownership, self-reliant industrial development

should be promoted. To overcome the concentration and centralization of capital, community ownership and/or community
control of the industries should be encouraged as well as new
forms of workers' management and ownership of the industries.
What is advocated here is not so much increased nationalization,
but the decentralization of capital. We shall return to this point
further on. The bishops recommend that Canada's labor-inten-
sive industries be saved. While it makes no sense to resist the
trend toward computer technology, it is dangerous to convert industry to the new technology without plans for the workers who
will lose their jobs. The bishops recommend the creation of an
appropriate industrial technology, one that takes into account
technological progress and the requirements of full employment.
The statement also suggests that greater efforts be made to develop renewable energy sources for Canadian industries. These
proposals are not intended as a definitive outline for an alternative model of economic development; they are rather proposals to foster a public debate on such models.

The Documents do not confine themselves to an analysis of
economic oppression, even though they make this their focal
point. They also recognize other forms of victimization in Canada, the subjugation of the Native Peoples, the marginalization
of non-white minorities, the neglect of the handicapped, the
aged, prisoners, and other groups in the margin. In many instances, these forms of injustice are linked to economic exploitation. Because in our society human beings are honored in
accordance with their economic productivity, people without
jobs are regarded as persons below the norm and hence little attention is paid to them. But the solidarity *of* and *with* the workers
includes these people. The Documents are perhaps not sufficiently sensitive to the woman's movement.

The Canadian Catholic bishops have repeatedly recognized
the peoplehood of French Canadians.[13] The bishops of Quebec
have written an important pastoral letter in which they defend
Quebec's right to self-determination.[14] But neither they nor the
Canadian bishops as a whole have tried to tell the Quebec people
how to respond to the project of sovereignty-association. In their
pastoral letter, the Quebec bishops insisted that the future of

Quebec must be decided by Quebec people themselves—the French majority as well as the Native Peoples, the English who have long been established there, and the more recent immigrants. Movements of national self-determination are acceptable from a Catholic point of view, the bishops write, only if they are not accompanied by a political ideology of national superiority and if they are effectively restrained by a commitment to respect the civil rights of the minorities.

Critical Social Theory

The emerging Catholic social theory adopts a conflict approach to the understanding of Canadian society. It regards as the dynamic element of society the movement of solidarity created by the workers and with them by all groups suffering injustice, joined by all citizens who love justice, a movement aimed at creating a society free of domination. The theory appeals to the experience of the various peoples, classes and groups that suffer under dominating structures. It proposes paradigms for interpreting these experiences, and it initiates the new members of the movement into a set of analytical tools that will allow them to link their local experience of injustice to the economic forces that define Canadian society and its relation to Third World countries. The theory is carried by an alternative vision of Canadian society, a utopia in the sense of Paul VI, which stands in judgement over the present order, reveals the ideological distortions of mainstream culture, and strengthens people's commitment to the movement of solidarity.

At the same time, the social theory remains incomplete. While it identifies the historical agent of social change, it does not indicate the manner in which this movement might transform the existing order. One reason for this, I think, is that this Catholic social theory, while reflecting the experience of grassroots organizations, has been formulated by bishops, by men whose high office in the Church prevents them from entering more directly into Canadian politics. The Documents are written in such a way that they allow several readings, in particular a reformist and a more radical one (cf. D4, n.18). Some Catholics committed to social justice think they follow the new Catholic teaching when they become engaged in the more or less established ways of political and social reform, while other Catholics, following a more radical reading, become more restless, more troubled, and more demanding. They involve themselves in struggles around particular issues, they join one or several action groups, they work in a political party if they detect in it radical possibilities, but their deeper political intention is the creation of a movement of solidarity, possibly through and around a political party, that aims at the transcendence of capitalism.

It can be argued, I think, that the emerging Catholic social theory is incomplete also for more profound reasons. By identifying the movement of solidarity as the agent of social change, the Documents leave to this movement the decisions regarding the way and the manner social change is to be brought about. The basic principle of the Canadian approach was formulated by Cardinal George Flahiff, Archbishop of Winnipeg, in his speech at the 1971 Synod of Bishops:

> I suggest that, henceforth, our basic principle must be: only knowledge gained through participation is valid in the area of justice. True knowledge can only be gained through concern and solidarity. . . . Unless we are in solidarity with the people who are poor, marginal, or isolated we cannot even speak effectively about their problems. Theoretical knowledge is indispensable, but it is partial and limited. When it abstracts from lived, concrete experience, it merely projects the present into the future.[15]

Because this principle has been observed, it is possible to speak of a Canadian Catholic social theory, different in emphasis and tone from Catholic social theories worked out elsewhere. At the same time, because of this principle, the Documents offer a social theory that is incomplete precisely because it is a critical theory (rather than a theory in the classical sense),[16] one that is guided by a concrete utopia, that initiates people into the critique of the existing order, that encourages solidarity among workers and other groups struggling for justice, and fosters solidarity with workers by all who share an emancipatory ethics, a theory, in other words, that defines an approach, a style or reflection, a method. It offers theoretical grounds for a movement of solidarity, but then remains open to the political ideas that such a movement will generate. Catholic social theory will then apply the same critical method to test the new ideas, retaining its focus on the ethical, spiritual, emancipatory dimension of the social struggle.

A number of Canadian economists have made public pronouncements in support of the bishops' statement, in which they interpreted the bishops' social message simply as a condemnation of the government's monetary policies and a strong support for a return, possibly an enhanced return, to Keynesian economics. They think, therefore, that the critics have been needlessly hard on the bishops: their statement had nothing to do with socialism. This interpretation is not totally convincing. It is true, a certain intended ambiguity allows the statement to be read both in a reformist and a more radical way; but if all it recommends is the return to Keynesian economics, one does not see the need for the emphasis on "the option for the poor" and the creation of a workers' movement of solidarity as agent of social change. The thrust of the statement points to a more drastic transformation of the Canadian economy. How else can one interpret the call for workers' management and ownership of Canadian industries?

While industrial strategy recommended in the statement calls for intelligent economic planning, we noticed that no mention was made of the nationalization of the industries. Since Pius XI's *Quadragesimo anno* (1931), Catholic social teaching has acknowledged the need for nationalization. According to this encyclical (n. 114), nationalization is necessary whenever private ownership puts so much power into the hands of an elite that governments can no longer protect and foster the common good. Yet the call for extended state ownership is not without its dangers. First, nationalization offers no guarantee that the industries will be used in the service of the laboring people. This point is made very forcefully in Pope John Paul II's *Laborem exercens* (n. 14). Extended state ownership, moreover, puts excessive power in the hands of the government. Pluralism and freedom thrive in society only if they are inscribed in the economic infrastructure. Without a certain economic pluralism, the praise of freedom and democracy is purely idealistic. Ideas are powerful only if they are carried by infrastructural requirements. For this reason, Catholic social theory calls for the decentralization of capital. According to the Documents, the necessary centralizing trend, the growing need for responsible and democratically controlled economic planning, must be counter-balanced by a decentralizing trend, the cutting down to size of the giant transnational corporations. In this context the Documents recommend various forms of community ownership and workers' ownership of the industries (D5, n.14, D6, s.6). The tension between centralizing planning and decentralizing social ownership promotes creativity and political freedom.

The bishops' social teaching is in continuity with the Canadian political tradition. The Cooperative Commonwealth Federation (CCF), founded in Regina in 1933, the Canadian equivalent of the British Labour Party, proposed a form of social democracy that from the beginning embraced the cooperative movement and cooperative principles. In the Regina Manifesto the CCF committed itself to the promotion of cooperative ownership. The fear of a powerful centralized state bureaucracy made the early CCF advocate various forms of social ownership, some federal, some provincial, some regional or local, and some cooperative. The CCF also wished to balance the centralizing trend of economic planning with a de-centralizing trend derived from the pluralism of social ownership.

In this context it is of interest to recall that socialism advocated by the CCF retained a particular ethical tone.[17] It clearly distinguished itself from so-called "scientific socialism" with its positivistic presuppositions. The CCF had been created by the union of several radical movements in Canada, including a strong influence of the Social Gospel, especially in the Prairie provinces. Emancipatory ethics remained an abiding principle in the CCF, which its leaders were not ashamed to invoke in their speeches. From this view, there is a good deal of similarity between the emerging Catholic social theory and the old CCF socialism.

Notes

1. The five documents, D2 to D6, are reprinted in G. Baum, D. Cameron, *Ethics and Economics, Canada's Catholic Bishops on the Economic Crisis* (Toronto: Lorimer, 1984).
2. G. Baum, *The Priority of Labor* (New York: Paulist Press, 1982).
3. Since D6 is not divided into numbered paragraphs, I shall number the subtitles, s1 to s6, and use them in my references.
4. For an account of the option for the poor, see the Final Document (nn 1134–40) of the Puebla Conference, in *Puebla and Beyond*, ed. J. Eagleson, P. Scharper (Maryknoll, N.Y.: Orbis Books, 1979), p. 264.
5. This controversial sentence was repeated and expanded by Pope John Paul II on his Canadian visit in 1984. Cf G. Baum, "Labor Pope in Canada," in this volume, pp. 88–103.
6. *Quadragesimo anno*, n. 65; *Mater et magistra*, nn. 91–103. For a collection of recent papal documents see J. Gremillion, ed., *The Gospel of Peace and Justice* (Maryknoll, N.Y.: Orbis Books, 1975).
7. In his *Octogesima adveniens* (1971), n. 37, Paul VI borrowed from Ernst Bloch and applied to Catholic social teaching the radical notion of 'utopia.' Cf. G. Baum, "Faith and Liberation: Developments Since Vatican II," in this volume, p. 18.
8. *Laborem exercens*, nn. 1 and 11.
9. For an analysis see J. Gremillion, ed., *op. cit.*, pp. 23–27.
10. *Witness to Justice*, Social Affairs Committee, Canadian Catholic Conference of Bishops, Ottawa, Canada, 1979, pp. 19–20.
11. Cf. John Williams, *Canadian Churches and Social Justice* (Toronto: Lorimer, 1984) pp. 77–87.
12. See C. Wright Mills, *The Marxists* (New York: Dell Publishing Company, 1962) pp. 72–80.
13. Cf. "A letter on the 100th Anniversary of Confederation," 1967.
14. "The People of Quebec and its Political Future," in John William, *op. cit.*, pp. 181–188.
15. Cardinal Flahiff's speech is published in the booklet, "Witness

to Justice," Canadian Catholic Organization for Development and Peace, no date, pp. 1–3.
16. Cf. Max Horkheimer, *Critical Theory,* (New York: Herder & Herder, 1972) pp. 188–243.
17. G. Baum, *Catholics and Canadian Socialism* (Toronto: Lorimer, 1980 and New York: Paulist Press, 1981) pp. 76–80.

5.
John Paul II's
Social Teaching in Canada

John Paul II's visit to Canada in September 1984 was a major religious and cultural event that affected the entire country. Because of his image as a conservative churchman, many Catholics were worried about his coming. Of course, they did not expect the Pope to change his mind on sexual ethics, women's ordination, priestly celibacy and democracy in the church. But would he come as the Pope of Vatican II? Would he promote the Church's renewal? Or would he utter warnings that would paralyze pastoral action? More importantly, would he support the Canadian bishops in their bold social teachings, worked out ecumenically over the last decade and crystallized in their 1983 message, "Ethical Reflections on the Economic Crisis"? This message had provoked a nationwide debate. One person who refused to support it was Cardinal Emmet Carter, archbishop of Toronto. Serious opposition came from government circles, the traditional political parties, the business community, the editorials of some newspapers, and economists of the mainstream. Where would the Pope stand?

Impact on Canada

In his very first talk in Quebec City, on his arrival, John Paul II presented himself as the Pope of Vatican II. He greeted the peoples of Canada, the native peoples, the French, the British, the later immigrants; he addressed the Catholic community, the Protestants, the Jews, members of other religions, and secular Canadians. He had come to Canada not to convert them to Catholicism, but to promote friendship and justice. John Paul II accepted our pluralistic society. He tried to formulate, in line with his encyclicals and in dialogue with contemporary theology, the Church's mission in this new context. In today's world the Church's mediation of the Gospel includes the promotion of the human, the demand for human rights, the call for social justice, and the dedication to peacemaking.

Millions of Canadians heard this message. The local churches received the Pope enthusiastically. Celebration followed celebration, generating an atmosphere that was both reverent and gay, expressive of inward peace and bursting with energy for action. Even thoughtful and critical people were greatly impressed by the mass demonstrations. What made the Pope so appealing, even to people who were not Catholic, even when they did not share some of his ethical positions, was—in my opinion—a peculiar twofold spiritual talent. He was a man whose faith in Christ made him trusting and cheerful, despite the great suffering he has seen; and at the same time he was the man who respected the consciences of others and came as a friend and lover of justice. Canadians admired the stillness in his personality: they felt united to him, and accepted by him, even when they disagreed with some of the points he made. Some Catholics were unhappy, it is true, because the Pope does not extend the same respect of consciences to dissident Catholics. But even many of them were won over by his powerful preaching of "the good news to the poor" (Lk 4:18).

This article will not attempt to analyze the twelve day visit of John Paul II, nor to summarize the teaching he proposed in his sermons and speeches. One unexpected impact of the papal visit was the creation of a new, more autonomous self-understanding of the Canadian Catholic Church. Since the Canadian Broadcasting Corporation televised the entire tour with artistic perfection, accompanied by intelligent commentary, and since each local church involved the Pope in imaginative, colorful celebra-

tions reflecting local styles and local problems, Catholics gained
a strong sense of being the "Canadian Church." The term was
hardly used before; now it is on everyone's lips. Since Canada is
a country without a strong sense of national identity, since we
have regional loyalties without much awareness of what the entire country is like, the papal visit, brilliantly televised, helped to
create a recognition of Canada's plural structure as well as its
cohesion. Canadians who were not Catholics shared this feeling.
Everything took place in French and English. People were getting
a sense that if it is unilingual, it is not Canadian.

The Pope gave loud public recognition to the native peoples.
He addressed three groups in different parts of the country. He
honored their culture and their religious tradition; he regretted
that the earlier missionaries had tried to wipe out their religious
customs; he supported the native people's present effort of self-
government. Who else in this country has ever given the native
peoples such visibility? For this alone, the papal visit was an important event in Canadian history. The Pope's speeches to the
Amerindians, especially the words that honored their religious
and ethical heritage and encouraged the idea of integrating these
values into the Christian life, had a significance far beyond Canada, especially since there has recently been some ecclesiastical
opposition to the "enculturation" of Catholic worship in non-
European traditions.

The Pope also greeted the more recent immigrants and their
children, speaking to them in their own language. He hoped that
Canadian pluralism—the bi-national character of the country
and the multi-cultural reality—if lived courageously and imaginatively, could offer the world a creative vision of society. Few
people in Canada can say such things with authority.

Before we come to the Pope's social teaching, two preliminary remarks are necessary, one doctrinal and the other historical. The Pope grounded his call to justice in his Christology.
Every sermon of his contained a social message. He never spoke
of God and Jesus Christ without drawing attention to the impact
of dogma on society. In line with his first encyclical, *Redemptor
hominis,* John Paul II presented a "transformist" Christology.
The self-revelation of God in Jesus Christ is for the Pope a dis-

closure of the divine mystery and at the same time an illumination of our ambiguous human reality and a thrust forward toward its transformation. Divine revelation illumines and transforms the world. Every encounter with God leaves us changed. John Paul II strengthened here the teaching of Vatican II that in Jesus is made manifest, in a definitive manner, God's design to transform the historical reality of men and women and to make humanity more authentically human. According to *Redemptor hominis,* this action includes the transformation of economic, political and social structures. For the Pope, dogma serves the humanization of the world. Christ's resurrection has transformist meaning for present history.

This is not, we note, "conservative" theology. The transcendent divine mystery is seen as mercifully present in people's historical struggle to become more human. There is no hint of a sacralist vision, according to which God's grace creates colonies of holiness, unrelated to people's earthly wrestling for justice and truth. The otherness of God includes God's making the world other. At the same time, John Paul does not pursue a monopolistic vision, according to which the entire humanity is destined to become Christian and human reconciliation in peace and justice can take place only within the Catholic Church. John Paul II acknowledges a pluralist world, with several religions, all of which he honors, and with several ethical traditions, from all of which he expects contributions to the building of a world more in keeping with the Creator's will. The Pope tries to find ways of preaching his transformist Christology in a manner that invites dialogue and cooperation with non-Christian people.

Ecumenism

The second preliminary remark has to do with the orientation of Catholic social teaching in Canada. Since the early 1970's, the Catholic Church has joined the other Christian churches in creating an ecumenical approach to social justice ministry. The churches established several inter-church committees with clearly defined tasks of research, action and public education. The churches also cooperated in the writing of reports on social justice in Canada, which were jointly submitted to the federal government. The social justice statements of one church were usually supported by leaders of the other churches. When the Canadian bishops published their controversial "Ethical Reflections," making more concrete the social message they had published over the last decade, they were supported by the leaders of the other churches.

In Canada, ecumenism and social justice have gone hand in hand in an altogether unique way. For Protestants this meant the return of the social gospel, possibly in a new key, and for Catholics it meant the emergence of a new orientation, influenced by developments in Canada and by ecclesiastical teaching coming from Latin America supported by the synods of bishops held in Rome. The Canadian bishops' "Ethical Reflections," a provocative statement summarizing this new trend, produced an uproar in Canada because it expressed solidarity with workers, employed and unemployed, and criticized the present orientation of capitalism. How would the Pope address himself to this situation?

To give the papal visit an ecumenical tone, the Protestant and Anglican Churches were generous enough to cooperate with the president of the Canadian Conference of Catholic Bishops in composing a joint pastoral letter, addressed to all members of the major Canadian churches, which extended an ecumenical welcome to John Paul II and presented his visit as a public witness to the Christian Gospel in Canadian society. I do not know whether such a joint ecumenical welcome ever took place in other countries.

Catholics involved in ecumenism feared that the papal visit could become an occasion for Catholic triumphalism. The Pope's dramatic presence easily makes Protestant church leaders invisible, even at ecumenical gatherings where Christians pray together and shake hands. Catholic symbols easily exclude the rest of the world. How would John Paul II act in this situation?

In his speeches, Pope John Paul II praised the ecumenical movement. He fully endorsed Vatican II's "Decree on Ecumenism." He participated in several ecumenical services. During the ecumenical service at St. Paul's Anglican Church in Toronto the

Pope lauded the orientation of ecumenism in Canada, encouraged it to go forward in imaginative and as yet untried ways, and in particular recommended continued ecumenical cooperation in the Christian ministry of social justice. He blessed the work of the inter-church committees and hoped that they would continue their work, even though they have been criticized by many because of their bold positions. Economics is in need of ethical evaluation. Faith offers a critique of culture and society—this was one of the Pope's main themes on his Canadian tour.

At the ecumenical service in Toronto, John Paul mentioned some ethical principles according to which we must examine the existing social order: "The needs of the poor must take priority over the desires of the rich, the rights of workers over the maximization of profits, the preservation of the environment over uncontrolled industrial expansion, and production to meet social needs over production for military purposes."

This sentence quotes verbatim, and then expands, the most controversial phrase of the Canadian bishops' "Ethical Reflections" of 1983. The Pope here placed himself behind the bold approach of the Canadian bishops. The original sentence, derived in part from the writings of the American social theologian, David Hollenbach, was shaped by the Canadian bishops to express the meaning of the "preferential option for the poor" in a Canadian context. It represented the guiding line of the Canadian Catholic approach to social issues. And it was precisely this sentence that was regarded by many commentators as dangerous, divisive, and ideological.

In 1983 several Liberal members of parliament, churchgoing Catholics, published a joint statement which accused the Canadian bishops of following a Marxist orientation. By dividing society into rich and poor, powerful and powerless, owners and workers, the bishops were supposedly fomenting class struggle. In reality the opposition between rich and poor in church documents is drawn from the prophetic tradition of Old and New Testament. The new critique of capitalism contained in the more recent Catholic social theory, I have argued elsewhere, has been generated by an extended dialogue of traditional Catholic social teaching with biblical prophecy, the experience of oppressed people and Marxist social theory. At the same time, the more recent Catholic teaching has created its own independent orientation and its own original vocabulary. In his Toronto address, Pope John Paul fully supported the Canadian bishops in their preferential option for the poor.

While in his encyclicals John Paul does not use the expression "the preferential option for the poor", he has created his own vocabulary for it in his *Laborem exercens:* there he speaks of "the priority of labor over capital", "the solidarity of workers and with workers", and even "the solidarity of the poor supported by the solidarity of all who love justice". In Canada John Paul dramatized the option for the poor. He visited the retarded and handicapped in several homes, he addressed himself to the problem of unemployment, he supported workers in their struggle for justice, he expressed his solidarity with the native peoples, he urged a halt to the growing gap between the rich North and the poor South.

The Pope did not mention women in this context, except briefly once or twice. Since he does not (as yet) regard the women's movement as a justice issue, it would not surprise me if the Canadian bishops had asked him not to speak about women at all. The bishops themselves plan to engage in a dialogue that will lead to ethical reflections on women and the demands of justice.

The Priority of Labor

A second speech of special interest to us was given by the Pope to the fishermen at Flatrock, Newfoundland, among whom there was much unemployment and great malaise. Large corporations were taking over the fishing industries. Since they made use of sophisticated technology, the new companies undermined the trade which the fishermen of Newfoundland had exercised for generations. At this time the fishermen have appealed to the government for protection. John Paul supported them in this. These are the Pope's words: "Prolonged failure to find meaningful employment represents an affront to the dignity of the individual for which no social assistance can fully compensate. The human cost of such unemployment, especially the havoc it brings to family life, has frequently been deplored by the Canadian bishops. I join with them in appealing to those in positions of responsibility, and to all involved, to work together to find appropriate solutions to the problems at hand, including restructuring the economy, so that human needs will be put before mere financial gain."

The Pope made concrete reference to the problems of the fishermen: "The fishing industry has been concentrated more and more in the hands of fewer and fewer people. Around the globe, more and more small or family fishing concerns are losing their financial independence to the larger and capital-intensive enterprises. Large industrial fishing companies run the risk of losing contact with the fishermen and their personal and family needs. They are exposed to the temptation of responding only to the forces of the marketplace, thus lacking at times sufficient financial incentive to maintain production. Such a development would put the distribution of the world's food supply into ever greater jeopardy if food production becomes controlled by the profit motive of a few rather than by the needs of the many."

John Paul II is here criticizing two trends of unrestrained capitalism. The first trend is the increasing concentration of capital in ever larger corporations which leads to the control of the market, including the labor market, and undermines the organization of production in small units and the more human conditions of labor associated with them. In the age of high technology, unrestrained capitalism produces massive unemployment. Second, the Pope argues that free enterprise under contemporary conditions is not the appropriate system for the production and distribution of food. He here underlines a point made by the Canadian bishops in their message on world hunger (1974) in which they express their doubt that the free market is the appropriate system for the distribution of food. Why? Because the market distributes food only to those who have the ability to pay, while all people in God's creation have the right to eat. In his speech at Flatrock, the Pope said, "The responsible stewardship of all the earth's resources, and especially food, requires long-range planning at the different levels of government, in cooperation with industries and workers."

The Pope had the nerve to make special recommendations for the fisheries of Newfoundland. He asked for "courageous decisions to overcome the negative consequences". He recommended "the promotion of cooperatives of fishermen, collective agreements between workers and management, some form of joint ownership or partnership". For him, "these are some of the possible solutions that would aim at ensuring that the workers have a voice in the decision-making affecting their own lives and the lives of their families."

While the Pope's words at St. Paul's Anglican Church supported the Canadian bishops in their "preferential option for the poor", his words at Flatrock supported them in the second fundamental principle of the bishops' social teaching, "the value and dignity of labor". What does this principle say? It claims that the value and dignity of labor are such that they entitle workers to participate in the decisions regarding the work process and the use to which the capital they produce is being put. In *Laborem exercens* the Pope called this principle the priority of labor over capital. To teach these matters in Canada is bold.

Imperialistic Supremacy

The third speech important in our context was given at Edmonton, Alberta. Here the Pope spoke on the North-South conflict. "Understand me correctly," he said, departing from his manuscript, "not the East-West conflict, but the North-South conflict." Raising his voice in moral indignation, the Pope said that the North is becoming increasingly wealthy while the South gets poorer and poorer. "Poor people and poor nations—poor in different ways, not only lacking food, but also deprived of freedom and other human rights—will sit in judgment on those people who take these goods away from them, amassing to themselves the imperialistic monopoly of economic and political supremacy at the expense of others." Newspaper reports claimed that this was the only time John Paul II expressed anger in public. According to Stanley Oziewicz, writing for the *Toronto Globe and Mail*, "the Pope's hands were trembling in anger, his face contorted in steely Slavic determination and his voice so loud that it made the huge outdoor speakers vibrate".

What does the Pope mean by "imperialism"? Is he invoking Marxist-Leninist categories? Already Pope Pius XI, in an encyclical of 1931, written during the Depression, condemned what he called "the new imperialism of money". (*Quadragesimo anno*, n. 109). Pius XI argued that the free enterprise system had given way to monopoly capitalism which controlled the production and distribution of goods as well as the flow of money. In many cases even governments, Pius XI said, had to obey the dictates of monopolistic power. Pius XI called this "economic dictatorship". He spoke of "the new imperialism of money", contrasting it with the older political imperialism of the colonial age.

John Paul II picked up this repudiation of imperialism. He mentioned it in his first encyclical, *Redemptor hominis,* in connection with other evils such as neo-colonialism and economic exploitation. In Edmonton he interpreted the North-South conflict in terms of imperialism and supremacy. This interpretation supported the Latin American bishops who at their conferences of Medellin (1968) and Puebla (1979) had used a form of dependency theory to account for the misery, poverty and powerlessness of their continent. Latin American economic decline is related to the economic progress of the industralized world. The gap between the poverty of the South and the wealth of the North is growing. That is why, according to John Paul II, the poor of the third world will sit in judgment on the wealthy first world. God is on the side of Lazarus against the rich man. The Pope threatens the center of the capitalist world with the wrath of God.

The Pope's reference to "economic and political supremacy" makes his condemnation more precise. It points to the two superpowers, in particular to the supremacy which the U.S. government claims over Latin America and beyond. Economic supremacy is exercised by transnational corporations, and political supremacy is exercised by the U.S. government when it protects the transnationals and intervenes in the affairs of Latin American societies and beyond with methods that include violence, the sale of arms, financial aid to right-wing groups, secret action of CIA agents, support for terrorists, and so forth. Political supremacy also describes Soviet domination of the Eastern European bloc. But in Edmonton speaking so close to the American border, the Pope addressed himself to the relation between first and third world.

Why did the Pope choose his Canadian trip to make this strong statement? The bold social teachings of the Canadian bishops have not used this radical terminology. Was this utterance a message to the Catholic bishops of the United States who were then putting the finishing touches on the first draft of the statement on the American economy? Did he offer them a strong sentence which he would like to see quoted and explained in their statement? Or was his declaration a response to Cardinal Ratzinger's Instruction sent to Latin America, warning against the excesses of liberation theology?

The Catholic Church, including the Vatican, is still wrestling with the proper Christian response to the struggles of the third world. Sometimes a cautious trend is allowed to express itself, and at other times a more radical current is given official recognition. The 1984 Vatican Instruction was excessively cautious. While it affirmed the validity of a liberation theology, clearly admitted that the Scriptures reveal God's promises to include liberation from economic and political oppression, and recognized the brutal nature of economic exploitation in Latin America, the Instruction laid the main emphasis on warning Latin American Catholics of the dangers of liberation theologies that were "excessively reliant" on Marxist concepts. Thomas Sheehan, writing in the *New York Times* (Sept. 16, 1984) called the Instruction "insidious". "The Vatican document grossly overestimates the importance of Marxist analysis in liberation theology. It also claims, quite dubiously, that the use of Marxist concepts—particularly that of class conflict—to analyze a given social situation necessarily entails swallowing the entire Marxist theory and practice. Such a straw-man attribution is an old tactic of the Vatican Curia. It consists in creating a heresy on paper, wrongly attributing it to selected theologians and then condemning them for positions they have never held."

When John Paul II was in Halifax, Nova Scotia, he seemed

to offer a defense of liberation theology. "Development and liberation have a place in the Church's mission," he said, "as long as the spiritual message remains at the center." At Edmonton, in the words quoted above, he offered his own adaptation of Marxist social analysis to the understanding of the North-South conflict. The Pope uttered a threat—as no Marxist could—to the power elite of the developed world. By invoking the New Testament parable of Lazarus and the rich man, John Paul warned the power elite, and all of us who are comfortable in the rich world, that we risk our eternal salvation.

Cultural Oppression

Perhaps even more important for Catholic social theory than the sentences uttered at Toronto, Flatrock and Edmonton was a theme to which John Paul returned many times, the faith-born critique of Canadian culture. While third world countries suffer primarily from economic oppression, developed countries like Canada are not subject to economic oppression in the same way. It is true that we suffer from mass unemployment and have growing pockets of poverty, but the principal oppression we experience is cultural. John Paul insisted that faith, Christian faith, illuminates culture: it brings out its dehumanizing impact as well as its humanizing potential. He warned us against three trends in the dominant culture. The principal damage is done by "consumerism". The Pope here adapted in a Catholic theological context the Marxist concept of "commodity fetishism". According to the Pope, we live in a culture, created largely by market forces, that makes us into consumers: we tend to define ourselves in terms of the goods we possess or consume. We become individualists and utilitarians, even when we claim belief in God. For everything has a price now. The exchange value crowds out the great moral values of loyalty, dedication, love and justice. Life is ruled by the logic of the market. We no longer conceive society as a joint project, in which we all cooperate and for which we are collectively responsible; instead we see society as a market system, a taken-for-granted given, in which each tries to get the most.

    This culture oppresses us because it makes us powerless to

overcome unemployment and other social ills from which we suffer. We have lost social solidarity and political will. We have lost the sense that we belong to one another and that we must assume joint responsibility for our future. We have become seekers of personal satisfaction in a world that increasingly deprives the majority of people of this satisfaction. This cultural captivity is made worse through two further trends: temptations offered by technology and surrender to idolatry.

Following his encyclicals, the Pope strongly affirmed technology as an ally of human beings, especially of workers, since it delivers them from drudgery. We are grateful to God for the human development of technology. But technology could become an enemy of humans. First, technology may be pursued and developed simply for its own sake. It may come to be regarded as the privileged mode of action by which people try to solve the problems of their society. Technology may become the metaphor of human existence; we then begin to understand ourselves in scientific terms alone, think of society as an apparatus which we have to manipulate, and detach ourselves from the ethical human quest. The disappearance of ethical reflections from public policy and economic expansion constitutes a threat to human well-being.

The second temptation offered by technology is one that would tie it "to the logic of profit and constant economic expansion without due regard for the rights of workers or the needs of the poor and helpless". The Pope here again supports the Canadian bishops who have insisted in their "Ethical Reflections" that conversion to high technology of factories and offices is ethical only if it is accompanied by plans for new employment of the workers. The Pope stresses here the need of critical reflection on the relation of technology and capitalism. The third temptation offered by technology is that it becomes "linked to the pursuit and maintenance of power, instead of serving as an instrument of freedom". Under this rubric the Pope repeatedly deplored that the technological help which the industrialized nations have extended to third world countries consisted mainly in the sale of arms and military technology.

Where shall we find the moral resources to resist these temptations? Since what these temptations offer us fits well into the consumer mentality into which we have been socialized, we tend to give in to them without even recognizing them.

There is, however, another dangerous trend. According to John Paul II human beings are incurably religious. Alive in us is a longing for total fulfillment, a desire to surrender ourselves to the absolute, a yearning for the truth that makes sense of it all. When this religious inclination is not steered in the direction of the true God, there is a danger that people will invest limited aspects of reality with absolute authority and make them into gods. As a consumer culture, we are especially vulnerable to idols. Money or power or personal gratification may become the supreme value in our lives.

In his encyclical *Laborem exercens,* the Pope presented an argument which he repeated on his Canadian tour. We are always tempted to interpret the real struggle in which we are engaged, for instance between labor and capital, in terms that claim universal validity. Theories that are helpful in a particular historical conflict become ideologies that claim absolute truth and universal applicability. The grave oppression which people suffer in many areas is not simply due to the contradictions in economic and political institutions, but also and especially to the ideologies, the absolute commitments, which guide their operation. Systems here become absolutes, false gods. Idolatry is the principal sin at work in imperialism, supremacy, political and economic oppression.

You have economic hardship and injustice in Canada, the Pope seemed to be saying, because you willingly endorse the economic order that produces these effects. One has the impression the Pope had read Antonio Gramsci. The present economic system is not imposed upon us by force, by the legislation of a powerful government; rather, it derives its stability from our consensus. The consumer mentality into which we have been socialized assumes that the present system is based on common sense and is the only possible reality.

The Pope's analysis of cultural oppression is the context for understanding his Puritanical view of human sexuality. For the Pope, sexuality in our society has become a consumer good. To the young people in Montreal he said, "Have the courage to resist the dealers in deception who make capital out of your hunger for happiness and who make you pay dearly for a moment of artificial paradise." Because sex is used in advertising, because the entertainment industries use sex to increase their profits, because the exchange value has affected our view of sexuality, people in our society tend to be excessively preoccupied with sex. The moral energy required for the reconstruction of society demands more self-discipline and self-sacrifice than we are accustomed to in the present culture.

While we may disagree with the Pope's view of sexuality, conceived almost exclusively in terms of procreation we do not want to reply to him too quickly. His Marxist critique of sex as commodity deserves honest reflection. Perhaps market values have gotten under our skin?

Yet John Paul did not deliver a message of despair! There are counter-forces in society. The Pope believes that the roots of our civilization are still alive. Many religious and cultural subcultures in Canada constitute counter-currents against the mainstream. They are still bearers of communal values. The Pope gave encouragement to all communities, be they religious, ethnic, or based on joint projects such as cooperatives. In his encyclical *Laborem exercens,* the Pope looked upon the labor movement as a counter-current, the bearer of communal values, the catalyst for social solidarity in society. John Paul II regards it as the particular task and mission of the Church to promote community, communicate symbols that bind people together, and awaken in all people a sense that they belong together, that they are one another's keeper, that they bear a joint responsibility for their future, and that a mystery of salvation is working itself out in their history.

The social teaching of the Canadian bishops put great emphasis on the creation of a movement of solidarity in Canada, built around the labor movement, yet reaching out to all the groups that suffer, the native peoples, the unemployed, the immigrants of color, but also the handicapped, the senior citizens neglected by society, the youth largely without job opportunities, and the women who in all these categories bear the greater burden. This movement must be joined by all who love justice, of whatever social class. Only such a movement could create an ethos of solidarity. If it succeeds in mobilizing the majority, such a solidarity movement could become the historical agent of radical social change.

Bibliographical note: For John Paul II's speeches delivered in Canada see *The Canadian Catholic Review*, 2(Oct., 1984)318–396. An excellent commentary on the papal visit is Dan Donovan's *A Lasting Impact: John Paul II in Canada*, Novalis, Ottawa, 1985. For the social teaching of the Canadian bishops see G. Baum, "Toward a Canadian Catholic Social Theory," in this volume, pp. 66–87.

6.
Liberation Theology Blessed

In the spring of 1986 the Vatican has given its blessing to liberation theology, provided it remains in dialogue with the entire Christian theological tradition. In a letter of April 9, 1986, addressed to the Brazilian bishops, a letter greatly applauded by them, Pope John Paul II approved of the critical socio-political positions adopted by the Brazilian hierarchy and praised liberation theology. "We are convinced, we and you, that the theology of liberation is opportune, useful and necessary." Yet this theology is faithful to the Christian tradition only if it preserves the primacy of the spiritual and sees itself as a new stage of Christian reflection, inspired by the struggle for justice and guided by the Church's social teaching.

A few weeks earlier, on March 22, the Congregation for the Doctrine of the Faith, had published a new Instruction, "On Christian Freedom and Liberation," signed by Cardinal Ratzinger, which elaborated in detail the kind of liberation theology that is receiving official blessing. This positive treatment of the theme of liberation had been promised in the previous Instruction, "On Certain Aspects of the Theology of Liberation" (August 6, 1984), the purpose of which was to warn Catholics of the dangers implicit in liberation theology. This Instruction was accompanied by repressive measures against Father Leonardo Boff, one of the most respected liberation theologians, influential among the Brazilian hierarchy.

The 1984 Instruction was not without its contradictions. In

a brief first part it recognized that the biblical promises proclaimed by the Church included the liberation of people from political, economic and cultural oppression. It recognized that the struggle for justice, which was one the characteristic "signs" of the present age, called for special theological reflection. In this context the Instruction warned against "an insufficiently critical use" of Marxism. Yet in the second and major part, we are offered warnings against the theology of liberation, because in certain of its phases it has entered into dialogue with Marxist thought. Relying on any element of Marxist thought is dangerous, we are told, because whether one likes it or not, such reliance necessarily leads to swallowing the whole of Marxism. In the second part, then, it appears that reprehensible is not only "an insufficiently critical use" of Marxism, but any use whatever. This was puzzling, especially since John Paul II, in his *Laborem exercens,* had engaged in such a fruitful, critical dialogue with Marxist social theory.

A New Instruction

The new 1986 Instruction is a positive statement recognizing the divine promises of liberation. In its treatment of the topic it has chosen not to mention the terms liberation theology and Marxism, even though it constantly alludes to them. The Instruction offers a summary of the most recent teaching of the Church on salvation and emancipation, including the radical positions found in John Paul II's encyclicals. Thus we read, for instance, that "the right to private property is inconceivable without responsibilities to the common good. It is subordinated to the higher principle which states that goods are meant for all" (88).

Let me give another example. "Solidarity is a direct requirement of human and supernatural brotherhood. The serious socio-economic problems which occur today cannot be solved unless new fronts of solidarity are created: solidarity of the poor among themselves, solidarity with the poor to which the rich are called, solidarity among the workers and with the workers. Institutions and social organizations at different levels, as well as the state, must share in a general movement of solidarity" (89).

The 1986 Instruction has five chapters. The first deals with the Western history of freedom and the Church's response, the second treats people's divine vocation to freedom threatened as it is by the tragedy of sin, the third spells out the Christian meaning of liberation, the fourth deals with the Church's liberating mission, and the fifth summarizes the Church's contemporary social teaching as guide in the struggle for liberation. The Instruction makes a beautiful little book, ideal for the classroom. It has, nonetheless, its unresolved problems, which I shall mention further on.

The struggle for liberation is a sign of the times. It is an almost universal human aspiration. Christians must interpret this sign in the light of divine revelation. In fact, the contemporary understanding of God's message to us is inadequate if it does not shed light on this phenomenon. The Instruction puts the liberation struggle of third world peoples into the context of the Western history of freedom, beginning with Renaissance and Enlightenment. The freedom which people sought was not without ambiguity. The Instruction offers a critical analysis of the "liberal" idea of freedom, freedom of the individual to do as he pleases and shrug his shoulders in regard to society. The Instruction presents a more sympathetic picture of the "socialist" ideal of freedom, people's "shared freedom" (29): "A just social order offers people irreplaceable assistance in realizing their free personality" (32). People are free when they stand together in solidarity and rely on one another and their society to unfold their personal gifts and talents. However even this secular ideal was flawed, the Instruction argues, because it abstracted people from the deepest ground of freedom, which is God.

While the secular Enlightenment project has had certain undeniable success—the abolition of slavery, the affirmation of human rights, the overcoming of certain diseases—it also led to new forms of oppression. The massive crimes of the twentieth century, including genocide, remind us daily of the ambiguity of the emancipatory struggle. Secular people failed to understand the dividedness of the human heart. They regarded God as an obstacle to human autonomy. And because they did not grasp that true human freedom was found in dependence on, not in independence from, God, they allowed their social struggles to be taken over by the lust for power. Moreover, the reliance on science, technology, economic management and social engineering made the struggles for emancipation indifferent to ethical imperatives. People believed that the reconstruction of society was possible without the conversion of the heart. These are some of the reasons that the Instruction gives for the tragic failures of the modern project.

What is then the Christian approach? Should Christians turn their back on the modern effort to create a just society beyond man's domination of man? Here the Instruction offers a positive reply. The Christian Church must be critical of secular Enlightenment projects; but because of the divine destiny of human beings as free and self-determining children of God, Christians must affirm the historical struggle, make their own critical and positive contribution to it, and seek common action with others in the effort to create a more just society.

The liberation promised in the Bible is first of all liberation from sin and death. It is spiritual. It is so overwhelmingly powerful that nothing on earth, no prison and no injustice, can take it away from people. At the same time, because the human being is a spiritual-bodily unity and because God is graciously operative in human history, salvation has a temporal, political dimension. Salvation and emancipation are distinct, but united in the same history. The claims of liberation theology are fully justified. God is indeed on the side of the poor and oppressed. God calls people to stand in solidarity with the marginated in society. God summons people to reconstruct their society to bring it into greater conformity with social justice and social solidarity. But liberation theology becomes false teaching if it reduces the divine promises to the arrival of a purely earthly realm. The spiritual has primacy: but because the spiritual is incarnate, inserted into concrete history, it has an earthly, liberating, transforming thrust.

In my judgment Latin American liberation theology has always been faithful to the primacy of the spiritual. It has been conscious of the ambiguous nature of the struggle for freedom and therefore stressed the need for spiritual openness to God, and the commitment to an ethic of love of neighbor. Rumor has it that after reading Gustavo Gutierrez' *A Theology of Liberation*, Pope John Paul II said that he found nothing against Christian faith in the book.

Practical Consequences

On the practical level the Instruction summons Christians to join others in an effort to reconstruct society. Oppression, poverty, discrimination, racism, all the structures that put unjust burdens on people's shoulders, are against God's revealed will. While sin in its primary meaning refers to voluntary opposition to God's will, in a derived sense social structures and institutions are "sinful" when they transform a group or class of the population into victims (74-75). What is demanded is a political effort to change institutions, accompanied by spiritual commitment. For while the change of institutions is necessary for the reconstruction of society, it is not sufficient: requisite is also a change of heart.

struggle for justice takes place with ethical means. The Instruction argues against the illusory myth of revolution. Many revolutions have led to oppressive regimes. Christians prefer dialogue and the exercise of non-violent power. "The Church's magisterium admits recourse to armed struggle as a last resort to put an end to an obvious and prolonged tyranny which is gravely damaging the fundamental rights of individuals and the common good" (79). Because of the new technology of terror, including torture, recourse to armed struggle becomes problematic even in these extreme situations. The Instruction recommends that Christians explore new strategies of non-violent resistance.

How does the Instruction differ from Latin American liberation theology? I shall mention three points. First, the Instruction only offers a cultural analysis of modern society: it denounces principally the false values that modern societies have chosen. And because they have chosen false values, it is argued, these societies have become oppressive. Latin American liberation theology does not stop at the false values: it offers a critical analysis of the economic and political systems that oppress the

people and for this reason engages in an extended dialogue with
social science, including Marxism. Liberation theology is contextual and concrete. It names the plague. And it advocates a commitment to policies that try to overcome the plague. The Vatican
Instruction talks about injustice and oppression in general. Liberation theology in each place mentions them by name, and for
this reason makes so many enemies.

The second difference is related to the first. Liberation theology is fully aware that many of the beautiful Christian words
such as love, common good, unity, harmony and respect have
been used as an ideology to defend the existing unjust order. This
is true especially in traditional Christian cultures. What is needed
therefore is an extended ideology critique. Only after the ideological use of these words has been recognized and negated can
we draw upon Christian symbols in a joint struggle for an alternative society.

The Instruction seems unaware of the ideological deformation of the Christian vocabulary. This takes us to the third difference, possibly the deepest. The Instruction presents the
Church, the Catholic Church, as somehow superior to history,
and hence as essentially innocent. According to the Instruction
the Church has been faithful to God's revelation and God's summons in history all the time. Occasionally it is admitted that there
were Catholics who opposed liberty and human rights and that
occasionally certain policy decisions of the Church may have
been lacking in wisdom, but the Church as such has always been
in favor of freedom and justice. Again, at times the Instruction
admits that there has been a development of the moral conscience, especially in regard to human rights, the equality of men
and women, and the universal call to social participation, but the
Instruction does not analyze who promoted and who resisted this
evolution. There is no attempt to analyze the Church's historical
position in society, the concrete legal, economic and cultural conditions of its presence in society. And hence there is no repentance, no change of heart, no firm resolve to renewal.

In recent years ecclesiastical statements on liberation and social justice, produced by episcopal conferences in the third world
and in Western countries, have introduced, as a new and unpre-

cedented note, analytical, self-critical reflections accompanied by repentance. The document *Justitia in mundo,* promulgated by the 1971 Synod of Bishops, demands that the Church as a human institution recognize its own involvement in secular institutions and hence its possible participation in the injustices of society. At Puebla (1979) the Latin American bishops recommended "the self-evangelizing" of the Church: the Church, they said, must test its own institutional life to see if it accords with the ideals it proclaims. This note is still lacking in the declarations of the Roman Congregations.

Still, despite several unresolved problems, the new Instruction offers support for liberation theologians in Latin America and other parts of the world, including the bishops and the bishops' conferences that have opted for solidarity with the poor and powerless. There is good reason to be grateful.

II
Theology and Emancipation

7.
Liberation Theology and "The Supernatural"

At the meeting of the Association for the Sociology of Religion (ASR), held in Toronto in August 1981, the church in Latin America and liberation theology were repeatedly discussed by sociologists. Listening to the speakers I had the distinct impression that it is difficult for sociologists to understand theological language, just as it is often difficult for theologians to know what sociologists are talking about. In particular, since liberation theology uses certain terms derived from Marxist or neo-Marxist social theory and understands itself as oriented toward social revolution, it is easy for sociologists to get the impression that liberation theology is a form of radical social theory such as Marxism and that in its heart is a purely secular passion for justice, freedom and independence. What theologians call the *via negativa,* the critical negation of the inadequacies of the Christian tradition, including spirituality and the concept of divinity, is all too easily understood by social scientists as repudiation of the historical Christian faith. Liberation theologians in Latin America argue that secularization is a European and North American problem, not a Latin American one, and for this reason they confidently address themselves to an audience that regards itself as rooted in the Catholic faith. They feel no need, therefore, to spell out in detail the "supernatural" foundation of their theology, i.e., its foundation in God's self-revelation in human history culmi-

113

nating in Jesus Christ. One might wish to argue that liberation theologians overlook the advancing secularization of Latin America and that it is an illusion to take for granted that people are familiar with the content of the language of the Catholic tradition. But that is another matter. Since powerful institutions in Latin America and in North America, for reasons of their own, accuse the radical church groups in Latin America of being fronts of secular, subversive, Marxist or even Communist movements, it is important to clarify the nature of liberation theology and bring out its supernatural status. At the Toronto meeting of the ASR only one speaker expressed the view that liberation theology is a secular revolutionary theory in disguise. Yet even sociologists sympathetic to liberation theology often had the impression that this Latin American theology was simply a theory of action, with little or no interest in either prayer or doctrine.

Stimulated by the discussion at the ASR meeting, I wish to clarify in this article the theological positions shared by the great number of Latin American liberation theologians. These positions, as I see them, are also found in the political theology produced by German theologians, especially J.-B. Metz, J. Moltmann and D. Soelle. Needless to say, any attempt to clarify the foundations of a theory is an interpretation; it is therefore controversial and may itself be questioned by liberation theologians. We note that there are two kinds of debates regarding liberation theology, one of them, the more fruitful one, taking place among Christians committed to a liberationist perspective, and the other involving participants some of whom are for and some against liberation theology. This article situates itself in the first kind of debate. Here then are the positions I wish to present.

1. *The De-Privatization of the Christian Message.* Over the last decade many Christians have discovered that the Gospel has social meaning. More than that, they have become conscious that in the churches in which they grew up and in the theology taught at the seminaries the Christian message was understood almost exclusively as addressed to individuals, as dealing with personal life, even though the churches as social organizations had a location in society and exerted cultural and even political influence. But in preaching and theology, salvation meant personal salva-

tion, sin meant personal sin, and conversion and new life referred to what happened to individuals. This privatizing trend existed in much of pietism in both its Protestant and Catholic form; it often existed in neo-orthodoxy, especially in North America, and in the Protestant and Catholic theologies influenced by existentialism. Liberation theology in Latin America and political theology in Germany sought to recover the social dimension of the Christian message. God's word was addressed to persons and their societies. It was J.-B. Metz who made the notion of "deprivatization" central in German political theology. He and his colleagues formulated their arguments mainly against the pietistic presuppositions operative in the churches and the existentialist influence on the theological community. In Latin America the recovery of the social meaning of the Gospel took place through the religious experience of ordinary Christians committed to the struggle against injustice.

Christians engaged in the struggle against oppression, united in small communities, experienced the call of the Gospel in a new and startling manner. The biblical stories they had always known suddenly revealed a new meaning. They read the Bible in a new light. Even the celebration of the Eucharist communicated a sense of social solidarity they had not known before. They became convinced, without the help of theologians, that God's promises revealed in the Old Testament, and confirmed and extended in the New, were addressed to them as a struggling people. God was on their side, on the side of the poor, in their quest for justice and truth. They discovered, for instance, that the Eucharist was not simply spiritual food given to believers on their individual journeys. The Eucharist was the divine manna given to Israel on its way to the promised land; it was the renewal of the covenant involving the whole of the people; it was the festive meal creating community among the participants; it was the banquet where all had enough to eat and none were hungry, symbol of the society for which God had destined them; it was the divine pledge joining bread to the Spirit, making all bread a spiritual reality, and the quest for bread to feed hungry children a material struggle with a spiritual dimension; it was for them the presence of Jesus Christ, persecuted, crucified and now vindicated by God, as the passage or passover through which they themselves now had to move; it was the divine promise, sealed in the risen Lord, that God in the long run will not allow the murderers to triumph over the innocent victim. These and similar spiritual perceptions enabled these engaged Christians to "de-privatize" the Eucharist and the Christian message.

The entry into liberation theology was new religious experience out of a situation of social struggle. The de-privatizing of the Gospel, we note, does not try to reduce the personal to the social. Political and liberation theologians recognize that the personal and the social are irreducible poles in some tension; they try to clarify how the two poles are interdependent, and they study how the structures of society affect personal consciousness and in turn how at certain moments a new spiritual perception influences the making of society and the course of history. Liberation theology never identifies liberation with salvation. Instead it tries to clarify the mutual interrelation between them. Since the secular left, be it Marxist or non-Marxist, has so little to say about the personal, the existential, the intimate, the spiritual, liberation theologians believe that as Christians they should be able to make a special contribution to social theory.

The recovery of the social dimension in the Christian message has been fully accepted by the Catholic magisterium, at least on paper. The significant text marking a turning point in the Church's official teaching is in the document "Justice in the World" produced by the 1971 Synod of Bishops; here we are told that the redemption Jesus Christ has brought includes the liberation of people from oppression.

2. *The Preferential Option for the Poor.* Political and liberation theologians are very much aware that any attempt to understand a society moves along a particular value perspective. There is no total objectivity in historical matters. If we compare American and Canadian history books used in high schools and colleges we find that the historical events that affected both countries are described quite differently. The American books take for granted that the American Revolution was a good thing, while the Canadian books are interested in the historical factors that have shaped the Canadian political and social reality. Is there a

specifically Christian way of looking at society? Does Christian
faith affect the way we read the social reality to which we belong?
Liberation theology answers these questions in the affirmative.
Christians must try to understand their society from the viewpoint of the poor, of the little people, the marginals, the outcasts,
the oppressed. Liberation theologians argue that it is impossible
to look at one's own society from a neutral position. Either historians or social thinkers choose a perspective from which they
examine society, or they adopt, possibly without knowing it, the
perspective of the social class or social group to which they belong. The claim to perfect neutrality usually means that social
thinkers have not brought to full consciousness their own axio-
logical presuppositions.

When theologians argue in this manner, they realize of
course that they are joining a classical controversy in the social
sciences. Is sociological research ever value-neutral? When liberation theologians defend their view on the relation between science and commitment, they are well aware that their position is
not only defended by left-wing sociologists, Marxist or non-
Marxist, but also by sociologists who have not been influenced
by Marxism, by scholars as diverse as Dilthey, Troeltsch and Weber. Weber himself, who strongly defended the value-free nature
of formal reason and hence of methods, procedures and demonstrations in the social sciences, recognized at the same time
that every social science project is undertaken from a value perspective, which, according to Weber, is freely chosen by the sociologist. Weber's value-neutral social science had nonetheless a
voluntarist basis. The reason for making these remarks is to refute the arguments sometimes proposed that the intimate connection between science and commitment is a Marxist position
and that anyone who accepts it, such as liberation theologians,
are by this fact adopting a Marxist perspective.

While the German political theologians have arrived at the
perspectival view of social science, and in particular at the preferential option for society's victims, through dialogue with the
Frankfurt School of social thought, the Latin American liberation theologians base themselves much more on their own personal experience. They tell us that once they joined the groups of

struggling Christians, they began to look at society from a wholly
new perspective. Most of the theologians came from a middle-
class background. They had been taught to understand Latin
American history and look upon their society in a certain way.
Once they joined the struggling communities out of compassion
and solidarity, they had the extraordinary experience of seeing
their own society in a new light. They discovered the structures
of oppression that keep the majority of the people in great misery
and the distorted cultural and religious traditions that legitimated and strengthened these structures, all elements of society
to which they had previously been insensitive. Their own personal experience, often accompanied by dramatic changes in
their personal lives, revealed to them that the approach to one's
own society is inevitably perspectival. Later they turned to dialogue with the social sciences to clarify and refine their own discovery.

Liberation theologians argue that their perspective, the option for the poor, is based on biblical revelation. God has revealed Godself as the one who takes the side of the oppressed,
the excluded, the outcasts, the despised. This, liberation theology
argues, is made known in the pronouncements of the Hebrew
prophets; it is highlighted by the divine election of Israel in the
exodus story and the ancient covenant; it is confirmed in the
psalms; it is lifted to new heights with the coming of Jesus, who
was poor himself, who stood with the little people, often in opposition to the religious and secular authorities, who suffered
persecution, crucifixion, resurrection; it is reconfirmed by the experience of the apostolic church, recorded especially in the apocalyptical passages of the New Testament which predict the
humiliation of the powerful and vindication of the poor. These
biblical themes are all well known. The poor struggling for justice read these themes together as constituting a single revealed
thrust, God's option for the oppressed.

In their biblical arguments Latin American authors sometimes express themselves as if they were literalists. They seem to
attach enormous importance to a few single passages. A more
careful study of liberation theology reveals a more sophisticated
hermeneutical approach. In general, liberation theology is less

concerned with the historical critical method which, following the sociology of knowledge, tries to establish what a particular message meant at the time when it was written. They are more concerned with a critical approach that brings out what the ancient texts mean today, what questions they ask, what demands they make, in which direction they point, what power they exercise over the listener, etc. Here the social and cultural location of the listener must be taken seriously. What liberation theologians must explain is why "God's option for the poor and oppressed" is being heard by sections of the Church today while it was not heard, or not heard in the same way, in previous ages.

The preferential option for the poor has been acknowledged by the Latin American bishops at their meetings of Medellín and Puebla. The texts of the episcopal magisterium do not attribute to this option the epistemological role it plays in liberation theology. For many bishops the option for the poor only determines the orientation of the Church's pastoral ministry. They are less concerned what this option means for scientific research, the social analysis of society, and political action.

Because of the nonsense that has been written on liberation theology it is important to emphasize that the preferential option for the poor is not derived from Marxism. Marx concentrated on the industrial proletariat as the universal class. He had little sympathy for the unemployables and outcasts in the cities, the *Lumpen* as he called them. For Marx the industrial workers had the special role in the revolution and the making of the new society because they were the ones who extracted the raw materials, produced the goods, and created the wealth of society. The *Lumpen* had no destiny in society. The Marxist position is, therefore, quite different from the Christian option for the poor. Christians argue, rather, that when they are confronted by a conflict between rich and poor (or powerful and powerless, or masters and slaves), then the Gospel demands of them that they side with the oppressed. This is basically a religious and a moral decision. In the various adaptations of Marxism to the conditions of the third world there are attempts to make the poor and disinherited the bearers of revolution. This subjects Marxism to major surgery. This transforms it into a social philosophy that embarrasses the official Marxism of Russia and the Soviet bloc. For Christians living in the third world it has become a matter of enormous importance that they participate in the creation of the social philosophy that orients the social revolution and directs the making of the new society.

We note that the preferential option for the poor constitutes a critical principle that remains valid and operative after the revolution. It provides critical insights for the new society. It draws attention to those who remain oppressed and discarded. The application of this principle prevents the new rulers from becoming oppressors themselves. The preferential option for the poor is a truly transcendent principle, rooted in the divine call, providing guidance before, during and after a revolution. I doubt if there is a purely secular principle of which the same claim can be made.

These considerations proper to liberation theology have been underlined by the position of Pope John Paul II in his encyclical on labor. The Pope affirms the need for solidarity among workers and other groups whenever they live under conditions of deprivation and exploitation. In solidarity they must wrestle for social justice and the transformation of society. This principle also holds for the dispossessed in the third world. "The Church is firmly committed to this cause for she considers it her mission, her service, a proof of her fidelity to Christ, so that she can truly be 'the Church of the Poor'. And the 'poor' appear under various forms; they appear in various places and at various times; in many cases they appear as a result of the violation of the dignity of human work. . . ." With his theory of "the poor" the Pope offers a dialectical transcendence of Marxist theory.

3. *The Primacy of Action.* Liberation theology is based on a particular epistemological approach. We have already hinted at this. Most of the theologians involved in this new theological movement were still trained in a theology which gave primacy to knowledge. First was the quest for truth; a second step was the application of the truth to practical problems. First was the scientific and/or theological search for a set of truths that were truly universal, and then, because these truths had universal validity, they were applicable everywhere, to all practical problems. This order is still embodied in many institutions of the educational

system. First we study medicine in a theoretic manner, then we apply it to individual people. First we study the laws of the physical universe, then we apply them in practical engineering. Liberation theologians question this order for the human sciences. They assign primacy to action. They argue, for instance, that their own knowledge of the society to which they belong became possible for them only after they had committed themselves to struggle for social justice. It was through action that they acquired the perspective, in the light of which society began to make sense and could be analyzed satisfactorily with the help of scientific tools. Without this perspective, the scientific tools themselves would not have led to the same insight. Action grounds the intellectual search for truth, and ideas in turn have an historical weight and must therefore be evaluated by their effect on people's lives. The ultimate norm of truth here becomes the transformation and emancipation of the human family. If a scholar, a social scientist, a thinker, a theologian is not committed to the emancipation of humankind, the knowledge which he or she generates will, no matter how brilliant the mind and how convincing the arguments, lead to the alienation of people.

Where does this new epistemological approach come from? Liberation theologians were undoubtedly involved in dialogue with some revisionist form of Marxism. But Marxism was not the only partner in this conversation. Already Hegel developed the position that reason itself is historically constituted, that consciousness varies from age to age, and that social location and hence social commitment have epistemological consequences. Marx followed this line of thought in his own way, but so did other left-wing Hegelians. The primacy of action is thus recognized in American pragmatism. In the Catholic theological tradition it was above all Blondel who, at the turn of the century, defended the primacy of action and for whom knowledge was reflection on action. Blondel believed that his own philosophy, while related to Hegel, was in keeping with the ancient Christian theme of the primacy of charity. There have always been Christian thinkers for whom charity was primary, not only in the sense that charity was the flowering of faith and the fruition of union with God (on this all theologians agreed) but also in the sense that charity was the ground from which truth became available. Unless you love, you do not know God. Commitment opens the access to truth. Liberation theology has worked out its stress on the primacy of action in dialogue with philosophers of praxis, including Marxists, but in doing so they have not separated themselves from the ancient Christian tradition. Truth is here seen not as the conformity of the mind to a given object, including the divine, but as the participation of the mind in the full entry into love and justice. The norm of truth is the praxis of love; truth reflects this praxis and in turn promotes and intensifies it. Liberation theologians like to say that the norm of truth is liberating praxis. This does not mean that they question or neglect the Church's dogma. In line with the primacy of action, they regard orthodoxy as true to itself only if it is sublated by loving and liberating action, by orthopraxis.

Liberating praxis for Latin Americans includes revolution. In other words liberation theology presupposes a revolutionary situation. What is meant by this demands careful definition. Liberation theology as such cannot be applied to the developed societies of the West. What is necessary is to apply some principles of liberation theology to the creation of a politically responsible theology for Western societies. One of the characteristics of a revolutionary situation (one shared by some other critical moments of history) is that in it those who love the good have only one choice. Either you opt for the struggle or you become a defender of an unjust order. *Tertium non datur.* There are a few moments in history when God reveals a single course of action. We have here the classical Joan of Arc question. While normally history remains ambiguous and offers several choices to those who love the good, Joan of Arc believed that for a moment history had become transparent and what was demanded of all Frenchmen was to unite in chasing the foreign occupiers off French soil. During World War II, the Dutch churches under German occupation believed that you either resisted or you became a collaborator and a traitor. *Tertium non datur.* Many Christians believed that the struggle against Hitler was a moment when history became transparent and God's will was clear. The Christian churches during the American Revolution believed that for a moment history revealed a divinely-grounded "must" and that there was no middle way between revolution and treason. Christians in some third world countries argue that theirs is such a revolutionary situation.

4. *Praxis: The Social Construction of Reality.* Liberation theologians refuse to acknowledge the world in which they live as a given, and truth as the conformity of the mind to this world. The world is too awful, too distorted, too unjust for this. On the contrary, they look upon the world as something made by people and hence also transformable by people. Here again, truth is not the conformity of the mind to the given, but the participation of the mind in the transformation and liberation of human life. As people build their world, they also constitute themselves as such and such people. Their making of the world affects them; they come to be in a certain way. This world-building process is often called "praxis".

Praxis has two dimensions. The first is "action", referring to people acting in the world, and the second is "theory", referring to the framework of ideas and symbols through which the world is perceived and through which people react to the world. Since some commentators have suggested that liberation theology is activist and hence anti-intellectual, it is important to point out that liberation theology attaches special importance to ideas and intellectual activity as the theoretic dimension of man's world-transforming task. There is the praxis of doing (Matthew Lamb calls this "agapic" praxis) and the praxis of knowing ("noetic" praxis). For this reason then, liberation theology produces critical studies of the various theologies and philosophies through which people understand their world and examines to what extent these ideas either confirm the conditions of oppression under which people suffer or promote the social struggle through which oppressed people reach out for their emancipation. Liberation theology not only provides critiques of the ideological deformations of Christian teaching and Christian spirituality; it also produces positive formulations of the Christian Gospel and records new forms of spirituality which express divine revelation as the entry of God into man's making of man, as the gracious principle of liberation and redemption. Again, the idea that liberation theology neglects doctrine is false. Instead, it interprets Christian dogma as the proclamation of God's redemptive and empowering presence, enabling people to become the subjects of their own history.

Liberation theology cannot be identified with Marxist theory that regards the economic infrastructure alone as the significant factor responsible for the transformation of society. It cannot be identified with any form of economic determinism. It holds on the contrary that infrastructure and consciousness are mutually interrelated. The process of world building begins with people's collective effort to satisfy their material needs. It begins with labor. But as soon as language emerges, it does not confine itself to the organization of labor; it also turns to issues of collective identity and breaks forth in songs and stories. The struggle for material existence remains the primary organic basis of society, but ideas, symbols, religions and spirituality are important factors because they either confirm and stabilize the existing social order, or they reveal the contradictions of society and turn people into agents of change. While classical Marxists wanted to get rid of religion since they perceived it simply as an ideology protecting an oppressive world order, liberation theologians, believing in the redemptive and liberative self-revelation of God in Jesus Christ, want to overcome ideological religion through a more authentic understanding of revelation as the good news of human emancipation. While liberation theology regards itself as "noetic" praxis, aimed at the transformation of history and as such this-worldly, it offers a defense of the Christian religion. It opposes modern secularism, it affirms divine transcendence, it points to the presence of this transcendence in the gracious passages of people from sin to holiness, from death to life, from oppression to liberation, and it contends that this divine passover is offered in the celebration of the Church's sacramental liturgy.

It is a superficial understanding of praxis that has led some writers to suggest that liberation theology is not concerned with contemplation.

5. *The Mystical Dimension of Politics.* Liberation theology recognizes the social construction of reality. People are engaged in building their world. This praxis includes labor and various

forms of organizations as well as the creativity of consciousness. Since an unjust social order is kept in its place by the political power of government and by mainstream culture, dominant symbols, ideological religion and certain forms of spirituality, political engagement to social change takes place on two levels, on the level of political action and on the level of cultural transformation. Culture and religion exercise a political function. The word "political" here does not have the narrow sense of involvement in public power struggles, but the wider sense, commonly used in liberation theology, of participation in the world-building process. Since the Church is not a community organized for political action in the narrow sense, the Church makes its contribution to social change (and hence exercises a political function in the wider sense) primarily through its promotion of cultural transformation. We saw above that liberation theology provides a critique of the ideological uses of mainstream Christian teaching and Christian piety. Liberation theology offers a critique of the culture in which the Church lives, it pays special attention to the new religious experiences of Christians committed to justice, and, by basing itself on these new experiences, it elaborates an interpretation of Christian teaching and sacraments that serves the overcoming of oppression and the transformation of society.

In this connection, liberation theology is particularly interested in prayer and spirituality. It presents critical studies of traditional liturgies and various forms of piety, bringing to light both the ideological and the utopian elements of Christian prayer. Liberation theology concentrates on the spiritual experiences of Christians in which the divine-human encounter manifests itself in the creation of solidarity and the empowerment to act in the world. Pietism in its various forms has become problematic. While at one time pietism was a vital and imaginative response to the formalism of the public religion, today the pietist concentration on God-and-the-soul tends to legitimate contemporary individualism. In pietism the soul discovers itself alone before God and seeks God's blessing. Other people are excluded from the encounter of the alone with the Alone. What becomes central here is private devotion, the spiritual journey and ultimately the salvation of the individual. Christians engaged in social struggles are suspicious of religious experiences that exclude the others, especially the oppressed others. For them the divine-human encounter reveals the problematic nature of the ego and the illusion of individualism; it bursts the walls of the self, creates a sense of solidarity with others, especially the poor, and makes people aware that they are embedded in a conflictual social matrix, the liberating movement of which is part of the mystery of divine redemption. Religious experience here does not strengthen the sense of man's aloneness; on the contrary it breaks down this isolation, reveals it as a consequence of sin, and inscribes the others, especially the oppressed, into the fibres of personal consciousness. It is no longer possible to know oneself before God without encountering the whole of the suffering people.

Christians committed to social justice are often shy of the language of spirituality. They believe that this language has too long been used to justify the private journey, admittedly on the highest possible level. Because of this distaste for traditional spiritual language, liberation theology is often understood by certain readers as standing for a wholly secular movement. It is true, of course, that liberation theology gives expression to this-worldly religion in Max Weber's sense of the term, but it is equally true that this commitment to this-worldliness is generated by an encounter with the transcendent: being overwhelmed by the divine call to justice, being turned inside out by the revelation of a new light on reality, being shattered and empowered by an authority not derived from human resources, being lifted up to a hope beyond human calculation, being taught to weep over the misery in the world and to rejoice in the modest happiness of the moment as a sacrament of the divine victory over evil. Liberation theology expresses a this-worldly religion produced by the encounter with the burning bush, with a fire in history, that is not limited by history. God transcends history, not in the sense that history is thereby made relative and given secondary importance, but in the sense that no historical establishment is ever safe. The God of compassion will not be tamed.

We conclude that if we mean by "the supernatural" the gratuitous presence of God in history and the lives of men and women, then it is clear that liberation theology, as the reflection of the Christian community on its struggle for justice, is not a religious ideology aimed at arousing political commitment, but in the strict sense of theology based on "supernatural" revelation. Liberation theology is specifically Christian. It could be argued that liberation theology presents a dialectical overcoming of Marxist theory. It reveals in an original manner, better than other theories, the errors of the Marxist system, and it corrects these in such a way that the true insights of Marxist thought are allowed to stand and, in the new context, reveal a power and relevance they did not previously have.

8.
Salvation and Emancipation

In recent years Christians have come to ask the question whether and to what extent the salvation brought by Jesus Christ rescues people from their earthly misery. Is it possible to regard divine salvation as a liberating force in human history? Is Jesus the author of human freedom? These questions have obliged theologians to engage in dialogue with the social sciences in order to clarify the forms that domination takes and the ways by which it may be overcome. In this article I wish to examine the interrelation between "salvation" and "emancipation."

The message of salvation stands at the centre of the Christian proclamation. God is savior. Jesus has been sent to save us. Through faith and commitment to Jesus Christ we are saved from sin and death. He is the savior of the world. Jesus has conquered sin and death. In him we find forgiveness for our sins and the grace to live a life of holiness. In him we have access to the Spirit. In him we have life eternal. When we die, the Christ life in us shall not perish. Through Christ we are united to one another and with God forever. This is the Church's message of salvation. There have been many different theologies of salvation, but until modern times they all expressed themselves in this essentially religious language inherited from the scriptures.

The notion of emancipation has come to us from the Enlightenment. In the modern age new, secular philosophies emerged that explained the world in purely rational terms and recommended the remaking of society in accordance with this rationality. The Enlightenment philosophies were closely connected with the rising class of burghers, the new middle class, engaged in a struggle against feudal and aristocratic society. The self-confident burghers sought liberation from the repressive structure of an *ancien régime:* they yearned for a society characterized by freedom. Enlightenment philosophy, in its different forms, regarded reason as the organ of human emancipation. In the traditional societies people were caught in prisons of various kinds, some of which were made of ideas and symbols, others of physical restraints. Enlightenment philosophy analysed these forms of oppression and argued that with reason as guide people were able to struggle for their emancipation.

Let us look at some of the prisons from which the enlightenment thinkers sought to release their fellow humans. Some of them, especially the great French "philosophes" wanted to emancipate people from the myths and fables of the past. They argued that people were caught in false, pre-rational ideas regarding the origin and the order of the universe. The inherited ideas made people slaves to the traditional hierarchies. The ancient legends prevented people from discovering their true powers as human beings to free themselves from oppression and live rationally in society. Many Enlightenment philosophers turned their anger against the Church and the Christian religion. They engaged in critical scholarship to show that the biblical and post-biblical miracles belonging to Christian history were unconfirmed legends at odds with a rational understanding of the universe. Many of them sought to establish that the metaphysics of the Christian religion had no rational foundation. The end of Christianity was for many the first step in the direction of emancipation.

Political and Economic Oppression

The enlightenment thinkers also understood emancipation as liberation from physical oppression. Some concentrated here on political domination. The feudal order, aristocracy and monarchy held wide sectors of the population in bondage. Freedom promised participation. Freedom meant democracy where all citizens participate in the shaping of public opinion and the making of public policy. Freedom meant the end of slavery and serfdom. These philosophers demanded civil rights. They argued for the brotherhood and equality of all men.

Following the same Enlightenment thrust toward emancipation, social thinkers of a later period concentrated on the analysis of economic oppression. They argued that political emancipation by itself was not enough. If you are hungry, you cannot eat civil rights. It was more important, therefore, that laboring people and the poor be able to participate in the wealth of society. Workers have a right to the products of their hands. Marx and other socialist thinkers produced a rational critique of economic and cultural domination associated with capitalism. Emancipation here meant the end of economic dictatorship.

The same Enlightenment thrust engaged scientists in a struggle against disease. They believed that sicknesses of various kinds had causes that could be analysed scientifically and overcome by appropriate treatment. This approach was extended to the mental illnesses. Emancipation promised to free people from the psychological complexes and compulsions that pushed them toward self-destruction. Freud and other depth psychologists after him discovered that behind every Dr. Jekyll was a Mr. Hyde, that outwardly conformist behaviour often masked profound, even if unavowed desires, and that unless these passions were recognized and confronted they would push people, against their better judgement, into destructive behaviour against others or, more especially, against themselves. Freedom here meant liberation from neurosis and entry into growth and creativity.

What these various strands of Enlightenment had in common was the profound conviction that humans were responsible for their lives, that reason was the significant organ by which they could analyse their oppression, enter upon a new practice, and move towards greater emancipation. Humans were meant to be subjects of their own lives, not objects determined by powers at odds with their rationality. For some thinkers, especially for the political democrats and the participatory socialists, this meant that people were to be the subject of their society, even of their entire collective history. Other thinkers, the humanists and the psychoanalysts, were more directly concerned with liberating people to become subjects of their own personal lives. Yet for all of them, whatever their orientation, the human world was not a given, static reality; it was rather a process, a development, a construction, one for which people were, to some extent at least, themselves responsible. In time, many scientists emphasized the rational *necessity* operative in this process and thus questioned human freedom, while others, remaining more faithful to the Enlightenment emphasis on *freedom,* insisted that the social construction of the human world passed through people's collective decisions. People are called to participate freely in their own historical self-constitution. But even the scientists who denied freedom were driven by the Enlightenment passion for scientific knowledge and rational control.

The Church's Response

How did the Church respond to this enlightenment movement? At first the Church rejected it. This was not surprising since the movement largely defined itself against the traditional order and its religion. Emancipation from pious fables turned against Christianity. At first the Church resisted all attempts to apply critical rational thought to its own foundational documents and institutions. Until recently, the popes repudiated modern biblical criticism. It was only at Vatican Council II that the Catholic Church fully reconciled itself to the new methods of biblical scholarship. Yet even today the ecclesiastical authorities are still cautious in regard to historical research dealing with the origin of dogmas, sacraments and church structures.

The emancipation from oppression, political or economic, was regarded by the Church as a threat to the existing order. The Church defended aristocratic society against liberal democracy in the 19th century, and later it defended bourgeois society and the rights of private property against the socialists in the 19th and 20th century. The emancipation from sickness and psychic bondage also seemed dangerous to the Church. When the Church reconciled itself to the natural sciences, it began to affirm medical research and the practice of modern medicine. But Catholics tended to regard the psychoanalytic discovery of the ambiguity of virtue as a threat to Christian holiness. Church authorities were disturbed by the idea that the repression of sexuality could become the psychic motor force leading to domination and lust for power. Again, it was only in recent years that the Church has entered into dialogue with depth psychology.

As a result of this negation of the quest for emancipation, the Catholic Church of the 19th and early 20th century came to emphasize ever more strongly the supernatural character of the Christian religion. Salvation was supernatural. It had to do with the invisible world. By widening the gap between the natural and supernatural order theologians were able to talk about salvation from sin and death as spiritual events that had no impact on the sociological and psychological realities of human existence. Yet this distance of the spiritual from concrete human life was no longer in harmony with the classical Catholic tradition, in which the gift of grace to sinful humanity had always been seen as spilling over into the concrete historical order. Grace was not only elevating people to the divine, it was also healing the human order. The unqualified "No" to modernity led Catholics to an impoverished grasp of their own Catholic tradition.

In contrast to the Catholic rejection of modernity, some liberal Protestants in the 19th and 20th century totally identified themselves with the Enlightenment movement. While the Catholic Church then said an unqualified "No" to the modern movement, they sometimes said an unqualified "Yes" to it. They affirmed human emancipation as the adequate expression of the salvation promised by Jesus Christ. A prophetic Christian conscience (demanding justice in society, truthfulness in the realm of ideas, and honesty in the search for self-knowledge) created in these liberal theologians such an enthusiasm for the Enlightenment that they interpreted the Christian message in accordance with ideas derived from this modern intellectual movement. In doing so they discarded central elements of the Christian message. For instance, they no longer knew what to do with resurrection and eternal life.

In our own day, many Catholic and Protestant theologians try to transcend the unqualified "No" and the unqualified "Yes" to the Enlightenment by carefully articulating a qualified "Yes," a "Yes" that *affirms emancipation yet does not empty out the meaning of salvation.* The Churches themselves are wrestling with this issue. It is my opinion that the Catholic Church has come to this qualified affirmation of modernity, has critically identified itself with the emancipatory movements in society, and has learnt to proclaim the salvation of Jesus Christ in a manner that includes the liberation of people from political and economic oppression. First there was Vatican II. Then, the 1971 Synod of Bishops meeting in Rome, in a statement entitled 'Justice in the World,' declared that Christian preaching included, as an integral part, the call to social justice and that the redemption which Jesus Christ had brought included the liberation of people from their oppressions. This was a startling development of doctrine. In his first encyclical, *Redemptor hominis,* Pope John Paul II declared that Jesus Christ has identified himself in a certain sense with every human being and that, therefore, the promotion and defense of human rights has christological significance. The Church's mission includes the promotion of social justice. Over against an older teaching which distinguished between the "supernatural mission" of the Church to convert people to Christian faith and the "natural mission," subordinate to the former, to improve social conditions, *Redemptor hominis* recognized a single mission defined by the inseparable bond between gospel proclamation and action for social justice. Salvation has an emancipatory thrust.

Salvation and Emancipation

At the same time salvation and emancipation are not identical. In the following pages I wish to clarify the bond and interrelation between salvation and emancipation. Let me trace the theological steps by which Catholic thinkers have moved from "No" to modernity to a qualified "Yes."

   In the 20th century, the Enlightenment tradition produced its own self-criticism. This is not surprising since many of the great Enlightenment projects have miserably failed. The struggle to liberate the mind of fables and superstitions made people abandon their religion only to become vulnerable to new myths,

often dangerous and destructive ones. The struggle to liberate society from political domination through democratic government
became wedded to capitalism and the quest for economic domination of the world. The struggle to free people from economic
domination through socialism and democracy in the factory led
to authoritarian movements and produced totalitarian governments that oppress their people. And the struggle to free people
from debilitating psychological compulsions through therapy
often led people to such a preoccupation with themselves that
they became indifferent to the wider realm of society and collapsed into self-centeredness. What has gone wrong? Why have
these fruits of the Enlightenment been so bitter?

Here is one answer that has been given. The Enlightenment
trusted in science, in scientific reason and technological control.
Eventually, it has been argued, the Enlightenment thinkers applied the scientific method to all aspects of human life; the entire
world became a machine for them which could be scientifically
known and technologically controlled; values, vision, freedom,
the quality of the human, all of these aims disappeared under the
pressure of technological rationality. What began with Enlightenment became positivism. The Enlightenment projects failed, it
is argued, because they were based on a behavioristic understanding of the human. Human problems were to be solved with
the help of a purely instrumental rationality. Reflection on freedom and the quality of human life disappeared. That is why the
Enlightenment projects led to domination. And because human
beings did not fit into a scientifically defined framework, they
often burst out in new forms of irrationality.

It is important to recall that scientific or technological rationality was not the whole of the Enlightenment. At the beginning
it was accompanied by a higher rationality, often called "practical reason," which had to do with human goals, with freedom,
with equality, with fellowship and participation. Practical reason
was understood as the human organ thanks to which society was
able to enhance human life, produce a qualitatively higher form
of existence, and discover the essence of what it means to be human. Practical reason touched upon morality. But throughout
the 19th and into the 20th century, scientific or technological

reason became stronger and repressed practical reason. Scientists remembered Kant's Critique of Pure Reason which equated true knowledge with empirical science, yet they forgot Kant's Critique of Practical Reason which sought to ground rationality in man's effort to live humanly. Practical reason tended to be forgotten: modernity defined itself increasingly in terms of positivistic science. Today the scientific Enlightenment has become an obstacle to freedom.

This Enlightenment critique of Enlightenment, first worked out by a group of social thinkers in the 1920's, often referred to as the Frankfurt School, had an enormous appeal for many Christian theologians, Catholic and Protestant. Thanks to the research done by the Frankfurt School it was possible to criticize and wrestle against the positivist thrust of the Enlightenment, which has become so powerful in the present age, and at the same time affirm, retrieve and strengthen the thrust of practical reason, reason as the organ of human emancipation. The Frankfurt School critique of Enlightenment allowed Catholic theologians to give a more positive meaning to the "No" to modernity, pronounced by the Catholic Church in the 19th century. At the same time, they urged that practical reason with its emancipatory thrust had a special affinity with the Christian message. What arguments did they offer for this?

Christianity and Emancipation

First of all, these theologians said, there is an emancipatory thrust in the divine promise recorded in the scriptures. The Exodus, the ancient covenant, the original paradigm of human redemption, records a history of liberation. God empowered people to free themselves from oppression. In the prophets of Israel and in the prophetic passages of Israel's poetry and wisdom, God remains the Holy One who rescues the poor, the persecuted and the oppressed: to believe in God is to do justice.

Jesus himself appeared as liberator. He preached liberation from an oppressive religious practice. While he affirmed Torah and the ancient promises, he offered a vehement critique of the religion promoted by the temple priests and some of the pharisees. He shook the foundation of the established order. Even though Jesus did not speak against the Roman Empire, by which his own people and other peoples surrounding the Mediterranean had been subjugated, his shaking of the foundation in Israel was regarded as dangerous enough for the Empire that he was condemned to die on the Roman cross. At a later time when Stephen blasphemed and shook the foundation of the official religion, he was stoned in accordance with religious law. Yet Jesus' execution was secular and political: he was crucified. It was feared that the religious liberation that he preached could justify disobedience to the imperial institutions. The Romans were correct. For Jesus did proclaim the coming judgement of God on the wicked world. He preached *metanoia:* people had the right to be disloyal to the institutions to which they belonged, turn in repentence to their God, and yearn for the coming of God's reign. Because of this preaching, the early Christians remained suspect. Their message too was religious, not political in the immediate sense, yet their religious faith liberated them to be disloyal to any and every institution. For it was better to obey God than men.

In the scriptures, then, it appears that humans are meant to be free and live in justice and that God inspires and empowers them to free themselves and to create a just society. This is the first argument that there is an affinity between the Christian message and the emancipatory thrust of practical reason.

The second argument is of a different kind. It is based on the public witness of Christian communities presently engaged in liberation struggles against colonialism and other forms of domination: their faith in Christ and eucharistic worship confirm and strengthen them in their struggle. They wrestle to free themselves from the bondage to the fables offered them by the powerful, free themselves from political and economic oppression, and free themselves from the psychological prisons into which prolonged colonialism has locked them. As they read the scriptures and celebrate the liturgy they do not hear, as their ancestors did, a call to obedience, humility, subservience, sacrifice, submission, crucifixion, and hope only for another world: they hear God's voice confirming them, they recognize Jesus walking with them, they experience the Spirit as empowerment. Their hope also touches upon this world. Salvation here includes liberation from oppression. Because of this historical experience of Catholic communities theologians have come to affirm the affinity between the Christian message and human emancipation. In fact, the biblical argument presented above is only valid if one reads the Bible from a perspective that is already touched by the new Christian liberation struggles. Even the grasp of the scriptures is founded in commitment and action.

We have taken a brief look at the biblical and historical foundations of the recent doctrinal development that includes in the salvation brought by Christ, the liberation of people from their oppressions. Faith and justice have become inseparable. The Gospel has acquired a socio-political thrust. Christian faith has become a social praxis. Divine revelation in Israel and in Jesus Christ is here understood as a gracious work of liberation and humanization. God is here understood as summoning and empowering people to become the subject of their own history. While in the past there was a tension between incarnational theology, stressing God's presence with us, and eschatological theology, putting the emphasis on God's fulfillment, the recent doctrinal development reconciles incarnation and eschatology. God is indeed present, but not as the stabilizer of what is, but as judgement on the present, as empowerment to change it, as orientation toward the future. God is present as the forward thrust moving a sinful world toward the justice of the future.

A Challenge To The Church

In this article I do not have the space to show what this remarkable development of doctrine means for the entire teaching and practice of the Church. Because salvation includes emancipation, every aspect of the Church's life acquires a wider and richer meaning. At the same time, this wider understanding of salvation poses serious problems for the Catholic Church. Some of these problems are internal. For the Church itself is governed by a highly centralized apparatus that prohibits participation and prevents regional churches from assuming responsibility for their own ministry, worship and mission. The Church, moreover, discriminates against women by excluding them from ordination, as it once excluded slaves. If the message of salvation includes the promise of emancipation, then it challenges the Church itself. The same development of doctrine has also created external problems for the Church. For while the Church at one time was expected to bless the existing order, despite its contradictions and injustices, the recent identification of the Church with the poor and oppressed greatly disturbs the holders of power in society. The most startling expression of the Church's new approach is John Paul's encyclical, *Laborem exercens,* which recognizes the labor movement as the dynamic element of contemporary society, defines social justice in terms of the priority of labor over capital, and calls for the solidarity *of* the workers and the poor as well as solidarity *with* the workers and the poor. The Church, according to this encyclical, is identified with the emancipatory struggle of the dominated classes.

What follows from this recent development of doctrine is that whenever salvation is proclaimed in purely personal terms or in a purely spiritual, non-historical language, the Christian message is being falsified. An individualistic understanding of the Gospel represses its social and historical dimension and hence distorts the Christian message. More than that, the preaching of an individualistic Gospel has political meaning: by neglecting its emancipatory thrust, the Christian message becomes a defense of the status quo. If sin is purely personal, and conversion is purely personal, and the new life into which Jesus initiates us is purely personal, then society remains untouched. The Christian message then pronounces no judgment on it. Christian life then seeks private virtue, not the creation of a just society. When we see the signs "Jesus saves" on our highways, we divine the right-wing political position that inspires them. For if Jesus is simply the savior of souls, then he does not condemn racism, nor economic oppression, nor empire building, nor even the arms race.

Salvation Transcends Emancipation

While salvation includes emancipation, it is very important to distinguish salvation from emancipation. On the surface liberation is a secular movement, it involves religious and non-religious people: if Christians simply equated salvation with emancipation, they would empty out the meaning of the Gospel. The specifically Christian would be lost—to the detriment of the world. How then does salvation stand apart from emancipation and remain in mutual tension with it? In my reply I confine myself to two remarks.

Without the Christian doctrine of salvation, the emancipatory struggles against domination appear as a Promethean project, as humans saving themselves. There are in fact Christian theologians who oppose the new liberation theology because it appears to them as a project of self-salvation or salvation by works. These theologians are quite right when they insist that we are saved by grace and that this grace is assimilated first of all by the surrender of faith; they are quite wrong, however, when they suppose that liberation theology abandons the gratuity of salvation. In the light of the Christian faith the struggle for justice, the longing, the perseverance, the sacrifices, all the hardships that are part of the struggle are the work of people, and at the same time the work of God present to them. The emancipatory struggle is not only *actio,* it is also *passio.* People suffer God's power coming into their lives. They become restless and critical, they reject the wisdom of the world, they dare to analyse their situation with honesty, they escape apathy and despair, they weave the bonds of solidarity with others, they expand their heart, they transcend their personal self-interest and identify with the struggle of their class or community, they experience the affirmation of the comrades, and even though the odds may be stacked against them, they live from hope. Their *actio* is grounded in their *passio,* in suffering divine grace. Even when Christians look at secular people dedicated to the struggle against domination, they marvel because they recognize in the release of vision and power among them the coming of God's reign. The Enlightenment dictum that humans are meant to be the subject of their own history can be affirmed by Christians because they believe, in accordance with the divine promises revealed in Christ, that God enlightens and empowers people to do just that, to become the subject of their history.

Because salvation includes emancipation and yet remains distinct from it, one Christian response to the struggles for justice in the world is gratitude and worship. We give glory to the God who will not be tamed, who loves justice, who is no respecter of persons, who makes people long for their freedom, who empowers them to engage in struggle, who is present to them, and through them to history, as the liberator of humankind. Again incarnation and eschatology are reconciled. Transcendence is here the mode of divine immanence. God's presence is explosive, unsettling, empowering, future-creating: it transcends all the prisons that humans have built for themselves and triumphs over all domination and injustice.

It is important to distinguish between salvation and emancipation, moreover, because the meaning and power of salvation remains with people even when a particular struggle for emancipation fails. According to the Christian message, God continues to sustain such people, heal them, console them, take away their despair and their bitterness, and rekindle their hope. God the liberator becomes God the counselor to people in prison, to people broken by life, to people sick and moving into old age. This comfort is not offered in the name of heaven, that is with reference to another world more important than this one. Since faith and justice are inextricably intertwined, it is this world, this history, that holds primary importance for the Christian. The divine comfort is here offered through God's presence in history promising the eventual deliverance of oppressed people from the powers of domination.

Salvation includes emancipation, but remains forever distinct from it. Christians have come to a critical affirmation of the Enlightenment (and join secular humanists in wrestling against positivism or the dominance of technological reason); at the same time they in no sense have abandoned their own self-identity defined through God's gratuitous gift in Jesus Christ.

9.
The Holocaust
and Political Theology

Before, during and after the Holocaust the Christian world remained silent. There were a few courageous men and women who spoke up or who acted. God was not totally left without witnesses in the church.

Belated Repentance

After the War several Christians, Protestant and Catholic, began to ask themselves whether and to what extent the Christian tradition itself had contributed to the genocidal mass murder. They recognised of course that Nazism was anti-Christian and that Nazi racism rejecting everything Jewish also repudiated Jesus and the New Testament, but they believed that the anti-Jewish teaching and symbols present in the Christian tradition had created a cultural world in which the anti-Semitic language and sentiment of the Nazis were able to spread so rapidly and where people had a vague feeling that the destruction coming upon the Jews was a providential punishment. Of great importance was the book *Jésus et Israel* (1948) by the French historian Jules Isaac, himself a Jew, which demonstrated that contempt for Jews and the denigration of Jewish religion were elements of Christian preaching almost from the beginning. While at first only a few Christians had the moral courage to study this material and confront the issue, their number grew; they organised, published their own reviews, established research centers, and eventually succeeded in influencing the leadership of the churches.

During the sixties, church councils and church boards, Protestant and Catholic, with varying degrees of honesty and repentance, made important public declarations that expressed their great sorrow over the giant evil inflicted upon the Jews. They repented of their silence, repudiated the anti-Jewish elements of Christian teaching, gave up proselytism in regard to Jews, and demanded instead solidarity with the Jewish people. In many churches these declarations led to the re-writing of catechisms, religious education material, liturgical texts, and theological treatises. Many churches, especially in North America, gave public expression to their solidarity with the State of Israel.

As Christians in ever greater number wrestled against the distortions in their own tradition, they discovered to their dismay how deeply the negation of Jewish existence was inscribed in the presentation of the Christian message. The Christian way was always presented as the supersession of the religion of Israel: with Jesus Christ, Judaism had lost its validity. Anti-Judaism, as Rosemary Ruether has formulated it, was here 'the left hand of Christology'.[1] Is it possible to proclaim the Christian Gospel in fidelity to Scripture in a manner that respects and honours Jewish religion? Taking seriously the Holocaust meant for some theologians the re-thinking of Christology. Jesus Christ became for them the Great Protector of humans, who stood against all the forces of death.

The Holocaust remains forever a principle of discontinuity for the Christian Church. No amount of rethinking and reformulating the Christian message and no amount of dialogue and cooperation with Jews will ever allow the Church to be reconciled with its past. As part of Western civilisation, the Church stands convicted by its silence. Holocaust is unique for Christians. The silence of the world may simply have been indifference to the suffering of others; the silence of the churches was more than indifference. It expressed a vaguely religious sense that the Jews were not our brothers and sisters, they represented something antithetical to the Christian vision of society, they bore the mark of Cain on their foreheads, and they were now visited by a mysterious providential act. Confronting the Holocaust, now Christians discover that there are no innocent bystanders. Confrontation with the Holocaust provokes discontinuity and restlessness in the Church. Christians can no longer be silent, even if their speaking reveals the complicity of their own Church. Christians must forever examine the ideological distortion of their own religious tradition.

Because of this double challenge, "Speak out against social evil", and "Examine your own complicity in this social evil," the belated Christian response to the Holocaust affects the Church not only in its relation to Jews but more universally in its relationship to the world.

The silence of Pope Pius XII has become the symbol of the Church's guilt. Hochhut's play *The Deputy* has given this symbol great cultural power. Since then the Church has begun to speak out on social evil. At one time, the Catholic Church regarded itself as protector of the inherited Christian civilisation. It spoke out on political matters only when its own institutional interests were at stake, or when modern, liberal society violated traditional ethical norms related, for the most part, to procreation and family life. The Church observed a respectful silence in regard to the conflicts between nations: at best, it offered diplomatic channels for peaceful reconciliation. Pius XII remained silent when Hitler invaded Poland, even though Poland was an ancient Catholic land. The German bishops also remained silent. The silence of Pope and bishops before the persecution and later the mass murder of the Jews is better known.

Public Witness to Justice

Since the Second World War, the Churches, including the Catholic Church, have begun to speak out against social evil. They have often done this out of a spirit of repentance over their silence during the mass murder of the Jews. In response to the Holocaust bishops have become spokesmen for peace, justice and human rights.

The Pastoral Letter on War and Peace (May 1983) published by the American bishops is, in my opinion, historically incomprehensible without taking into consideration the Holocaust and the Church's silence during the Second World War. The American bishops at this time believe that their own country is moving in the direction of mass destruction, the dimensions of which stagger the imagination. The world is driven toward self-destruction through the logic of the nuclear arms race—a demonic evil. Traditional just war theories no longer apply to nuclear weapons. Because of their enormous power and the uncontrolled nature of their destruction, they exterminate whole populations. They make total war against innocent people. There can be no moral justification for nuclear bombing. Americans must not forget, the bishops argue, that they were the first country to produce the atomic bomb and the only country ever to drop it. They now ask the Catholic people to influence public opinion so that it becomes possible 'for our country to express profound sorrow over the atomic bombing in 1945'. 'Without this sorrow', the bishops add, 'there is no possibility of finding a way to repudiate the future use of nuclear weapons'.[2] It is hard to find parallels in church history for a declaration made by the bishops of a superpower that offers resistance to the crimes of empire.

Since the Holocaust the churches have begun to examine their own complicity in social evil. In theology this is known as 'ideology critique'. The German and North American theologians who, under the name of 'political theology', have engaged in ideology critique as an indispensable step in the clarification of the Christian message for our age, have all been profoundly affected by the encounter with the Holocaust. This is true especially of the German theologians Metz,[3] Moltmann,[4] and Soelle.[5] It is also true of North American political theologians, such as Robert McAfee Brown,[6] Francis Fiorenza,[7] Matthew Lamb,[8] and Rosemary Ruether.[9] It is no coincidence that the term 'ideology critique' is derived from the Critical Theory of the Frankfurt School, which engaged in an extended critique of anti-Semitism before the War and which, especially in the writings of Adorno and Horkheimer,[10] dared to face the judgment on civilisation implicit in the Holocaust. It is in obedience to the challenge of the Holocaust that Christian thinkers, and in some cases even Christian churches, have taken sides with the victims of society and truthfully examined the hidden complicity of Christianity with the forces of oppression.

Liberation Theology

In this context it is necessary to mention another historical event, one of an altogether different nature, that also had a profound effect on the self-understanding of the Christian Church. It also generated the twofold challenge, 'Speak out against social evil', and 'Examine your own complicity in this social evil'. The event I am referring to is the breakdown of Western empire. In the past the churches had legitimated the rule of Western empires over other peoples and continents, first when it took place through military conquest and commercial exploitation and later when it was exercised through the extension of the Western economic system. The Church accompanied the colonial expansion of Western powers to extend its mission and plant Christian communities in the distant lands. Now it is precisely these churches of colonial origin that accuse of complicity the churches identified with empire. The former colonial churches are now exercising a mission in regard to the churches of the West. Thanks to their critique, the churches have discovered to what extent their message, their piety and their institutions have been distorted by colonialist ideology.

The churches in Third World countries strive for a Christian Gospel that expresses solidarity with the poor, the hungry, and the dispossessed, with the masses who have been robbed of their human dignity. They want a Gospel that is not allied with the powers of domination. The best known expression of this Christian quest is Latin American liberation theology. Similar liberation theologies exist in all parts of the formerly colonised world. Many elements of this liberation theology have been taken up into the Church's official teaching, especially at the Latin American Bishops Conferences at Medellin (1968) and at Puebla (1979). The so-called 'preferential option for the poor', the decision to look at society from the viewpoint of the victims and to give public witness to solidarity with them, has since been integrated in the Church's official teaching even at the Vatican.[11]

While impressive church documents have been produced, the Christian leaders and theologians who take them with utmost seriousness are still a minority. The Christians in the West who have been most open to liberation theology and the ecclesiastical 'option for the poor', are precisely those who had learnt ideology critique and the need for public witness from their anguished encounter with the Holocaust. In one and the same argument they defend the right to self-determination of the colonised people and the existence of the State of Israel as a place of refuge, a house against death, for a persecuted people. The public policy statements of Christian churches in the United States, including the Catholic Church, affirm the right of Israel to exist in safe borders and all of them, without exception, demand at the same time, human rights for Palestinians and recognise their claim to a homeland.[12] This position is not without its difficulties.

Many Jewish leaders in North America have found this position unacceptable. They have argued that Christians have not sufficiently confronted the Holocaust: they have not yet discerned in themselves their hidden anti-Jewish impulses; they still remain prejudiced in their criticism of Israel; and their defence of Palestinian rights is even-handedness, forgetful of the mortal danger in which the Jewish people find themselves after the murder of the six million. There are undoubtedly Christians who fall into this category. Others do not.

Some Jewish religious leaders have expressed their puzzlement and sometimes even their dismay, at the new political stance taken by the churches in their identification with Latin American liberation movements, with protest movements in the formerly colonised world in general and with the Native peoples and other oppressed groups in North America. In several church documents, the new option has led to a critique of the world capitalist system which protects political freedom and material well being for vast numbers of people at the centre, but which widens the gap between rich countries and poor countries, i.e., creates dependency and misery in the Third World, and even produces ever growing pockets of poverty in the Western industrialised countries.

Emil Fackenheim, the great Jewish religious thinker, who makes response to the Holocaust central in his philosophy and theology, has recently adopted a very critical approach to Christian faith; he has recognised nonetheless the continuity between the Christian response to Auschwitz and the emergence of political and liberation theology.[13] After Auschwitz, he argued, Christians could no longer emphasise the completeness of redemption in Jesus Christ. In the face of the Holocaust, Christians moved into a new sense of unredemption. They recognised the brokenness of the Church, yearned for peace and justice and put their hope in the eschatological promises. Christians began to feel closer to the traditional Jewish longing for the messianic days. Fackenheim's analysis is persuasive. John Pawlikowski has even spoken of a "contemporary re-Judaisation of Christianity," by which he meant the emergence of an earthly and communal yearning for the fulfilment of the divine promises in history.[14]

The reader will have noticed that this article is written from a North American perspective. It reflects, moreover, my involvement in theological education, located on the whole in the white middle classes. Oppressed groups of people, including oppressed Christians, are likely to look upon the Holocaust quite differently. The Blacks of South Africa who suffer under the brutal system of apartheid and Latin American peasants of Native stock threatened by genocidal action are likely to see in the Holocaust a climactic symbol of the evil powers that now threaten to devour them. Neither the Blacks of South Africa nor the dispossessed Natives of Latin America belong to those who lost their innocence through compromising silence. They were held down as voiceless masses. The Christian preaching they had received was ideologically distorted, including incidentally the anti-Jewish bias; but the main thrust of this ideology was directed against their own group, keeping them tranquil in their house of bondage. The grain of anti-Jewish bias in this preaching must eventually be corrected: but the urgent task of oppressed people is the struggle for their own liberation from Pharoah's domination and the longing for the liberation of all the dominated. How would the Native peoples of Canada react to the Holocaust if they were asked to do so? How do Palestinian Christians react to the Holocaust? How do the Black people of the United States respond to it? How closely do the offspring of African slaves identify with the civilisation that enslaved them? It seems to me more likely that those who are in various ways oppressed look upon the Holocaust as a terrifying event, a fear-creating historical signal, symbolising the extent to which oppressors may go to execute their plans. Samoza had white napalm dropped on his own people in his own city.

The perspective on the Holocaust taken by the oppressed is very close to the position defended by the philosophers of the Frankfurt School. For Adorno and Horkheimer, Auschwitz is not an aberration from Western progress but an exaggeration of present trends operative in Western civilisation, in capitalist societies and in State socialism.[15] Auschwitz gives cruel visibility to the violence built into technological society that produces integration and identity by negating, and if need be, eliminating those who do not fit. For these philosophers Auschwitz contains a judgment on positivistic society. Since Adorno and Horkheimer are not Christians, they have no hesitation in saying this. Christian theologians hesitate to endorse this interpretation because it disguises the part which the Christian tradition has played in the Holocaust.

Dilemma over Double Standard

Western Christians of the mainstream are here led to an agonising dilemma. Their encounter with the Holocaust has led them to repentance and great sorrow: they recognise that they must speak out against social evil and examine the complicity of their Church and this social evil. They desire to protect Jews wherever they are endangered. At the same time, the entry into this new self-understanding has compelled them to listen to the voices of all the oppressed. The Christian churches in North America support Israel's right to exist within safe borders and at the same time defend human rights and self-determination for the

Palestinians. In this perspective what is needed is an extended ethical debate on policies of compromise.

Many Jewish thinkers in North America have found fault with Christian critics of Israel. They have argued that Christians tend to apply 'a double standard' in their evaluation of Israeli policies. They judge the policies of Israel by a high standard of Jewish and Christian biblical ethics, while they judge the policies of Arab nations and Arab political organisations by purely secular standards defined by the *Realpolitik* of the world. Christians may think that they honor Jews by looking upon the State of Israel as a religious biblical reality: but their use of the double standard in fact damages Israel and may well hide an unacknowledged, hidden, anti-Semitic resentment. Even complete evenhandedness is detrimental to Israel, it is argued, because it does not sufficiently recognise the danger in which the State and the Jewish people find themselves in this age.

The accusation certainly applies to many critics of Israel and Israeli policies. But it does not apply to all of them. In particular, the Christians who have reacted to the Holocaust in a manner described in these pages have come to feel uneasy about a totally different ethical 'double standard' that determines their approach to Israel. They have qualms of conscience because they do not apply to Israeli policies the norms by which they judge their own government. When their own government sells arms to Latin American dictators or strengthens its ties with South Africa, these Christians speak out in protest and join pressure groups to persuade the government to change its mind; yet when they read in the press of similar policies adopted by the Israeli government, they tend to remain silent. Christians in the USA and Canada have recently supported the struggle of the Native peoples to gain human rights and have their land claims recognised; yet the same Christians hesitate to be vocal in support of the disinherited Palestinians. Does the discontinuity brought by the Holocaust demand that one live with such an uneasy conscience? Is it a desire for unauthentic continuity to search for ethical principles that strain after universality?

Let it be said that a growing number of Jewish men and women in North America feel equally uneasy about this kind of 'double standard'. They too wish to enter upon an extended ethical debate. While Christians may not feel free to join this discussion, they want to follow it and learn from it.

Rabbi Arthur Hertzberg, an important progressive Jewish spokesman in the United States, has presented an interesting ethical argument to justify this double standard. He recommends that we apply to Israel a policy that in contemporary American legal language is called Affirmative Action.[16] Affirmative Action is a public policy designed to rectify age-old social injustices and discrimination. To correct the exclusion of Blacks or Mexican Americans (or women!) from opportunities to participate and succeed in American institutions, including politics, universities, commerce and industry, Affirmative Action legislation requires that these institutions give preference in hiring to these formerly excluded peoples, even if this inflicts a certain injustice on candidates of the mainstream who are better prepared for the position. To rectify a grave historical evil, Affirmative Action reconciles itself to minor forms of injustice inflicted upon individuals. It is right and just, Rabbi Hertzberg argues, that the West apply Affirmative Action to Israel. But he adds immediately that Affirmative Action has ethical limits. How long should it be applied? And how great are the injustices that may be tolerated?

The Making of Public Policy

At present these ethical issues are being debated in Israel. An Israeli organisation, Oz VeShalom, Religious Zionists for Strength and Peace, has introduced this discussion at the heart of Jewish orthodoxy.[17] 'Citizens of Israel, it is up to us to decide what we want', they announce. Then they put the following questions: 'A Jewish State governed by biblical values, just laws and reason OR a garrison state characterised by chauvinism, institutionalised injustice, and xenophobia? A democratic society, flourishing within small borders, in which the Arab minority enjoys full human dignity and human rights OR all of Eretz Yisrael at the price of repressing the political freedoms of one million Palestinian Arabs? Mastery of our collective destiny, in harmony weapons and money needed to wage war? Mutual recognition and co-existence between Israelis and Palestinians OR escalating destruction and loss of life?'

In North America this ethical debate is just beginning in the Jewish community. Because it has come so late, many Jewish writers demand a return to ethical reflection with great vehemence. In this context I am not thinking of Jewish authors such as Noam Chomsky and I. F. Stone who have always been critical of Zionism and excluded themselves from conversation with the Jewish community. I am thinking, rather, of Jews who are lovers of Israel and as such demand an ethical debate about public policies beyond the double standard. Rabbi Reuben Slonim, a Canadian Zionist, has always criticised Israeli policies and defended Palestinian rights on a Jewish, ethical basis. Thanks to a recent publication he has come into greater prominence in the Jewish community.[18] Earl Shorris, a Jewish novelist, has published a book, *Jews Without Mercy: A Lament*,[19] in which he establishes that Jewish religion has always called for justice and mercy, and then offers a lament that a significant sector of the American Jewish community has turned to the political right, adopted social views contrary to justice and mercy, and allied itself with similar forces in the State of Israel. What he calls for is an ethical debate on public policy. Another Jewish author, Arthur Waskow, also a lover of Israel, is involved in reviving the messianic strain in Jewish religion.[20] He too calls for a critical, ethical debate based on Jewish religious grounds. Some secular authors who define themselves in terms of the Jewish ethical tradition have recently come out with vehement protests. R. S. Feuerlicht's *The Fate of the Jews*[21] accuses the Jewish community of having abandoned ethical thinking in favour of blind loyalty to the Israeli government and therefore of sharing responsibility for the political direction taken by this government, which may ultimately prove to be self-destructive. Many of these critical voices, religious and secular, come together in an organisation of recent origin, the New Jewish Agenda.

The debate on ethical imperatives has taken place in Jewish religious literature in terms of the appropriate response to the Holocaust experience. For Jewish religious thinkers the Holocaust has a never to be relativised singularity, a uniqueness that will mark Jewish self-understanding forever. They resist the social scientific tendency to compare the Holocaust with other mass crimes in history—other genocides, mass bombings, and planned famines—as if the Holocaust were just one horror among a list of horrors. The Jewish thinkers resist this as an attempt to disguise the full demonic power revealed in the Holocaust and make less grave Western responsibility for the event. For Jewish religious authors the summons coming from the Holocaust says, 'Never again!' For some this means, Never again shall the Jewish people be humiliated and destroyed, and for others it means, never again shall the Jewish people nor any powerless people be humiliated and destroyed. The difference between the two is considerable.[22] The latter group of thinkers argue that the unparalleled, never-to-be relativised singularity of the Holocaust gives rise to a Jewish response that has universal implications and provides ethical guidelines for public policies. The Jewish religious authors for whom the summons, 'Never again!' refers exclusively to the future of the Jewish people tend to remain silent on the urgent contemporary issues such as the nuclear arms race, world hunger, the genocides of Native peoples in Latin America, apartheid in South Africa, and so forth.

The philosopher Emil Fackenheim has not resolved his own ambivalence on this topic. He insists that there shall be no relativising of the Holocaust and argues that Jews must resist a universalist ethical approach that would weaken them in their stubborn, faithful struggle for survival. He feels no urgency to take sides in the ethical debates on such issues as nuclear war, world hunger, or military dictatorships. He tends to evaluate historical events, in obedience to the summons from the Holocaust, in terms of the effect they have on the security of Israel and the Jewish people. At the same time, he speaks repeatedly of the present as the 'age of Auschwitz and Hiroshima'. In a moving passage he declares that Jews cannot say 'May the horror that has come upon us never come upon you,' to accomplices of the Holocaust nor to the silent by-standers, but they 'can and must say [this] to those upon whom it, or something resembling it, has come— starving African children, Gulag slave labourers, boat people roaming the seas.'[23] Here Fackenheim does not think that speaking of it, or something resembling it', implies a relativisation of the Holocaust. On the contrary, it is for him a starting point for more universal ethical reflection.

In recent years Jewish authors have been greatly concerned about the abuse of Holocaust language. They fear that contemporary political issues are often resolved not by a rational debate on ethics and strategy but by remembering the Holocaust and reacting to the present as if it were the past. Such abuse has become very widespread. The Western press has often described the Israeli occupation of the West Bank and the more recent Israeli invasion of Lebanon in terms drawn from Nazi aggression during the Second World War, implying that Jews have become like the Nazis who persecuted them. Jewish and some Christian voices have protested against this. The same unfortunate trend, however, is also found in the State of Israel. Mr. Menachem Begin set the tone for this. In his public utterance during the summer of 1982, Beirut became 'Berlin', and his military campaign set out to destroy 'Hitler' in his 'bunker deep beneath the surface'.[24] During the war in Lebanon, even the debate in Israel itself deteriorated to name-calling that drew upon Nazi memories. In the pro-Begin Likud attacks on the Peace Now Movement, the murdered peace demonstrator Emil Grunzweig was compared to Horst Wessel, a member of the Hitler Youth murdered by communists who was made into a martyr of the Nazi movement. The opponents of the Begin government also occasionally used analogies drawn from the Nazis. Thus some opposed the Jewish settlements on the West Bank as creating a *Herrenvolk* democracy.[25] In Jerusalem and Tel Aviv swastikas are occasionally painted on house walls by Sephardic militants or ultra-Orthodox groups as a protest against the Israeli police.[26]

In response to these abuses Abba Eban has insisted that since the Holocaust is an altogether unique event, it is not licit to use analogies drawn from this event in debates dealing with contemporary policies. 'Under Mr. Begin Israeli relations with other countries have ceased to be regarded as similar to other international relations, whether concerned with co-operation, opposition or even confrontation. With Mr. Begin and his cohorts, every foe becomes a 'Nazi', and every blow becomes an 'Ausch-witz'.[27] Other Jewish voices have complained that Holocaust lan-guage is used to justify contemporary political policies. The Nachum Goldmann, one time president of the World Jewish Congress and the World Zionist Organization, said that 'the use of the Holo-caust as an argument to justify politically doubtful and morally indefensible policies is a kind of *hillul hasham,* a banalisation of the Holocaust.'[28] Abba Eban has asked for the end of Holocaust language in the political arena.

Today some religious thinkers in Israel have questioned whether the Holocaust should be at the center of Jewish theology at all. While the mass murder of the six million must never be forgotten and fade from Jewish consciousness, the Holocaust cannot be the foundation for a religious revival of Judaism.[29] A similar point of view has been defended by some Jewish religious thinkers in the United States and in Britain.[30] The Holocaust does not summon forth the kind of inspiration and ethical commit-ment a people need to define their collective identity and their historical future. Jewish religious renewal must be grounded in the Mount Sinai experience, God's covenant with the people of Israel. Jews who assign a central place to the Holocaust argue that this uniquely evil event has introduced discontinuity in hu-man history, and that it is illusory and even dangerous for Jews to aspire to an ethical religion of universal meaning as if nothing had happened.

What does the discontinuity produced by the Holocaust mean to Jews and to Christians? Are there some continuities that must be defended against inappropriate shattering? Christians at this time are involved in a theological debate over the relation between biblical faith and public policy. It seems to me that Jew-ish religious thinkers are moving to a similar debate among them-selves. Can it be said that Jews and Christians have become brothers (sisters) in a new way because in their own communities they wrestle with similar issues?

Notes

1. Rosemary Ruether *Faith and Fratricide,* (New York 1974).
2. *Origins, NC Documentary Service,* vol. 13, no. 1, p. 27. In the debate Bishop Hunthausen said that the Trident located in his diocese can destroy as many as 408 separate areas, each with a bomb five times more powerful than the one dropped on Hiroshima. The Trident and the MX missile have such accuracy and power, he said, that they can only be understood as first-strike nuclear weapons. "I say with deep consciousness of these words that Trident is the Auschwitz of Puget Sound." (Jim Castelli *The Bishops and the Bomb,* Garden City, NY 1983, p. 28.)
3. J. B. Metz 'Oekumene nach Auschwitz' in *Gott nach Auschwitz* ed. Eugen Kogon (Freiburg 1983). pp. 121–144.
4. J. Moltmann *The Experiment Hope* (Philadelphia 1975).
5. D. Soelle 'Theology and Liberation' in *Political Theology in the Canadian Context,* ed. B. Smillie (Waterloo, Ont. 1982), p. 113.
6. R. McAfee Brown 'The Holocaust as a Problem in Moral Choices' in *When God and Man Failed* ed. H. Cargas (Philadelphia 1981), pp. 81–102.
7. F. Fiorenza *Foundational Theology* (New York 1984).
8. M. Lamb *Solidarity With Victims* (New York 1982).
9. Rosemary Ruether *Liberation Theology* (New York 1972), pp. 65–94.
10. M. Horkheimer & T. Adorno *Dialectic of Enlightenment* (New York 1972), pp. 168–208.
11. See G. Baum 'Faith and Liberation: Development Since Vatican II' in the present volume, pp. 8–26.
12. A. Solomonov *Where We Stand: Official Statements of American Churches on the Middle East Conflict* (The Middle East Consulting Group, 339 Lafayette St., New York, N.Y. 1977). See also 'The Middle East: The Pursuit of Peace with Justice,' National Conference of Catholic Bishops, Washington, DC 1978.
13. Emil Fackenheim *To Mend the World* (New York 1982), pp. 285–286.
14. John Pawlikowski *Sinai and Calvary* (Beverly Hills, Ca. 1976), p. 222.
15. See M. Lamb *Solidarity With Victims* (New York 1982), pp. 38–39.

16. Proceedings of the 5th National Workshop on Jewish-Christian Relations, Texas, 1980 (tapes).
17. *Oz VeShalom* (P.O. Box 4433, Jerusalem, Israel 91043), English-language bulletin no. 2, November 1982.
18. R. Slonim *Grand to be an Orphan* (Toronto 1983).
19. E. Shorris *Jews Without Mercy: A Lament* (Garden City, NY 1982).
20. A. Waskow *These Holy Sparks: The Rebirth of the Jewish People* (San Francisco 1983).
21. R. S. Feuerlicht *The Fate of the Jews: A People Torn Between Israeli Power and Jewish Ethics* (New York 1983).
22. G. Baum *The Social Imperative* (New York 1979), pp. 39–69.
23. E. Fackenheim, *To Mend*, p. 306.
24. M. R. Marrus 'Is There a New Antisemitism?' *Middle East Focus* 6, no 4 (November 1983), 14.
25. *Ibid.*
26. *Ibid.*
27. *Ibid.*, pp. 15–16.
28. R. Slonim, *Grand* p. 152.
29. David Hartman 'Auschwitz or Sinai?' *The Jerusalem Post*, Oct. 12, 1982. See *The Ecumenist* 21, no. 1 pp. 6–8.
30. Jacob Neusner *Stranger at Home: The Holocaust, Zionism and American Judaism* (Chicago 1981). Dow Marmur *Beyond Survival: Reflections on the Future of Judaism* (London 1982).

10.
Three Theses on Contextual Theology

In this paper I wish to deal with the social context of theology from a theological point of view. I wish to show that by entering upon dialogue with sociology, theologians do not abandon theology but remain guided throughout by a theological perspective. Each of the three theses I propose deserves an extensive treatment. All I can do here is to indicate the direction the argument should take. The three theses are the following: 1. Theology must analyze and reflect upon its historical context for reasons that are properly theological. 2. Theology affects the choice of the sociological approach for analyzing the social context. 3. In the Canadian context theology must be based on an act of preferential solidarity.

Thesis 1

Theology must analyze and critically reflect upon its historical context for reasons that are properly theological.

While the concern of theologians for their historical context has been largely generated through dialogue with sociology and certain pastoral experiences of the Church, the imperative calling theologians to critical reflection is derived from theology itself.

157

The search for a contextual theology does not represent a surrender of theology to social science but arises out of the essential dynamics of the Christian faith.

It was undoubtedly dialogue with sociology, especially with the sociology of knowledge, that convinced many thinkers, including theologians, that it is impossible to grasp the meaning and power of ideas until their relationship to the social context has been clarified. Ideas, symbols, moral imperatives and theological concepts do not float above history; they are grounded in certain historical situations, they are uttered by people who wrestle with the concrete conditions of their existence. Unless their *Sitz im Leben* is analyzed and taken into consideration, their meaning cannot be fully clarified. Traditional thinkers, especially philosophers and theologians, liked to think that ideas transcended the historical situation, that they were universal, that they were true or false quite independently of their social location, that they were beyond politics and the social struggle. The sociology of knowledge has questioned this. Dialogue with sociology and Enlightenment criticism has forced philosophical and theological thinkers to confront the largely hidden involvement of their ideas in the historical struggle of their time. Thoughts, ideas, theology—all have inevitably political meaning: they have weight and power in history. They may not be reduced to their political impact, but they also may not be understood apart from it. Ideas may confirm the cultural mainstream, or they may encourage the forces of reaction, or they may express a new imagination that promotes the building of a better society. Even the affirmation that Christian faith is pre-political, i.e., that the believer's encounter with God in Jesus Christ is independent of his or her socio-political location, has political meaning.

After World War I and the collapse of the monarchy, the Evangelical Church of Germany, still deeply caught in the monarchical tradition, found it almost impossible to accept the Weimar republic. The Church remained faithful to the older order. When Karl Barth proclaimed that God was wholly other, and that the encounter with God was therefore quite independent of culture and politics, he was accused by the conservative theologians of the Evangelical Church of legitimating and supporting

Weimar. They understood correctly that the affirmation of the pre-political nature of faith in their situation was a reproach addressed to the Evangelical Church and a pastoral effort to free Christians to break with the past and become open to democracy and pluralism.

It would be interesting to examine the socio-political meaning of the neo-orthodox affirmation in other historical contexts. When a Christian church is under the influence of the social gospel and makes the demand for social justice an integral part of Christian proclamation, the neo-orthodox affirmation that faith is pre-political aims at taming the Church's prophetic engagement and thereby protects the political status quo.

To understand the practical meaning of the Church's message, theologians have entered into dialogue with social science. They were willing to learn that religious statements and theological theories are always incarnate in historical situations and become bearers of political meaning that often escapes their authors. Fidelity to the Gospel demands of theologians (a) that they clarify this hidden political meaning and (b) that they evaluate this meaning in terms of Gospel values. Theology must assume responsibility for its socio-political impact. Pre-critical theology is no longer adequate for the present age.

The theologians who opened themselves to critical reflection of this kind quickly realized that the preaching of the Gospel in the Churches has become quite individualistic over the centuries. Sin has come to mean personal sin, conversion a turning away from personal sin to Jesus the Savior, and the new life the regeneration of individual believers in the Spirit. This "privatization" of the Gospel has questionable political consequences. For one, it sanctions the individualism of modern society. If sin is understood largely in personal terms, then the judgment of God pronounced on us does not touch society at all. The preaching on sin does not involve the preacher in critical reflection on political and economic institutions. Yet according to the Scriptures, sin is both personal and social. In its self organization Israel often sinned against the Lord. Jesus' judgment on the religious parties in Israel had to do with the collective deformation of their religious consciousness. And if sin is both personal and social, then conversion and redemption too have personal and social aspects. The new life into which Christians are initiated has social consequences. Thanks to the impact of this theological trend, the Synod of Bishops held at the Vatican in 1971 published a statement *Justice in the World* which recognized the reality of social sin and declared that the redemption which Jesus Christ has brought includes the liberation of people from the condition of oppression.

What follows from this is that Christian theologians who clarify the meaning of sin and redemption today must attend to the historical context in which the Church and the theological community find themselves. To proclaim Jesus in truth we must name the sin from which he saves us and the new life toward which he calls us—and this naming includes the socio-political order.

This is the theological method to which theologians have been led by the pressure of historical events and the dialogue with the sociology of knowledge. Is this approach in keeping with biblical revelation? Does the entry into critical theology lead to an estrangement of theology from its own substance and inspiration? Or does it, on the contrary, express a new fidelity to theology's own nature and mission? Thesis 1 of this paper affirms that the demand for a critical contextual theology is properly speaking theological.

In the Scriptures, faith is always presented as an encounter with God's Word as judgment and new life. Faith has therefore a dynamic structure. It implies the acknowledgement of the divine judgment, the recognition of sin, repentance and a turning away from sin to the Author of mercy; and it leads to a new perception of reality, a new orientation of life, and a new openness to the future. According to biblical teaching, the recognition of sin itself is a divine gift. People cannot enter upon self-knowledge relying on their own resources. It is the encounter with the divine Word that leads people to self-knowledge, reveals the hidden elements of sin and discloses the as yet unrealized and unexplored possibilities of the present situation. The old Protestant-Catholic controversy whether we are saved by faith alone or by faith and works tended to obscure the true dynamics of biblical faith,

namely conversion and entry upon new life. Faith has an operational thrust. Faith is a praxis. Faith is discipleship.

Christians wish to remain open to God's continued address:
they are ready to discover new levels of sin and destructiveness
operative in their lives. They listen to God's Word speaking to
them in Scripture, in the Church's preaching, in conversation
with others and in historical experiences. Conversion in this
sense is an ongoing obedience to God's Word, even when we
should be addressed by secular voices. When the native peoples
of Canada speak to us, we discover how deeply our communities
have been identified with conquest and domination. Yet listening
to them we hear more than their voice; we hear a transcendent
summons. The critique of religion that comes to us from the Enlightenment has power over us to the extent that it can be grafted
upon the prophetic tradition of the Scriptures and thus mediates
a summons that comes from God.

In the Scriptures the operational thrust of faith had to do
with the neighbor and with the life of the community. At a few
exceptional moments, the people of Israel, then a small agri-
cultural people, believed that they were collectively responsible
for their societal life. God's Word addressed to them through
the prophets had immediate political meaning. But in most situations, the ancient Jews, imprisoned as they were in imperialistic institutions, did not think that they were collectively
responsible for their society. Society was a structure that had
to be borne with patience. There were some moments when
people praised their social organization. There were other times
when social structures were so oppressive that people longed to
be delivered from them and yearned for the coming of a new
age. In all these situations, the operational dimension of faith
related believers to their neighbor and to the believing community.

It was only in modern times, through the industrial and
democratic revolutions, that people discovered their power over
the processes of nature and society and hence experienced a new
sense of collective responsibility for their world. It was then only
that the life of faith touched upon the political order in a critical
way. In the present situation, the encounter with God's Word as

judgment and new life includes the entry into self-knowledge, the recognition of sin in its personal and social dimension, repentance, and the raising of consciousness in regard to the destructive trends operative in one's world. The new life that it offered unfolds the as yet undiscovered and unexplored possibilities of the present on the personal and social level. The dynamics of faith in contemporary society has a political thrust. The critical concern of Christian theology for its social context is, therefore, due to the very structure of Christian faith.

Thesis 2

Theology affects the choice of the sociological approach for analyzing the social context.

As theologians want to come to a better understanding of the social context to which they belong, they turn to sociological studies. Thesis 2 proposes that in choosing a sociological approach theological reflection is involved. The choice has to do with scientific considerations but it is for all that not a purely secular option. The entry into self-knowledge and the recognition of sin is never simply the work of flesh and blood; it is guided by the Spirit, or it cannot take place at all. Science alone cannot reveal to us the sin in which we live. Thesis 2 proposes that in turning to sociological science, the theologian continues to operate out of Christian faith.

I wish to discuss three types of social theories that present a sociology of evil applicable to contemporary society, even though they are not all of the same importance. The *first* one in particular has little support among social scientists. It is found, for instance, in the book *Identity and the Sacred* by the Canadian sociologist Hans Mol. Mol argues that the principal threat to the survival of our civilization is the undermining of personal and social identities and consequently of human well-being. Today society is being threatened by chaos. Today the rate of social change has reached a maximum. Nothing remains stable, nothing dependable, nothing sacred. People lose their sense of identity, they no longer know who they are, they are no longer nourished by their roots, they begin to float and in doing so destroy their civilization. To counter this great danger it is necessary to strengthen order in society. Mol's sociological analysis sanctions the law-and-order emphasis found in political society and some conservative churches. Mol regards principles of social justice, cultural critique and biblical research as the ideology of the intellectuals, a liberal subgroup in society. Truth for him is simply the truth of the positive sciences; truth for him has nothing to do with self-criticism, with social justice, with human freedom. Restraint on the recommended law-and-order policies is solely derived from practical considerations of whether they will work.

Mol's social theory is an almost indecent exaggeration of classical functionalism, according to which the well-being of individuals is promoted by the stability and equilibrium of the whole society. Whatever endangers this social equilibrium must be counter-balanced by new social or cultural forces so that the well-being of society as a whole remains protected. Sociological functionalism, however, has been concerned with personal freedom in society. It has tried to clarify the social conditions under which greater adaptability becomes available to individual persons. According to Mol functionalism has been too much concerned with adaptability. What present society needs are social policies that concentrate on stability and security.

Mol's social theory is not highly regarded among sociologists. Admittedly, it points to serious problems in our society that deserve analysis and attention. But to regard social change as the principal cause of social evil is a theory that does not stand up when challenged by rational arguments. What is most objectionable to me is Mol's positivism, his limitation of reason to scientific methodology, his total disregard of matters of truth in religion and matters of justice in society.

The reason why I mention his social theory in this context is that it expresses the viewpoint of many people in our society who are not students of sociology. The emergence on the political scene of peoples and classes who have previously been subjugated and who now demand their rightful place among the nations threatens the stability of our societies and the sense of security of the middle classes. For this reason we are witnessing new cultural trends, secular and religious, that put greater emphasis on security and try to reconcile people to the existence of an unjust world. Let us not get all excited about social justice, let us resist the changes for which so many restless people clamor, let us defend our own security and stability. This cultural trend exists today even in the Christian churches. Mol's sociology fits into this new cultural trend.

The *second* theory I wish to mention, a famous one this time, locates the dehumanizing trends in modern society in the growing power of technology and bureaucracy. Max Weber spoke of the increasing "rationalization" of modern society which, according to him, led to the decline of culture and the disenchantment of the world. Human life was becoming rational, programmed, utilitarian, defined by material needs and the work necessary to satisfy them, leaving no room for human creativity and self-expression. This social theory goes back to the nineteenth century when social critics began to analyze the impact of modernity on society; and it is still defended by contemporary social thinkers, Peter Berger for instance, who try to give it greater scientific clarity.

Peter Berger argues that the malaise of modernity, source of restlessness and despair, is people's impotence in the face of the mega-structures in which they are caught, whether they be big government, big corporation, or big labor unions. Human life is becoming ever more controlled by technology and bureaucracy, "technocracy" in the jargon of the 1960's. Profound frustration enters into people's hearts whether they be rich, middle class, or poor. Berger argues that socialists have misinterpreted the malaise of modernity: they have tried to make people believe that injustice and inequality are the principal causes of human suffering. They falsely believe that greater social justice will produce a more human society. Large-scale industrialization, Berger argues, leads inevitably to technocracy, whether the economic system be capitalist or socialist. The modern malaise is here to stay. The only way to protect humanity from total depersonalization is the creation of communities, small enough that members come to know one another by name, in which people spend their time away from work. These mediating structures, as Berger calls them, will protect and promote man's humanity. Berger argues that the Christian churches should abandon their preoccupation with social justice, especially the support they give to third world liberation movements, and instead place new emphasis on the experience of the sacred and the local congregation built around this experience. In this way the churches would multiply mediating structures and help people save their humanity in an industrial society.

. Technocracy as principal enemy is a social theory that has been attractive to many theologians eager to contextualize their theology. The best known author is here Jacques Ellul who argues that modern society has become simply speaking the technological society, a kind of mega-machine, in which all social processes, including communication, alienate and distort the authentically human. In contemporary society all talk about truth becomes propaganda. While Ellul's theological passion summons forth admiration, in my opinion the French theologian vulgarizes Weber's sociology. For sociologists, technocracy is a paradigm or, in Weber's terminology, an ideal type, in the light of which they engage in empirical observation and examine the extent to which technology and bureaucracy have affected the lives of people in society. For Ellul, technocracy is no longer a paradigm or ideal type that guides observation; it has become simply the image of society and the metaphor for understanding contemporary culture. Ellul does not search for the existence of counter trends in society: in fact his method makes these trends invisible. If Ellul were right and all social processes and forms of communication in modern society were distorted and distorting, then the typesetting, printing and distributing of his own books would be indistinguishable from propaganda. Ellul does not offer sociological categories that account for his own activity in society. Frankly, this is bad sociology.

Jacques Ellul's theology has a following in North America. It allows Christians to create a theology that takes the social context seriously and reveals an important aspect of contemporary alienation. Yet if technocracy is the principal cause of human degradation, then economic exploitation and political oppression become minor issues. Why? First, because the dehumanization produced by technological society affects people in all classes, be they rich or poor, and, second, because the social struggles to overcome exploitation and oppression, being part of modern society, are seen as instruments that deepen alienation even further.

The theories of alienation proposed by sociologists such as Weber and Berger deserve most careful attention. No sociological theory of modern society can afford to disregard them altogether. But as such they are inadequate. The work of Jurgen Habermas has convinced me that theories of alienation based on the impact of technocracy are exaggerations: they magnify certain trends in society and disregard others. Technology and bureaucracy have a multiple impact on society, they generate a variety of cultural trends, some of which are indeed alienating while others on the contrary promote communication and cooperation among people. Here is an example. A gathering of church people and theologians involves many levels of technology and bureaucracy—think of the telephone system, the mail service, the modes of transportation, the printing of texts, and so forth—yet there is no good reason why we should exclude the possibility that true communication will take place. The theory of technocracy exaggerates existing trends in society; it is therefore incomplete and ultimately unreliable. Sociologists like Weber and Berger, moreover, assume that the relentless increase of the technocratic impact is derived from the nature of technological rationality while there are good reasons for holding that the impact of technology and bureaucracy also depends on the powers that plan it, organize it, and use it for their own purposes.

Apart from these sociological arguments against the technocratic theory of alienation, Christians are likely to be suspicious of it for two reasons. For one, there is a deterministic element in the technocratic theory. Modern society is here seen as inevitably oriented toward the mega-machine. Weber spoke of "the fate" of modernity and Berger of "the inevitability" of modern alienation. Christians do not accept deterministic theories; for them history remains a wrestling, a struggle, in which man's freedom is involved and in which the *novum,* God's gracious gift, remains a possibility. Secondly, Christians feel that the technocratic theory excessively relativizes the plight of the poor, the hungry, the marginal, the exploited. They fear that this theory helps the middle class to become reconciled to the existing structures of oppression. Weber's cultural pessimism, endorsed by many other German thinkers before World War I, exercised a certain ideological role: it weakened the resistance to the political ambitions of the German empire and provided a brilliant argument against the socialist movement. Because of this suspicion, contemporary Christian churches have not adopted the theory. For the World Council of Churches, and for the major Christian Churches, including the Roman Catholic Church, the cause of contemporary misery has been oppression and domination.

This takes us to the *third* social theory that offers us a sociology of evil. Here the sources of dehumanization are the structures of oppression and domination, built around the economic process of production and distribution. Economics is central because people must eat—and in a world of scarcity this leads to conflict. To live human beings must produce food, shelter, protection, social organization and symbols of self-definition, and it is in this process that oppression and domination occur. Some groups of people are made to bear the burden of labor; some groups of people (often the same) are excluded from the resources and the wealth produced; some groups (often the same) are prevented from participating in shaping society and from defining themselves. Economic exploitation is not the only form of oppression; there are others, for instance ethnic, racial, sexual, and religious discrimination. But these other forms of oppression are usually made to serve an economic interest and hence exercise a function in the system of production and distribution.

This theoretical approach to society is sometimes called "conflict sociology." Society is here perceived as a conflictual reality, divided between a power elite that controls the economic system and the dependent classes and groups that have little control over their lives. Marxism in its various forms presents us with conflict sociologies. Dependency theory offers a conflict sociology. There are conflict sociologists who do not regard themselves as Marxists, just as there are socialisms that are not inspired by Marxism.

The reaction of Christians to this sociology of evil is divided. Since the Christian churches in the West have on the whole belonged to the successful sector of society, and since in modern times they have usually been identified with middle class interests and perspectives, this social analysis of evil appears threatening to many Christians.

At the same time, the sociological theme of oppression is closely related to the biblical story. In the Bible the great metaphor of redemption is the exodus, the liberation of the people of Israel from injustice and oppression. This theme is replayed in a multitude of ways in the Old Testament. The Hebrew prophets demanded social justice in their own land by reminding the people of the oppression experienced by them in the land of bondage. "Remember when you were slaves in Egypt." Only if we look at society in solidarity with the oppressed do we recognize its true character. While the redemption Christ has brought has often been understood in purely spiritual terms, in terms that do not touch the structures of society, the apocalyptical passages in the New Testament certainly understood the coming of God's reign in historical terms and expressed eager longing for God's judgment on the oppressors and the gift of new life for the ordinary people. These are the reasons that many Christians in our day, relying on Jesus' promise of the kingdom, have an antecedent sympathy for a sociology of evil that focuses on the structures of oppression and domination.

Sociology of oppression exists in a variety of forms. It is important to examine their validity from a scientific point of view; but it is equally important to examine their anthropological implications. Some of the conflict sociologies are very rigid. They leave no room for the concerns expressed by Mol (identity and self-definition) nor for those expressed by Berger (cultural dehumanization through mega-structures). Some forms of Marxism are positivistic (they acknowledge only quantity and formal reasoning, abstracting totally from the qualitative dimension); some forms are deterministic (they see the course of history de-

termined by economic factors and hence subject to scientific pre-
diction); some are reductionist (they pay attention only to the
material infra-structure, overlooking the creativity of human
consciousness). Orthodox Marxism, especially as defined in
Eastern Europe, is positivistic, deterministic and reductionist.
But there are forms of Marxism that do not share these characteristics. There are, moreover, conflict sociologies that do not regard themselves as Marxist at all. In the face of the contemporary
women's movement, the ecological challenge and new forms of
oppression based on technological developments, a conflict sociology that wants to clarify the structures of oppression today
must be original, open and flexible.

There is no space to examine these conflict sociologies in detail. What is highly significant is that the Christian churches in
their official teachings have followed some form of conflict sociology. The principal evil in society is injustice, marginalization,
i.e., exclusion from access to power, wealth, and honor. Injustice
is a category that has structural and moral significance. The
structures of oppression are sinful. And since Jesus Christ has
come to deliver us from sin and death, from the demonic powers
that destroy human life, Christian redemption includes the liberation of people from the structures of oppression. On a previous page, I have mentioned that this is the conclusion drawn
by the 1971 Synod of Bishops held in Rome. A significant section
of the Catholic Church has come to acknowledge "the preferential option for the poor." Since society is a conflictual reality
to which we ourselves belong, it is an illusion to think that we
can examine society from a neutral point of view. From what perspective then should Christians look at the social reality? "The
preferential option for the poor" means that Christians should
understand society out of an identification with the poor, i.e.,
with the oppressed and dependent sector of society. It is argued,
correctly I think, that Jesus looked upon his society from the
viewpoint of the powerless, the little people, those who were
marginalized by the dominant institutions.

In a recent encyclical, *Laborem exercens*, Pope John Paul II
offers his own interpretation of what oppression and domination
mean in present-day society. He argues that the basic conflict in

the contemporary world is between labor and capital. Economic oppression and economic crisis are due to the fact that capital has been organized against labor. The encyclical vehemently defends the priority of labor over capital. Capital, it is argued, is simply the accumulation of labor; it is therefore united to labor and for this reason must serve labor. And how can this be achieved? Only through the workers' struggle for social justice. All working people must organize in solidarity to transform society, and their movement must be supported by all who love justice. The encyclical here makes use of a conflict sociology to understand contemporary evil. Social sin is analyzed with the help of sociological tools that clarify the structures of economic oppression.

It is possible to find similar if not equivalent social theories in the documents of the Protestant churches, especially the World Council. May I add that while Catholic ecclesiastical documents have condemned Marxism—that is to say, Orthodox Marxism—many times, they have recently admitted the usefulness of "Marxist analysis," the analysis of social evil in terms of the contradictions of the economic system, as long as such an analysis does not lead to reductionism. Even Cardinal Ratzinger objects only to an "insufficiently critical use" of Marxism.

It is impossible to offer in a few pages a detailed proof of Thesis 2 that "theology affects the choice of the sociological approach for analyzing the social context." Yet the above remarks at least indicate the steps that must be taken in such a demonstration. While the validity of the sociological theories must be examined in sociological terms, the value perspective is never absent. The theologian makes a sociological judgment as theologian.

Thesis III

In the Canadian context theology must be based on preferential solidarity.

Before explaining the third thesis, a few reflections are in order. It is easy to convince people that conflict sociology and the option for the poor apply to certain third world countries such as the Philippines or Latin America. In these countries a fairly small power elite linked to international capitalism stands over against the vast majority of the people, dependent workers and, in greater number, the marginalized excluded from production altogether. In these countries, a single oppression built around the economic system marks every aspect of cultural life, and even the people who suffer from other forms of oppression, be it racial or sexual, have hope for greater justice only if the primary oppression is overcome. Here one may speak of a revolutionary situation.

In these countries, the revolutionary situation is the social context of church and theology. In the past, the Catholic Church was identified with the traditional power elite; more recently, the Church has taken the side of the liberal modernizers represented by middle class democratic parties. In the first context there existed a piety (and an appropriate theology) that was other-worldly and emphasized the sphere of the sacred. This helped people to bear the burden of the oppression and yet tended to make them passive. In the second context, a more worldly piety, accompanied by a new theology, promoted diligence and ambition, and enabled people to fit into and do well in industrialized society. These pieties and their appropriate theologies sanctioned social projects that benefited only a minority of the people.

Today a significant sector of the Church analyzes the social context out of an option for the poor, for the vast majority. Christians committed to this option understand the Gospel as a judgment on social sin, on the structures that marginalize the majority, and as a promise of new life for the people. In this context, Christian theologians regard it as their task (a) to demonstrate from the Scriptures that the God of Jesus Christ is on the side of the poor and oppressed, (b) to clarify how traditional religion and the traditional theologies, consciously or unconsciously, have legitimated the social structures of injustice, and (c) to present the Gospel of Jesus, freed from the inherited ideology, as God's entry into people's lives, enlightening and empowering them as a community to recreate their world in greater justice.

But does this sort of approach apply to Canada and other

developed capitalist countries? Canada is not divided between a small power elite and the great majority of the people living in misery. In Canada people's relationship to the system of production and distribution covers a very wide spectrum. The patterns of domination that do appear are multiple. On the surface at least, they do not seem to be structured around the economic system. In Canada we find oppression of native peoples, economic dependency on American capital, regional disparity, refusal to recognize the peoplehood of Quebeckers, and racism and discrimination against certain ethnic groups. In Canada women find themselves in positions of subordination. We have unemployment and inflation. We have marginal people in the country and the city, injured workers, old people, the handicapped, people destroyed by the struggle for existence. While there is suffering among the victims of Canadian society, the total picture cannot be compared with third world oppression. Some might wish to argue that conflict sociology, which sees society divided between a power elite and the dependent classes and groups, is not a useful tool for analyzing Canadian society.

Many Canadians are of the opinion that social evil in Canada is constituted by a set of unjust conditions that are only loosely related to one another. Commitment to social justice in this context means dedication to reform: wrestling with citizens to overcome some of the oppressive conditions and supporting the groups that are actually suffering. Concern for social justice here means involvement in a wide set of social issues. Many Christians who love justice understand the Church's social ministry in this way. What we need is an activist church and activist Christians. For them the commitment to social justice has very little to do with cultural criticism, intellectual activity, and theological reflection.

I wish to argue against this position. I wish to show that the approach of conflict sociology does apply to Canada. Many forms of oppression in Canada, unrelated to one another on the surface, are in fact built around the present economic system. Since there is no room here for a detailed analysis, I will simply draw my argument from recent ecclesiastical documents that have adopted a conflict sociology approach.

In a pastoral message on unemployment, written by the Canadian Catholic bishops in 1980, it is argued that the causes of unemployment lie in the changing structure of capitalism in this country. Because this is not understood by many people, they falsely blame the innocent for the present calamity. Some say that the workers themselves are at fault; they simply do not want to work. Others blame the arrival of immigrants or the entry of women into the labor force. Such superficial views give rise to dangerous prejudice. What is necessary, the bishops argue, is to analyze contemporary capitalism. The pastoral message mentions first the concentration of capital in an ever smaller number of giant corporations that operate on an international level. These corporations have become so powerful that they prevent governments from pursuing an industrial strategy. The pastoral message does not go into details, but the details are easy to find. The international structure of these corporations allows them to move production to regions where labor and raw materials are cheap. They are able to move capital from one country to another in the quest for more profitable conditions. Manipulations of this kind can have more influence on the destiny of a nation than the power exercised by the elected government. Many of these giant corporations have their head office in the United States. Some of them have their seat in Canada. Through these Canadian corporations certain economics in the third world are brought into subservience.

The pastoral message also mentions the centralization of capital. For the sake of efficiency and increased profit, industrial and financial institutions concentrate in certain urban centers dividing countries, and the whole world, into metropolis and hinterland regions where hinterlands suffer from underdevelopment and generalized poverty. The regional disparities in Canada have to do with the logic of capitalism. A 1979 pastoral letter, published by the Catholic bishops of the Maritime Provinces, explains the poverty of the region largely in terms of the concentration of capital in central Canada. The unwillingness to recognize Quebec as a people is also related to the protection of certain economic advantages.

The pastoral message on unemployment, moreover, mentions the high percentage of foreign ownership of the Canadian industries. Decisions that affect the lives of Canadian workers are here made by people who have no reason to be concerned about the well-being of Canadians. The pastoral message also explains that the Canadian economy, because of its colonial location, has always relied on the export of natural resources rather than the development of production. Canada is, therefore, in a special situation of dependence. Canada has still an economic structure characteristic of colonies. Finally the pastoral message mentions the fact that new industrial projects make use of such a highly developed technology that they employ few laborers. Here again, in the interest of efficiency, expansion and profit, decisions are made that do not benefit Canadian working people. In a pastoral letter on northern development (1975), the Canadian Catholic bishops argue that the decisions regarding the development of the north are made by institutions that define themselves in terms of the maximization of power and profit and hence tend to disregard the concerns of the native peoples.

These few explanations drawn from ecclesiastical literature indicate that the oppressive conditions in Canadian society are closely linked with the structure of the economic system. This structure produces unemployment and regional disparity; it motivates the domination of various peoples in Canada, the native peoples and to some extent Quebec; and to the degree that its influence remains unanalyzed, it leads to false explanations of unemployment in racist and sexist terms. It encourages, moreover, the exclusion from well-being of those people who no longer work (the old, the injured, and the broken) because in capitalism the worth of a person is defined in economic terms.

These few remarks suggest that the multiple set of injustices operative in Canadian society actually fit together rather well in a single sociology of oppression built around the economic system. It is appropriate, I conclude, to make use of the conflict sociology approach to understand social sin, and the social context of church and theology, in Canada. Even in this developed country, social justice demands that people choose between solidarity with society's victims or the defense of the existing order. What is called for is "the preferential option for the poor." Christians are called to preferential or partial solidarity. Sometimes this is called a class option. Since most theologians belong to the middle class, they have to opt against the perspective of their own class.

In some third world countries, solidarity with the poor draws people into a single historical project, the revolution. This is not true in Canada. There exists no joint project for recreating Canadian society. Because of the complexity of society and the interstructuring of various forms of oppression, Canadians in solidarity with the poor are united in their counter-cultural commitment but divided in their political struggles. There exists no political movement in Canada that embodies the aspirations of society's many victims. Committed Canadians are politically divided. Some Canadians committed to social justice even think of themselves as marching in the wilderness. It is not clear to them what movement they should join. Still their class option has important cultural consequences and hence exercises a political function in the long run.

How is the present economic system, which causes injustice in Canada and promotes exploitation in the third world, held in place? It is defended by the large political institutions, and it is sanctioned by the cultural mainstream. I wish to focus especially on the cultural mainstream. The cultural symbols of Canadians, mediated by various cultural institutions, including the mass media, the schools and the impact of the market economy, disguise the structures of oppression; they make invisible society's victims and legitimate the inherited economic order. For vast numbers of Canadians of middle and working class background, the national experience since World War II has been one of economic development and increasing prosperity. Capitalism has proven itself capable of overcoming the great depression. These Canadians believe that Canada has no class divisions. There are the few who are super-rich and powerful, and the few who live in destitution, but the great majority, it is believed, belong to the middle class stretching from successful business people to workers and farmers.

Mainstream Canadian culture persuades Canadians to entertain this perception of themselves. We come to think of ourselves as alike in our dreams and aspirations. We see ourselves as a business civilization. We are surrounded by cultural symbols that promote economic individualism. Society tends to be seen as a collection of private projects loosely linked through certain common institutions, not as a social project, not as an adventure of a people that struggles to assume responsibility for their own future and the future of the world. While the nationalist symbols of the United States leave Canadians indifferent, they are greatly affected by the American economic vision of humanity. In addition to this, the colonial background has often made Canadians timid and reticent; they are used to having their head office outside the country. They are often quite willing to be dependent, relieved when they can follow the decisions made by others. Mainstream symbols, disguising as they do the oppressive features of society, nourish a culture of injustice.

Christian theology in Canada must be countercultural. It must examine the cultural presuppositions of Canadian society and inquire to what extent they have influenced the life and piety of the churches and the theology taught at seminaries and divinity schools. Theology must introduce an element of rupture in regard to the dominant culture. It must be based on solidarity with the victims. As in Latin America, theology in a Canadian context must demonstrate from the Scriptures that God is on the side of the poor and judges mainstream culture; second, theology must engage in a systematic critique of the inherited spirituality and theology; third, it must present the Christian message in such a way that people are drawn toward solidarity *of* the poor and *with* the poor, and move toward seeing society as a social project for which they are responsible.

Theology becomes counter-cultural by recalling the critical memories of the Canadian experience. (Douglas Hall has developed this in his *Canada Crisis*.) There is the history of the Canadian social gospel. The subversive memory of Jesus has not always been neutralized in the Canadian churches. Theology must recover the prophetic elements of the Christian religion. Then there are the working class struggles and the socialist movements in Canada which constitute the historical roots on which to graft contemporary efforts to reconstruct society. Then there

are the historical struggles of the native peoples and French Canadians for juridical recognition and equality. There is the courage of the British pioneers who, coming to Canada at an early
date, often labored under conditions of colonial exploitation, for
instance being assigned land grants too small to sustain their
families. There is the struggle of European and Asian immigrants
who survived under conditions of economic exploitation and social discrimination. Theological counter-culture is also nourished
by Canadian painters, poets and novelists, the artists whose love
of truth and courage to be disloyal made them prophets in society.

Theology in Canada must learn to speak confidently of Jesus
Christ as the one who reveals to us our sin, personal and social,
who calls us to conversion, to repentant self-knowledge, personal
and social, and who initiates us into new life, a promise that has
personal and a social meaning. Jesus is here interpreted as "trans-
former of culture" (Richard Niebuhr). We must clarify what discipleship means today. We must learn to speak confidently of the
trinitarian God, the Ground of love out of which humanity is
born, the Word of truth that judges and enlightens us, and the
Spirit of hope that empowers us to remake the broken world. We
must develop a theology of the sacraments that shows them to
be moments of disclosure that reveal the culture of injustice to
which we belong and create a new yearning in us for a just society. To be Christian in Canada means to belong to a counter-
culture and be on the side of the lower classes and groups. Quebeckers speak of "les classes populaires" and of "l'église populaire." We cannot be fully at home in the middle class world to
which we belong. We need a powerful language of divine transcendence, one that expresses a rupture with present society. God
language must announce transcendence over mainstream culture. For God as "the Other" becomes available to us in faith
only through solidarity with "the others," especially with the oppressed others. The acknowledgement of divine transcendence
cannot be simply an act of the mind, a leap of abstract faith; it
must rather be a gesture of faith that resituates us in society and
changes our social perspective. Faith demands a price: we have

to give up our attachment to sin. And since Canadian theologians belong for the most part to the middle class, acknowledging divine transcendence means transcending the interests of their own class. Theology is here based on preferential solidarity—"une théologie populaire."

III
Critical Social Theory

11.
The Social Context
of American Catholic Theology

In this paper I wish to examine the impact of the social context on Catholic theology in the United States. In the first part I shall discuss several characteristics of American Catholic theology and then relate them to historical experiences that are properly American and not shared, at least not in the same way, by European and Latin American Catholics. In the second part of the paper I wish to raise a critical question in regard to American Catholic theology. Has this theology been generated out of an unreflected identification with the middle class? American Catholic theology is challenged by the perspective taken by the social teaching of the American bishops, a perspective largely derived from their solidarity not with the middle class but with the poor and powerless in society.

I

1. A distinctive American Catholic theology is something new. It is a post-conciliar development. It began while the Council was still in session. Prior to Vatican II, the theology taught at seminaries was largely derived from neo-scholastic manuals produced in Europe. It was taught under obedience and received under obedience. At that time Catholic theology did not represent an intellectual adventure. It did not excite the students nor was there

a response from the laity. Catholic theology did not engage in fruitful conversation with the Church's tradition, with early Christianity, the Patristic Age, the medieval debates, nor the wrestling of Catholics with modern thought. It did not introduce students to American Protestant theology; it did not even communicate to students the significant religious thought that had emerged in English-speaking Catholicism. For most students of theology, John Henry Newman remained an unknown. There was no attempt on the part of theology to communicate the theological insights contained in the imaginative literature produced by Catholics in Britain and America. Nor was theology related to American culture.

We note that the situation was quite different in Europe, at least in France and Germany and a few smaller countries like Holland and Belgium. Here creative Catholic theology had not been completely pushed aside by the neo-scholastic manuals. It had remained in touch with its classical sources and the innovative thinkers of the nineteenth and twentieth centuries. It was after all European theological developments that laid the foundation for the doctrinal renewal of Vatican II. And since European theology had never forgotten the historical dimension, Vatican II did not appear to Europeans as a dramatic dividing line.

Why was the American situation so different? Why was so little attention given to theology in the American Catholic Church? This question has been amply dealt with by historians. While in the first half of the nineteenth century the Catholic Church was in dialogue with American culture and sought full integration into American society, in the second half of the century the bishops decided, after a long and heated debate, to give pastoral priority to the immigrants who at that time arrived in great numbers from the Catholic parts of Europe. The Catholic Church, following a preferential option for the poor in its day, decided to become the Church of the immigrants. The Church now gave up its dialogue with American culture. In this context little attention was paid to theology. What resulted was a certain sectarian anti-intellectualism, a cultural mood carried forward right into the twentieth century.

With the convocation of Vatican Council II in 1960, the cultural and intellectual aspirations of Catholics, especially of educated Catholics, changed almost overnight. Americans began to devour the writings of European theologians, they invited the famous theologians to cross the ocean for lectures to the widest possible audiences. American Catholic theologians began to think and write themselves. New publishing houses were set up to promote theological literature. North American theologians became travelers: they were invited to give lectures in church settings and academic environments all over the country. American theology was being born.

Why did the American Church respond so enthusiasticaly to the intellectual liberation ushered in by Vatican II? Andrew Greeley has persuasively argued that the reason for this sudden explosion was an important historical development in the American Church.[1] Since after World War II, Catholics entered higher education and were joining the middle classes, they were beginning to feel uncomfortable with the pastoral style and lack of intellectual sophistication characteristic of the immigrant Church. Even if Vatican II had not taken place, Greeley proposes, there would have occurred something of an explosion in American Catholic life. Catholics were burning to enter into dialogue with American culture and be integrated into the American mainstream.

There was a certain analogy to this development in Holland. In Holland, Catholics lived mainly in the south of the country. They constituted a small-town and country population. When they moved to the industrialized part of Holland, they became laborers. Since World War II, however, Catholics had entered higher education, joined the middle class, and participated in the mainstream of Dutch life. As one writer put it, the new generation of Catholics were so creative because they combined the fervor of the minority with the self-confidence of those who have arrived. This combination is explosive. Of course, this mixture only lasts for one generation. For the children of these active and imaginative Catholics will not inherit the fervor of the minority: they now belong comfortably to the dominant culture.

There are historical reasons then, why American Catholic

theology (and possibly Dutch Catholic theology) is conscious of Vatican II as a turning point. This is when American Catholic theology started. So great was the jump from manual to contemporary theology that American Catholics acquired a strong sense that there were moments of discontinuity in the Church's tradition. Because of this peculiarly American experience, American Catholics, including their theologians, readily contrast the preconciliar and the post-conciliar Church. American Catholics tend to believe that the Church's teaching is subject to change.

In one of his public remarks, Cardinal Joseph Ratzinger has criticized the approach to recent church history that regards Vatican II as a watershed. He emphasized instead the continuity of the Church's teaching and theology. After a public lecture given by him in Toronto in April, 1986, Cardinal Ratzinger consented to participate in an open discussion at the Toronto School of Theology. We asked him many difficult questions. "In your public lecture you have spoken of the guiding function of the magisterium," one theologian said, "but you did not mention that the magisterium itself underwent transformation. North Americans," this theologian suggested, "remember in particular that in the fifties, John Courtney Murray was in trouble with the Roman magisterium over his defense of religious liberty and that a decade later he was invited to help draft the conciliar declaration on religious liberty. If we had an appropriate theory of development," the theologian proposed, "might we then not recognize that at certain times the dissent of theologians exercises a positive role in the evolution of Church teaching?" Cardinal Ratzinger agreed that we are in need of a theory of development applicable to the magisterium. But he did not like the word "change" applied to the Church's teaching, even in the case of religious liberty. Change suggests that modifications are due to external pressure of alien cultural influences. Cardinal Ratzinger preferred the word "development" which suggests a gradual unfolding of the inherited truth under new historical circumstances. The Church's teaching, he argued, never changes.

American theologians, according to my analysis, have a greater sense than European theologians and certainly than Cardinal Ratzinger, that the development of Church teaching, however continuous and self-identical, includes moments of discontinuity. For American Catholics, Vatican II was such a moment. American theologians sympathetic to Charles Curran's theological positions are not bothered by the fact that they differ from the teaching of the magisterium. I am prepared to argue that even American Catholics who desire the condemnation of Charles Curran's positions worry that the magisterium might even change its mind. They too have a sense that Vatican II was a turning point, and that they can no longer count on an unchanging Church. If Rome actually condemns Charles Curran's moral theology, these Catholics will remain afraid that Rome will pull another John Courtney Murray on them and in a decade invite Charles Curran to help formulate more appropriate norms for sexual ethics.

The passionate interest in theology, generated by Vatican II, has led to the creation of many new teaching institutions. We shall have more to say of these institutional changes further on.

2. The second characteristic of American Catholic theology is its openness to ecumenical dialogue. The almost total separation of pre-conciliar Catholic theology from Protestant intellectual currents was overcome very rapidly through the impact of Vatican II. In Europe, certainly in France and Germany, Catholic ecumenism preceded the Council. Thanks to the rapid post-conciliar evolution in North America, Catholic theologians have come to be engaged in constant dialogue with their Protestant colleagues: they cooperate with them in many joint theological and practical projects, and have come to enjoy personal friendships with many of them. Catholic theologians readily admit that they have learned much from their Protestant colleagues, and they recognize that Catholic theology in turn has had an impact on American Protestant thought. American Catholic theologians find dialogue and collaboration with Protestants unproblematic.

At the same time, this ready dialogue has not tempted Catholic theologians to move in a direction at odds with the Catholic tradition. It is my impression that Catholic theologians have remained very faithful. What they have learned from Protestants they have revised in the light of Catholic experiences and integrated into the Catholic tradition. They have been helped in this by the fact that the Catholic community enjoys a certain sociological identity. Catholics constitute something of a tribe, a tribal community, in America, defined by certain cultural traits that may not be easy to identify but that are often perceived intuitively. It is not just that Catholic theologians drink more than their Protestant colleagues. They do seem to reflect a different style, a different ethos, a different cultural memory.

The dogmatic foundation of the easy acceptance of ecumenism on the part of Catholic theologians remains somewhat unclear. While the conciliar Decree on Ecumenism recommends mutual respect, joint prayer, sustained dialogue and practical cooperation, it presents an ecclesiology that sees the Catholic Church as the unique embodiment of the Church of Christ and leaves the status of the other Christian churches somewhat vague. The Decree recognizes many ecclesial gifts of Christ in these churches but it considers them ordained toward their fullness in the Catholic Church. The Decree says that ecumenical dialogue must be carried on "on equal footing" (*par cum pari*), but does not spell out what precisely this parity, this equality, means. The ecumenical practice among American theologians transcends the ecclesiology of Vatican II. Americans often feel, in line with the philosophy of pragmatism, that a new practice, in this case a new ecclesial practice, in keeping with new religious experiences, will actually lead to a more appropriate perception of the truth.

American Catholic theology has also been open to Jewish religious thought. Catholic academic institutions often hire Jewish theologians, Catholic publishing houses publish Jewish theology, and Catholics engaged in dialogue with Jews do not hesitate to join with them in Jewish worship. Here again the practice precedes a clear doctrinal foundation. John Paul II's recent visit to the Roman synagogue gave universal recognition to a development fully embraced in North America, even though the dogmatic basis for joint worship remains obscure. It could be argued, I think, that the Church's recognition of the spiritual status of Jewish religion is the most dramatic example of doctrinal turnabout in the age-old magisterium ordinarium.

The rapid entry of American Catholics and, in particular, American Catholic theologians into ecumenism is related to the very structure of organized religion in the United States. Alexis de Tocqueville, visiting America in the first part of the nineteenth century, was the first to notice that the pluralistic structure of religion in America fulfilled an important social function.[2] Religion had adapted itself to the needs of people in a vast land, in a society marked by an as yet unheard-of horizontal and vertical mobility. While in Europe the churches tended to embrace entire nations and offer the overarching symbols that protected their unity, the churches in America constituted a plurality of communities, none identified with the whole, which allowed people to feel at home where they lived and when they moved to another place, to become quickly integrated in their new location. The plurality of religious organizations provided Americans with a sense of belonging in their vast land. Tocqueville's observations on American religion have been elaborated by subsequent sociologists. No one has written as persuasively as Andrew Greeley on the pluralistic, or more precisely, on the denominational character of religion in America.

The sociological distinction between church and sect has been useful for the study of religion in Europe.[3] Churches understood themselves as embracing an entire people, as co-extensive with a given culture, as the inherited, privileged, historic religion. Churches therefore sought an accommodation of the gospel with society. Sects, on the other hand, understood themselves as minority movements, as gathered communities, as made up of converts to the faith. Sects had no intention of embracing the totality. They did not desire integration into society. They emphasized rather the distance between the gospel and the prevailing culture.

Many sociologists have argued that the church-sect distinction was not useful for the study of religion in America. Richard Niebuhr observed that in America, churches tended to become sects and sects churches.[4] In America, the churches that arrived from Europe no longer aimed at representing the entire society: they became willing to see themselves surrounded by others. And the sects that arrived from Europe or were organized in America rapidly established themselves. They grew in membership, their people moved into the middle class, they acquired education and wealth, and instead of distancing themselves from society, they too tried to accommodate the gospel to the cultural mainstream. To designate the organizational form of religion in America a new term was required. In his *The Denominational Society,* Andrew Greeley, following Talcott Parsons, proposed that religion in America exists in denominations. Denominations resemble churches to the extent that they cooperate in the building of society. Denominations are worldly. But they also resemble sects to the extent that they see themselves as minorities surrounded by others. Denominational religion is pluralistic. A certain competition between denominations does not prevent them from cooperating with one another in the exercise of their social responsibility.

In the first half of the nineteenth century, the Catholic Church in the United States began to see itself as a denomination, as one church among many. Tocqueville marveled at the accommodation of the American Catholic Church to democratic institutions and democratic sentiments.[5] But when in the second part of the century the Catholic bishops decided to make their community the Church of the immigrants, they steered the Church away from assimilation and integration. A minority movement in the Catholic Church continued to seek full participation in American culture and its democratic tradition, a movement that was eventualy repudiated under the name of "Americanism." To remain apart from society, the American Catholic Church acquired certain characteristics sociologists of religion designate as sectarian: standing apart from culture, refusing to participate in the intellectual life, and cultivating visible signs of apartness, for instance observing Friday abstinence at public occasions. In the twentieth century, especially after World War II, the more access Catholics had to the middle class and the more integrated they became in American culture, the more they longed to participate on equal terms in the pluralistic society. Existing Church teaching forbad this participation. When Vatican Council II, in the Decree on Ecumenism, recognized other Christians as Christians and as other churches as Christian communities alive in the Spirit, American Catholics and especially American Catholic theologians quickly redefined their relationship to the pluralistic pattern of American religion. In sociological terms, Catholicism in North America became denominational religion, one church among others, faithful to its own tradition but ready to cooperate with others and assume joint responsibility for society with them.

This rapid development was quite different from the responses of European Catholicism to the new ecumenism. In Germany, ecumenism demanded the negotiation of a new equilibrium between two established churches. In Germany, ecumenism becomes very quickly a political issue. In France, Protestants were a minority, often a cultural elite, and ecumenical dialogue tended to remain confined to specialists. In England, Catholics were ill at ease with the privileged position of the Anglican Church and often preferred to remain aloof. In Holland, the entry into ecumenism was rapid, as in the U.S.A., but on very different social foundations: here ecumenism produced a new fellowship by bringing together two historical communities in a joint effort to influence the mainstream of public life. Only in America (and possibly in former overseas British Dominions) does the category of denominational religion apply. This is the reason why in America even the synagogues can be integrated into the cultural mainstream.

Andrew Greeley attributes the formation of denominations to the genius of the American churches. They adapted the inherited religion to the needs and aspiration of American society. This creativity, he thinks, explains the strong presence of Christianity in American society. There are, however, sociologists who have a more critical view of the denominational society. Richard Niebuhr in his *The Social Sources of Denominationalism* argued that it was the failure of the Christian Church to live up to the Christian message that resulted in the formation of the denominations.[6] The churches found it impossible to transcend the cultural tensions in American society, first between North and South, then between the urban East and the Western frontier, then between White and Black, and finally between the well-to do and the poor. The denominations resulted through assimilation to unredeemed America.

These explanations of denominationalism do not necessarily

exclude one another. Historical developments are complex. What follows from Niebuhr's critical observation is that the rapid entry of Catholic theologians into ecumenism was a development not necessarily without ambiguity. Did it imply accommodation to middle-class values? More of this later.

3. Another mark of American Catholic theology is its pluralistic structure. It is pluralistic from several points of view. First, Catholic theology is taught at many different kinds of institutions. It is, of course, taught at Catholic seminaries and theological faculties. Most of these, thanks to ecumenism and a more open approach to American intellectual culture, have moved closer to the university campus. This has led occasionally to new institutional arrangements. In some instances Catholic theological faculties have cooperated with Protestant divinity schools to constitute ecumenical unions or consortiums, schools of theology, which bring into dialogue and interaction distinct Christian traditions, all of which are respected and loved. There is no attempt in these new theological unions to create a theological interdenominationalism. The purpose of the interaction is to foster among the participants fidelity to the best and most authentic elements of their own traditions. As I mentioned earlier, the ecclesiology implicit in this practice has not been fully spelled out.

But Catholic theology is also taught at other institutions. Many Catholic colleges have created theology or religious studies departments where Catholic theology is made available to lay students. In some of these colleges students are able to major in theology and even obtain academic degrees in it. This is a postconciliar development. Before the Council, Catholic colleges did not offer courses in theology. The courses in religion that were available treated the topic mainly from a pastoral viewpoint. In those days, it was the philosophy department, committed to neothomism, that regarded itself as the soul of the college and the guardian of its Catholicity. The commitment to scholastic philosophy, called for by ecclesiastical authority, often made the philosophy department uncomfortable with the return to the Bible and the new approaches to theology encouraged by Vatican Council II. Sometimes tensions occurred in Catholic colleges between the philosophy department and the newly created theology department which emphasized biblical studies and a historical approach to theology and its philosophical presuppositions. The theology department tried to articulate in a new way the meaning of Catholicity.

Yet Catholic theologians also teach at many other academic institutions. We find them today teaching Catholic theology at Protestant divinity schools, at interdenominational seminaries, and in religious studies departments at secular colleges and universities. We find them at centers of religious educations, at mission schools, and at other pastoral institutes. The institutional base of Catholic theology has become very varied. We notice that many Catholic theologians teach at academic institutions where they are no longer subject to Catholic ecclesiastical authority. This is a phenomenon not without significance.

A second aspect of the pluralism of American Catholic theology is the diverse character of its practitioners. The membership of the Catholic Theological Society of America (CTSA) gives witness to this development. Theology is taught by men and women. The presence of women on theological faculties is only at the beginning, but the large number of women graduating in theology must make one hope that their number will also increase on the teaching staff of theological schools, despite certain hesitations on the part of the Vatican. What is remarkable is the body of literature of feminist theology that has been produced by American women theologians, Catholic and Protestant. This literature is unique in the world Church. American feminist theology is today being translated into many languages. Compared to other countries and other cultures, the participation of men and women in American theology is remarkable. But compared to the requirements of equality, the limited presence of women in American theological faculties is still lamentable.

The pluralism of Catholic theology also includes practitioners identified with sectors of society and cultural traditions that have been marginalized by society. There is an impressive Black theology, mainly in the Protestant tradition, though not altogether absent in Catholicism. A theological movement is emerging in the Mexican American community and more generally among Hispanic Americans. There are significant efforts to develop an approach to Catholic theology that is critical of middle-class culture and represents action groups in solidarity with segments of people, at home and abroad, that suffer oppression by the American empire. These new theological movements have achieved a certain institutional presence in the Theology of the Americas Conference, founded in 1975, which brought together theologians beyond the mainstream, representing third world Christians, women, racial minorities and labor socialists.[7] While these movements are still at the margin, they have had some influence on mainstream theology. This is true above all of feminist theology. Academic theologians who respond positively to Latin American liberation theology and understand their task as creating an appropriate political theology for North America, try to strengthen the impact of the new theological trends coming from the base. Their influence may not be strong in the CTSA, but it exists among us and may become more important. We are only beginning to understand what "the preferential option for the poor" means for the exercise of Catholic theology. What follows from this is that while American Catholic theology has a remarkably pluralistic character when compared to European theology, its pluralism is nonetheless marred by the structures of inequality proper to America.

David Tracy has argued persuasively that pluralism properly understood is one of the special contributions of the American cultural experience, a contribution that has become fruitful in American Catholic theology.[8] Catholic theologians have been in dialogue with several philosophical approaches and engaged in conversation with different currents of the social sciences. While these various intellectual currents, reflecting the secularism of the enlightenment, have often defended positions inimical to theology, they have been subject to self-correcting trends and sometimes achieved an openness that offered points of entry for theologians concerned with the meaning and power of the Christian message in the contemporary world.

Tracy recognizes that European thinkers are often suspicious of pluralism. Some think that pluralism implies a relativism that empties out the very notion of truth. Others see pluralism in the realm of thought as a reflection of the market, or better the supermarket, where customers choose what is most appealing to them. Radicals often criticize pluralism as an ideology that disguises the significant conflict in society by inserting it into the endless differences of opinion based on personal preference. Tracy argues that pluralism understood and practised at its best brings into conversation partners who are faithful to their own traditions and philosophical approaches, who respect the intellectual position of the others, who try to understand their point of view, allow themselves to be challenged by these others, and seek to respond to this challenge through enriching their own tradition either by retrieving a forgotten insight or by imaginatively drawing out of the inherited symbols relevant meaning as yet unexplored.

Pluralism thus understood does not imply relativism, compromise, or fuzzy thinking. Instead dialogue among several partners creates fidelity, imagination and innovation.

Allow me, nonetheless, to add a word of caution from a sociological point of view. The conversation involving two or more participants is only fruitful if there exists a certain equality of power among them. The call for dialogue between the powerful and the powerless easily becomes an ideology that aims at making the powerless happy without a change in their social position. Dialogue, pluralism and hermeneutics point the way toward universal reconciliation: this is true. But the commitment to pluralism must have a political thrust: it must aim at transforming institutions to increase equality of power among the participants.

4. I wish to mention a fourth characteristic of American Catholic theology, even though I am unable to clarify it completely in my own mind. In America, Catholic theology has a strong public presence. By this I mean (a) that the Catholic public regards theology as relevant and follows reports of what theologians are saying, and (b) that even the wider secular public recognizes the importance of religion in American society and hence shows a certain interest in theological developments.

During and after Vatican II, the Catholic public showed an enormous interest in the evolution of Catholic theology. Theological books sold well, public lectures by theologians were well attended, theological study days and workshops sprouted in every corner of the country. Even though this intense involvement of lay people with theology has declined, a widespread interest remains. Catholic theologians continue to have a sense that they speak for a community and to a community. This link to the Catholic community has given American Catholic theology a pastoral sense. Catholic theologians feel very strongly that theology, even when highly theoretical, is not abstract because it always has to do with peoples' lives and the decisions they make regarding the crucial issues.

But even the wider public, I wish to argue, has a certain interest in theological developments. The Catholic Church has a strong presence in American society. The significant controversies in the church and important theological developments are reported and discussed in the public media of communication. While there is often attention to the sensational, it is hard to deny that many excellent newspaper reports, radio and television programs, and analytical articles in magazines reveal a serious interest in theological questions and the meaning they have for the Catholic community and American society as a whole.

The social foundation of theology's public presence is not hard to find. Religion has been a success story in the U.S.A. While in European societies industrialization and entry into modernity were accompanied by the waning of religion, this did not happen in America. To interpret their own historical experiences many European sociologists have proposed the so-called theory of secularization.[9] According to this theory there is an intrinsic contradiction between modern society and religion. The more people become involved in industrial processes and participate in the technological mindset, the more detached they become from the churches and the more secular their philosophical outlook. In Europe there is much empirical evidence for this theory. However all sociologists, including the European, recognize that the theory is not verified by the American experience. Industrialization and the growth of the cities in the latter part of the nineteenth century did not lead to the waning of religion. On the contrary, religion fulfilled an important social function among all sectors of the population, including the workers. Vast numbers of workers were immigrants for whom the church remained the important community that protected their identity and trained them to survive and even do well in their new country. While secularization represents a significant trend in American society, especially among intellectuals, religion remains a powerful cultural force.

What is the reason for the success of religion in America? Sociologists have offered different explanations for it. Andrew Greeley has argued that American Christianity, thanks to its own resourcefulness, adjusted itself to the conditions of the new world and the emerging industrial society so that it was able to contribute to the social well-being of the people. Denominational religion provided people with a local identity linked to a national community: and it offered people caught in the pragmatic, this-worldly atmosphere of a business civilization with a transcendent purpose that gave meaning to their lives. Other sociologists have been less positive. They have argued that religion in America compromised with modern, secular culture by becoming secular itself, concerned with its social function rather than with the sense of otherness. Religion has become part of the American way of life. Religion in America, some European observers claim, has become part of an American ideology. Good Americans attend their church or synagogue at least occasionally. America stands for God against the atheist foe.

Whatever the reasons, religion is an important cultural factor in American society. As a consequence, American theology, Catholic and Protestant, has a strong public presence. Theology, moreover, is conscious of its public role. American theologians, especially the Catholics among them, tend to take for granted that religion is a dimension of human existence on the personal and social level.

II

So far we have looked at certain characteristics of Catholic theology in America and related them to particular historical conditions. We have mentioned (1) the sense that Vatican II was a new beginning, (2) the openness to ecumenism, (3) the institutional and sectional pluralism of the theology, and (4) its public presence in church and society. And we have not disguised the ambiguity resulting from the assimilation of Catholic theology to the national culture.

There are two quite distinct social sources for raising critical questions in regard to the development of American Catholic theology. The first such questioning comes from the Vatican, the institutional center of the Catholic Church, responsible for its worldwide unity. That Vatican thinks of itself as supreme guide protecting regional theologies from becoming too contextual and from neglecting the universal dimension. Yet observers of the Vatican easily have the impression that this call for universality and the warning against excessive cultural incarnation are based on the Vatican's own unconscious identification with a particular cultural phase of European history. While the Vatican suspects American theology of "Americanism," Catholics from North America, Latin America, Africa and Asia detect a certain pan-Europeanism in the documents emanating from the Vatican.

Recent events show that sectors of the Vatican are seriously worried about the development of Catholic theology and Catholic pastoral action in the United States. The reprimand of Charles Curran must be seen in the context of other public gestures on the part of the Vatican that express distrust of American theological literature, religious education, pastoral programs and democratic styles of ecclesiastical organization. These measures are supported by small Catholic organizations in this country with good connections in Rome, organizations that interpret Vatican II as if it had brought nothing new. They are unhappy about the new ecumenism, they oppose the puralistic character of Catholic thought and practice, and they resent the public impact of Catholic theologians on church and society.

Why does the Vatican pay so much attention to these groups? It is hard to avoid the impression that the Vatican at this time fears the farther decentralization of Catholic life and hence aims at greater centralization. Out of this policy comes the displeasure with the relative independence of recent American ecclesiastical developments. Involved in this may also be a certain European arrogance that looks upon America as a derivative culture, a watered-down Europe, destined to remain under the tutelage of European teachers.

There is, however, another source of critical questioning, one that deserves close attention. It is located in Latin America and other Third World churches as well as in Christian communities representing the marginalized sectors of American society. Here the question raised is whether post-conciliar American Catholic theology has surrendered to liberal values and the liberal political philosophy associated with the American dream? In the preceding pages, I myself mentioned the ambiguity associated with contemporary American Catholic theology. Has a certain sense of discontinuity made post-conciliar theologians forget the cautions against liberalism contained in pre-conciliar theology? Has the entry into ecumenism and the new denominational self-understanding encouraged Catholic theology to join the cultural mainstream? Has the theological affirmation of pluralism led theologians to a liberal, pluralistic political philosophy which sees society as the balance between various communities and interest groups that may need occasional correction but does not constitute a prison, an oppressive system, for any of them? Does the public presence of theology encourage the conformity of theology to the major cultural trends in society? Is American theology (and the theology of Canada and other NATO countries) generated out of an identification with the middle class? The question must, therefore, be asked: whether and to what extent American Catholic theology has become part of the liberal ideology that legitimates American society as the land of freedom and offers it as a model to the rest of the world?

With other social critics, I see in the United States three politico-philosophical approaches.[10] The first one corresponds to the orientation of the Reagan administration. It is often euphemistically called neo-conservative. It represents a peculiar union between monetarism and militarism. The neo-conservative political philosophy regards the free market as the essential principle of society, assuring economic growth, personal freedom and the relative justice of equal opportunity. Neo-conservatism wants to remove the influence of the public on economic institutions, shrink the welfare system, weaken labor organizations,

reconcile people with existing levels of poverty and unemployment, and foster indifference to the plight of the impoverished
nations. Neo-conservatism sees America as the outpost of freedom in the world. And because American society is the highpoint
of human cultural evolution, it is argued, the enemies of the free
market, the socialists, the people under the power or the sway of
the Soviet Union, try to humiliate the American people. What is
necessary, therefore, is a new love of country, a new nationalism.
To defend itself against its enemies, reluctantly, America has
taken on the role of a military empire.

Let me say that with few exceptions Catholic theologians do
not follow this political philosophy. It is to the honor of the
Christian churches, the mainline denominations as they are often
called, that they have resisted this trend to neo-conservatism. On
the highest level of their ecclesiastical institutions, the American
churches have expressed their commitment to a different political
philosophy. I shall say more of the courageous stands taken by
the Catholic bishops further on.

The second political philosophy in the United States is critical of monetarism and militarism. It represents the liberal tradition. It proposes reform. This political philosophy favors a
government-sponsored industrial policy to guide the privately
owned corporations and promote industrial growth that will create employment. It wants to see the welfare system strengthened
and organized in a more human fashion; it demands the respect
for labor organization, it opposes discrimination and fosters
equality of opportunity, and it calls for greater generosity toward
Third World nations. This political philosophy does not see
America as an empire but as a nation among nations and hence
calls for the cooperation of America with other nations to solve
the problems of the world. Liberals rely on Keynesian economics,
that is a national economy in which government subsidizes the
industries and intervenes in the market to overcome the periodic
slumps and depressions associated with capitalism. Liberals remember Roosevelt's New Deal of the thirties that set the economy on a new course, a course that eventually led to increasing
prosperity for the widest sectors of American society.

What has gone wrong in American society, according to this

liberal philosophy, is the decline of morals. Americans have become selfish, narcissistic, concerned only with themselves and their self-promotion. Gone is the traditional American spirit of social responsibility, gone the ideal of the citizen embued with loyalty to the community. Americans have begun to make use of public institutions almost exclusively for what they can get out of them. Because of this decline of morals, Americans no longer support the social ideal implicit in the New Deal. Instead they have turned to individualism and self-promotion. Many delude themselves that the well-being of society as a whole will be served if each individual eagerly labors to improve his or her economic status.

Robert Bellah's recent *Habits of the Heart* is the classical expression of the liberal's lament. In the past, Bellah argues, the American eagerness to succeed was tempered by a strong sense of civic responsibility. Thanks to this civic sense Americans desired a land of freedom and justice for all. But over the last decades, especially since the sixties, the civic virtues have been neglected. What is left is an almost universal individualism which expresses itself on a purely material level as utilitarianism or on a spiritual level as the search for self-fulfillment or what Bellah call expressive individualism.

Yet, according to Bellah's analysis, there are still some alternative languages left among Americans, languages that retain the love of community and foster fidelity to tradition. If healing and reform are to come to the American republic, Bellah thinks it will have to come through a cultural conversion to the traditions, secular and religious, that are bearers of community values.

There is however a third more radical politico-philosophical approach to American society. Here poverty, unemployment, discrimination, marginalization, the fragmentation of community and indifference toward third world nations are not seen as unfortunate accidents in an otherwise acceptable system nor as the unintended result of increasing cultural individualism: they are seen rather as the consequences of a politico-economic order created by the rich and powerful to enhance and protect their own privileges. Here the decline of virtue is interpreted as the result of an economy that relies almost exclusively on market forces and hence fosters a culture of self-promotion, competition, individualism, quantification and consumer gratification. Such a radical political philosophy is often proposed by Latin American social philosophers and liberation theologians, and by left-leaning social analysts in the U.S.A. identified with various marginalized groups, including a significant sector of the women's movement. What is remarkable is that this critical analysis has recently been adopted in important ecclesiastical documents, including the social messages of the Canadian Catholic hierarchy.

If this radical analysis is correct, then the liberal social philosophy outlined above disguises the real ills of American society, prevents people from recognizing the causes of the economic decline and the breakdown of their communities, and encourages them to entertain the false confidence that greater virtue, cultural conversion and the renewal of the old institutions will deliver them from the ills under which they suffer. If this radical analysis is correct, then the liberal social philosophy turns out to be an ideology in the pejorative meaning of the word, a set of ideas and ideals designed to legitimate existing power structures and disqualify the critics of the system as irresponsible extremists.

I am prepared to argue—though I may be wrong—that a good deal of American Catholic theology, innovative, ecumenical, pluralistic and effectively present among the people, has joined the cultural mainstream and expresses a liberal social philosophy. Vatican II itself recommended a new openness to modern, democratic, capitalist society. Vatican II itself offered a rather hopeful view of modern, liberal society. Vatican II itself put a new emphasis on the dignity of the person, on human rights, on moral conscience, on personal freedom. Vatican II itself reflected something of the cultural optimism characteristic of the North Atlantic middle-class societies, the countries from which the important liberal bishops and theologians came. It is my impression that American Catholic theology, reacting against the pre-conciliar indifference to personal experience and personal rights, has greatly emphasized personal worth, personal conscience and personal growth, all understood as fruits of the Holy Spirit. American Catholic theology has been less concerned with the common good than was traditional Catholic theology. The biblical message of salvation, the doctrines of the church, and the sacramental liturgy, all elements of the Christian tradition, were only too readily seen as gifts of grace, meaning and power, given to individual Christians and their communities.

American Catholic theology, as I mentioned above, tends to repudiate the neo-conservative trend in American society. But the critique of society which Catholic theologians provided has often been exclusively a critique of culture. In this context, psychology and psychotherapy appeared as helpful resources for analyzing the ills and projecting the remedies. My own book, *Man Becoming,* published in 1970, reflected this trend. What was required was a cultural transformation that would lead people to greater openness to others, greater acceptance of their own bodies, and greater generosity towards society.

Radical critics of American society would argue that focusing on a cultural analysis allowed theologians to dispense themselves from making a structural analysis of the economic and political forces with their link to the military. By calling for a cultural conversion, theologians left unsaid that without commitment to structural change cultural conversion means very little. What is required is both, the reconstruction of society and the renewal of virtue.

While liberal theology prefers to ground its reformist social impulses in the doctrines of the Incarnation and the universality of grace, political theologians recognize that social reconstruction implies a long struggle against powerful forces and hence prefer to ground their theology in the eschatological promises, God's judgement on a sinful world, God's coming through tribulation and vindication, God's reign as critical norm of all historical processes. Liberal theologians—and this includes most of us—engage in dialogue with contemporary culture to explore the salvational meaning of Jesus, God, grace and the sacraments, and then only, under the rubric of practical theology or social ethics, touch upon the structures of domination. Political theology, on the other hand—if I understand it correctly—supposes that we can articulate God's self-revelation in Jesus Christ only in the context of a social analysis that clarifies the sin into which we are born and the forms of new life that are concretely and historically possible.

It is my impression that the American equivalent of German political theology and Latin American liberation theology exists among American theologians only as a minority trend. We are grateful to Orbis Press and other publishers for offering us English translations of the important Latin American literature. Books on liberation theology even sell rather well. Courses in political and liberation theology are offered in many colleges and some seminaries. But the conscious rethinking of these important theologies and a responsible application of the radical perspective to the American situation remain confined to a fairly small number of theologians. I do not wish to mention them by name for fear of leaving out some. An important impetus comes from women theologians who situate the struggle of women in a movement critical of all forms of domination. It is only a slight exaggeration to say that the difference between the liberal and the radical trend in American theology is symbolized by the distance between two institutions, the thriving CTSA to which we belong and the faltering Theology of the Americas Conference. As I proposed earlier in this paper, we are only beginning to understand what the preferential option for the poor as hermeneutical principle means for the exercise of Catholic theology in America.

While a radical critique of modern society is found only in a minority of American Catholic theologians, it is found much more frequently in ecclesiastical documents on social justice, including the U.S. pastorals on peace and economic justice. The impact of the Latin American Church, especially the Medellin and Puebla Conferences, is here undeniable. The radical critique of capitalism (and communism) has been endorsed and further developed in John Paul II's remarkable *Laborem exercens,* however difficult it may be to reconcile his teaching with some of his practical policies. This new trend was very quickly supported by the Canadian bishops.[11] In writing their messages, the Canadian bishops relied on a network of small groups in the church which had opted for solidarity with the powerless and marginalized and looked upon society from their perspective. More recently the same trend has influenced the American bishops. Their pastoral letters on peace and the U.S. economy were composed in an ongoing dialogue with many sectors of American society, with special attention given to the marginalized and the radical Christian groups in solidarity with them. The same trend is reconfirmed in the most recent Vatican Instruction on Christian Freedom and Liberation (March 1986).

The tension between liberal and radical trends in American Catholic theology finds dramatic expression in the U.S. bishops' pastoral on economic justice. Both perspectives have had an impact on the pastoral letter. It is easy to criticize this lack of internal harmony. One may well argue, however, that the only way to get the support and the vote of an entire episcopal conference for a radical proposal is to insert it into a document that can also be read in a liberal perspective. Because I have the impression that the American Catholic bishops are more progressive in their social analysis and social vision than the majority of American Catholic theologians. I wish to present a brief analysis of the contrasting trends, liberal and radical, in the U.S. pastoral.

Much of the U.S. pastoral sounds like a call for a new New Deal. What the bishops ask for, in the name of justice and compassion, is a capitalist society in which government assumes special economic and social responsibilities. Government must stimulate, direct and stabilize the economy; it must plan for full employment, work for greater distributive justice, legislate against discrimination of women and people of color, and overhaul the welfare system in accordance with the dignity of those in need. In this context, "the preferential option for the poor" is an ethical principle that must be followed in the making of public policy on every level.[12] Decision-makers in all institutions must ask themselves what impact their policies have on the poor and what policies they could and should introduce to improve the lot of the powerless. Many of the concrete policy proposals contained in the U.S. pastoral follow this reformist thrust.

In reliance on *Laborem exercens* and on radical Christian voices in the American Church, the U.S. pastoral also contains bold proposals that go far beyond a New Deal Revisited. These proposals are summed up in the call for "a new American experiment."[13] The first American experiment, the revolution, created institutions to protect and promote the political rights of the people. Now that America has become the most powerful nation in the world, a nation and a world in which poverty abounds, the time has come, the bishops argue, for a new American experiment, one that will extend democracy into the economic realm. The economy is to be by the people and for the people. To achieve this, the bishops recommend structural changes for which there exist no precedents in the history of capitalism. They demand the creation of institutions that guarantee people's economic rights: the rights to food, shelter, health and work.[14] They advocate workplace democracy; they recognize the rights of workers to be the subjects of industrial production, that is, responsible agents sharing in the decisions that affect the work process and the use of surplus value produced by them.[15] Finally, the bishops propose that the market economy operate within a plan, a national plan, aimed at the service of the common good and controlled by the democratic process.[16]

The pastoral recognizes that a new New Deal or the new American experiment, or something in between, can come about only through the cultural conversion of the majority, through the commitment to a new consensus. The ethical and in fact the religious dimension is here primary. But in the context it is quite clear that the moral conversion offers a solution for present ills only if it is accompanied by bold structural changes. The pastoral follows the old adage of Pius XI, "Two things are necessary for the reconstruction of society, the reform of institutions and the conversion of morals."[17] What the pastoral does not recognize as clearly as other ecclesiastical documents is that contemporary individualism and utilitarianism, the respectability of economic greed and the indifference to inequality and poverty, are to a large extent the result of an economic system that relies almost exclusively on the free market. Still, in my judgement, the U.S. pastoral has a clearer sense than the major trend of American (and NATO) Catholic theology that the problems of personal spirituality, personal ethics, and personal well-being cannot be understood and overcome without an analysis of the material factors of domination and an historical commitment to emancipation.

At the end of this paper, then, I see myself arriving at an improbable conclusion. If American Catholic theology were to follow the radical analysis of the contemporary situation, including the arms race and the quest for empire, contained in contemporary ecclesiastical teaching, American Catholic theology would move more resolutely in a new direction, in line with political theology, and explore the meaning of the preferential option for the understanding of divine revelation.

Notes

1. Andrew Greeley, *The New Agenda* (New York: Doubleday, 1973) 42–43.
2. Alexis de Tocqueville, *Democracy in America,* vol. 2, revised by P. Bradley (New York: Random House, 1945) 9–13, 21–29, 104–18, 129–35.
3. Ernst Troeltsch, *The Social Teaching of the Christian Churches,* vol. 2, trans. O. Wyon (New York: Harper & Row, 1960) 331–43.
4. H. Richard Niebuhr, *The Social Sources of Denominationalism* (New York: Meridian Books, 1957) 17–20.
5. Tocqueville, *Democracy,* 30–31.
6. Niebuhr, *Social Sources,* 21–25.
7. S. Torres and J. Eagelson, eds., *Theology in the Americas* (Maryknoll NY: Orbis Books, 1975).
8. David Tracy, *Blessed Rage for Order* (New York: Seabury Press, 1978) 1–14.
9. Gregory Baum, *Religion and Alienation* (New York: Paulist Press, 1975) 140–60.
10. In this section I follow the analysis presented in the as yet unpublished manuscript, "The U.S. Bishops on Capitalism," by my colleague, Professor Lee Cormie.
11. Gregory Baum, "Toward a Canadian Catholic Social Theory," in this volume, pp. 66–87.
12. For a comparison between the meaning given to 'the preferential option' by the American and Canadian bishops, see G. Baum, "A Canadian Perspective on the U.S. Pastoral," *Christianity and Crisis,* 44 (January 21, 1985) 516–18.

13. Pastoral Letter on Catholic Social Teaching and the U.S. Economy, paragraphs 295–297.
14. Ibid., pars. 79–80.
15. Ibid., pars. 103, 104, 300, 303.
16. Ibid., pars. 315–317.
17. *Quadragesimo anno,* 77 in W. J. Gibbon, ed., *The Great Encyclicals* (New York: Paulist Press, 1963) 147.

12.
Humanistic Sociology, Scientific and Critical

When I began my studies in sociology at the New School, after having taught theology for many years, I was greatly impressed by the sociological critique of positivism. The writings of Max Scheler and Karl Mannheim were my guides at the time.[1] While their sociological and political views differed considerably, they were united in their lament over the effort to assimilate the social sciences to the natural sciences. They objected to a sociology that understood itself as a scientific enterprise to explain social action by discovering the laws operative in collective human behavior. They were critical of the claim that sociology was value-free and objective. They regarded this as an illusion. Both of them, even though in different ways, developed a sociology of knowledge which showed that the knowledge of the social reality involved the knowing subject, and that this knowledge was affected by the subject's social location and value orientation. Scheler and Mannheim had respect for the scientific method. But if sociology restricted itself to this method it had to reduce the complex human reality to measurable categories and thus confine itself to examining the external aspect of social action. In particular, positivistic social science had to abstract from the interior dimension of human existence.

Beyond Positivism

Positivistic social science has a reductionist impact on modern culture. Positivism persuades people that the only reliable truth is scientifically demonstrated truth, that values are soft, and that ethics is a purely private affair. Science and technology here easily become the metaphor of human existence. People begin to conceive of themselves as part of a system that operates according to fixed, impersonal laws. In this understanding society is neither an organic given held together by shared values, as Scheler supposed—in line with the conservative tradition—nor is society a social project in which people are involved according to their own creativity, as Mannheim supposed—following the liberal tradition. Both sociologists were convinced that positivism had dangerous cultural consequences. It excluded ethics from public life and from the debates over public policy.

Mannheim and Scheler were also concerned about the political consequences of positivism. For as the investigating subject in the natural sciences is superior to the object under study and entitled to manipulate and, if need be, destroy the object, so will positivistically inclined social scientists regard themselves as superior to the object of their studies, i.e., human beings acting in society, and be tempted to manipulate them and engineer their future. Human beings here count less and less. Positivism appears here as an ideology that fosters domination.

From the beginning of my studies, then, I was convinced that sociology must be humanistic, it must take into account the entire human being, it must respect persons in society. I was therefore pleased to learn from Max Weber that social action, the object of sociology, was constituted by two dimensions, by behavior and meaning, by an external aspect which was measurable, and an internal dimension which was not measurable but which sociologists could understand through appropriate interpretation. Sociological science is both scientific and hermeneutic.[2]

Max Weber's formulation prevented me from going overboard in my reaction to positivism. As a theologian I had my own reasons for being unhappy with positivistic social science. Many studies of religion looked upon religion simply from the outside, simply in terms of religious behavior, without a serious effort to understand the meaning this behavior had to believers and the believing community. Religious people are often offended by positivistic studies of religion because they do not recognize themselves in these studies.

At the same time, I also met theologians engaged in sociological studies who were grateful to positivistic scholarship because it delivered them from legends regarding the Church and the history of Christianity with which they had been brought up and which they later in life found difficult to swallow. There were moments in history when positivism was liberating. I remember a sentence in the writings of Mannheim in which he acknowledged the liberating role of positivism in historical situations where false and socially dangerous ideas promoted by those in power were exploded by the application of the scientific method. Thus positivistic research has invalidated various theories that tried to divide humanity into superior and inferior races. However much one argues against positivism, it is important that one does not reject empirical, quantitative research. Humanistic sociology must remain scientific.

The positivism which Scheler and Mannheim castigated was not simply a scientific and philosophical theory; it was also an intellectual atmosphere at the university and a mood of modern civilization. Many social scientists who do not regard themselves as positivists in the technical sense engage in sociological research out of a set of practical presuppositions that are in fact positivistic. They understand sociological research as objective, value-free, and demonstrable by the scientific method. And vast numbers of people in society who have never heard of positivism believe that the problems in society can be analyzed objectively by social science and solved by the appropriate office through the implementation of a value-free, scientifically demonstrated policy. Social problems can be solved, people think, without reference to values, without ethical reflection, without wisdom and virtue.

Criticism of positivism has led some thinkers to the repudiation of the scientific dimension of sociology altogether. When I began my studies in sociology, I read the works of Alfred Schutz who brought phenomenological sociology to North America.[3] He exerted considerable influence on the discipline. A particular reading of Max Weber led Schutz to the idea that the social reality was created by the meaning which people assigned to their actions, by the shared meaning through which they constituted their common world, and that for this reason it was in the language of everyday life that these meanings were negotiated and established. To gain an understanding of society we must investigate our daily consciousness of acting with others in the creation of the life world. We must unpack the implicit and unthematized knowledge contained in the language of every day. The life world is the primary world to which we belong: the more specialized studies of this world, for instance in sociology, are derived from this life world and never transcend it. Sociological research constitutes a special subworld in the primary world constituted by people through shared meaning. This approach reduces the scientific status of sociology if it does not cancel it altogether. Sociology is here mainly concerned with the analysis of consciousness and the roles which people play in the world constituted by them. The influence of Alfred Schutz is found in Peter Berger's sociology which presents itself as anti-positivist and humanistic.[4] Schutz's influence is also found in ethnomethodology.

There are other social thinkers who repudiate the scientific character of sociology. Some thinkers reject altogether the modern project, defined by the Enlightenment. According to them it was a grave error to conceive of human reason as an instrument of human liberation, promote science and technology and the control of nature, and struggle for a more rational, scientific, and responsible society. This sort of romantic reaction is found in some philosophers. I am more familiar with religious thinkers who repudiate the modern project. Both Neo-Thomism in Catholicism and Neo-Orthodoxy in Protestantism can be read in this way. The most influential contemporary theologian who defends this approach is the French Protestant thinker, Jacques Ellul. In his many books Ellul argues that the Enlightenment project is dehumanizing. Science and technology have transformed the human milieu into a machine, a technological society, in which even the best efforts at reform promote the manipulation of people, their subordination to technical ends, and the systematic distortion of public communication.[5] Making use of Max Weber's concept of "rationalization" and "disenchantment of the world," Jacques Ellul argues that "la technique," the dominant model orienting truth and values in modern society, inevitably produces a dehumanizing culture. Technology is so powerful that no force can stand against it: there is hope only for individuals who stand apart from it, who step into the margin, who refuse to play the game. Christians are called to stand apart.

Ellul has had considerable influence on certain Canadian thinkers. George Grant and Douglas Hall have learned from the French theologian.[6] While Ellul is a dedicated, thoughtful Christian who deserves great respect, it is my impression that he vulgarizes the sociology of Max Weber. Apart from certain polemical passages in which Weber expressed his fear of the future, the German sociologist used his categories, including "rationalization," as ideal types, as paradigms, to observe how far certain trends have gone in society. Weber's categories including "rationalization" pointed to currents in society; they were not meant to designate the laws that define society. Weber never denied that dominant structures and trends were opposed by countervailing movements in the same society. But by making an ideal type created by Weber the conceptual image of modern society, Ellul makes invisible counter-trends in society and hence leaves no room for explaining the purpose of his own publishing activity. For if in technological society all communication is transformed into propaganda, then this would also apply to his own books, printed, published and distributed by technique. Despite my respect for Ellul's spiritual stance, I feel that he offers the reader bad sociology.

I oppose the effort to defend the humanistic character of sociology by excluding the scientific method altogether. There is no reason to despise hard data, measurement, and demonstration. When the U.S. bishops in their pastoral on economic justice announce that a feminization of poverty is taking place in American society, I want to know whether it is demonstrable that the number of unemployed and poor is growing at this time and that among them the percentage of women, especially women heads of households, is in fact increasing. The pastoral provides the appropriate data.[7] Of course, sociology is concerned with more than the analysis of class structuration. It is concerned with causes. Why is it that unemployment and poverty are growing at this time in North America? And why is the heavier burden among oppressed groups placed on women's shoulders? Again, a proposed explanation must be demonstrated. At the same time, it would be unrealistic to suppose that the important debates in social science, the debates that touch the heart of our society, can be settled simply by the scientific method.

Allow me to offer an example of a debate that the scientific method alone cannot solve. In the first draft of the American pastoral on economic justice the bishops raised the questions of why unemployment and poverty were growing, why the gap between the rich and the poor was widening, why ever larger sectors of society were being pushed into the margin and excluded from participation. The bishops told us that the social scientists they consulted were divided on the issue.[8] Some argued that major changes had taken place in the structure of capital and the orientation of the economy, and that for this reason repairing the damage and overcoming present injustices would demand major structural change. Other social scientists argued that the present decline was not dramatic, that it did not indicate a significant break with the past, that it was due to unwise policies adopted by government and certain industries, and that it could therefore be incrementally overcome by the adoption of the appropriate policies. The bishops mentioned another problem which the scientists consulted could not resolve. The bishops wanted to know whether the economic collapse and the widespread misery in third world countries was produced by developments in these countries to which the developed nations of North America were simply onlookers, or whether it was produced by developments in third world countries that were in fact related to the growing wealth and power of the developed nations.[9] Because the scientists consulted could not agree, the bishops refrained from offering their point of view. In this case, it would seem, the scientific method alone was not sufficient. Social scientific research, as we shall see, involves more than the scientific method.

It is interesting to note that while the division among social scientists prevented the American bishops from making up their mind, the Canadian bishops resolved the question in their own pastoral messages.[10]

The Hermeneutic Dimension

Before we explore this inquiry into causes any further, let me return to Weber's position that social action is behavior-plus-meaning. To the extent that social action is behavior it can be quantified, but the meaning dimension cannot be quantified. Meaning demands understanding. Sociology includes the task of interpretation. Weber spoke of *verstehende Soziologie*. We must interpret the meaning of the action in the social setting, determined by commonly held expectations, "the shared meaning," and we must interpret the meaning that the action has to the actor, "the expressive meaning." It is this interpretative process that positivism has suppressed. Positivism looks only at behavior: it is behaviorism.

How does the sociologist go about understanding the meaning of social action? The scientific method is here not enough. What is necessary is to lay aside the cultural presuppositions of one's own class and society and enter into the thought world of those whose social action is being studied. One must enter their mental universe. What is required here is empathy for the people who are being examined, accompanied by growing self-knowledge. For the interpretation of the meaning which actors assign to their action must be humanly credible to the researcher. By putting themselves in the historical situation of the groups under study, the researchers explore their own self-understanding and discover new possibilities and powers within themselves. Sociological research calls for more than scientific reason, it calls for expanded awareness, openness to new experiences, imaginative identification with others. If this analysis is correct, sociologists need more than training in methodology: their training must en-

CRITICAL SOCIAL THEORY

courage them to become educated persons, persons of culture and imagination.

It seems to me a point worth making that since sociology aspires to insights into human action and the life of society, it cannot simply rely on the scientific method. Scientific reason alone cannot arrive at a deep understanding of human beings. Marx, Durkheim and Weber were philosophers as well as scientists. There is no substitute for wisdom. Researchers want to remain in dialogue with the classical sociologists whose work continues to act as guide and provide inspiration for understanding the social reality.

How can the proposals made by scientific, interpretative sociology be verified? They must stand up to critical examination of the community of scholars. Like all truths in the natural and the human sciences, they must be validated by evidence. In sociology it must be shown that the interpretation makes sense, that it takes into account the available data, that it sheds light on connected phenomena, and that it explains relations that were hitherto obscure. Daring proposals of interpretative sociology become acceptable if they give rise to creative approaches in other areas of inquiry. As I write this paragraph on how to demonstrate theses proposed by interpretative sociology, I inevitably think of the many ways in which Max Weber demonstrated his thesis that the affinity between the Puritan ethic and the spirit of capitalism affected the rapid spread of modernity in Europe and North America. Weber's thesis gave rise to many research projects into related areas of inquiry. He himself examined the economic ethos (Wirtschaftsethik) of the world religions. Many researchers after him have recognized cultural heritage as an indispensable factor in the sociology of economic development. Development proposals in third world countries are doomed to failure if the cultural factor, the ethos of the people, is not taken seriously.[11]

For Max Weber scientific, interpretative sociology was still an objective, value-free scholarly enterprise. He emphasized the value-neutrality of social science against the German government that wanted sociologists at the university to provide arguments in support of its own policies. Weber accepted the Kantian distinction between fact and value. He realized of course that sociological research was always carried on from a particular perspective and that this perspective in some way influenced the result. But he thought that this perspective was freely chosen by the social scientist. The social scientist chooses the question to be studied, chooses what aspects are to be examined and what aspects are to be left out. Still, once the issue and the orientation have been chosen, social science intends to be value-free and objective. The results of the inquiry must be demonstrated and stand up before the court of scholars, whatever their values and their political vision may be. Scientific rationality, Weber argued, was universal. We note, however, that Weber's distinction between fact and value differed from the similar distinction made by the positivists. For Weber the facts, the historical data, included intentionality, i.e., the subjective dimension.

While Weber defended the value-free nature of the social sciences, he wanted them to be value-relevant.[12] He thought that civic responsibility demanded that sociologists use their scientific skills to examine the impact of present social and economic policies on the population and study what would happen if these were replaced by alternative policies. What sector of society would be helped if this or that policy were adopted by the government? Would the burden on the poor increase or be relieved if this or that public measure were introduced? While sociology as a social science must abstract from ethics, it could nonetheless be helpful to those engaged in political life. Sociological research could enable politically responsible persons with an ethical vision to decide whether certain politices would actually help people and fulfil their political expectations.

When I studied Weber at the New School I was puzzled by his deterministic conclusion in regard to modern industrial society. He spoke of "the fate" of modernity. He lamented that the disenchantment of the world had become ineluctable. He predicted the end of utopia. These were polemical positions, basically at odds with his sociological approach which presumed that society always remained open to human agency. My first essay, later published as an article, examined whether there was empirical evidence in contemporary culture (the sixties) that the world

was not totally disenchanted, that utopias had not totally disappeared, that overcoming alienation was not necessarily an unrealistic dream.[13] I have always been convinced that Weber's
deterministic-sounding judgment on modernity was part of a
particular German ideological trend that associated industrialization with vulgarity and the decline of high culture.[14]

Weber's sociology was scientific and humanistic: for the significant human facts which sociology studied included subjectivity. Weber was not a determinist. Despite his lament about the
inevitable fate of modernity, his sociology respected the freedom
of persons as effective agents in the social process.

As a Christian theologian I had sympathy for this point of
view. History remains open to human intervention. At the same
time, I recognized that following Max Weber was opting for a
particular sociological paradigm among several others. There
were sociologists who saw individual persons and groups of persons more closely integrated into society and who therefore interpreted social action largely in reference to the function it
exercises in society as a whole. Something bigger than the persons involved worked itself out through their social action. Both
Marx and Durkheim understood society as a close fit, the former
in a conflictual and the latter in an organic mode. Both of them
understood social action as an expression of major forces operative in society as a whole. Max Weber did not believe in total-
ities. For him society was not a close fit. It was not held together
by the harsh bonds of exploiter/exploited relationships legitimated by an all-pervasive ideology, nor was it held together by
shared values, shared vision, shared symbols and rituals. For Weber the nation state was not a close weave. What held modern
society together was largely the power (Herrschaft) of government to make people conform to law and order. Weber took seriously the exploiter/exploited relationships in society and not
only in the sphere of economics; he took seriously as well the various forms of cultural legitimation that defended the existing order. But he did not think that this domination produced a closed
system: for him there remained room for countervailing trends
sparked by the enterprise of imaginative individuals and pro-

moted by movements inspired by them. Weber entertained a pluralist understanding of society.

Students of sociology learn very quickly that they must
choose one among several sociological paradigms. Should they
follow the functionalist approach? Should they prefer a Marxian
conflict sociology? Should they opt for Weberian pluralism? Or
should they turn to symbolic interactionism? How do sociologists choose the approach they wish to follow? The choice is first
of all a scientific task: sociologists want to choose the paradigm
that is able to take into account all the data, that remains open
to new research and new discoveries, that proposes causal relations that seem credible in the situation, and that has been used
successfully in important scientific studies by other sociologists,
especially by sociologists one admires. But the choice of a paradigm is not purely an exercise in scientific rationality. The option
also includes a philosophical dimension. All sociological theory
has implicit in it a philosophy of human life. Researchers turn to
a particular school of sociology because they have an intellectual
affinity with it, because they approve of its implicit philosophy,
or less reflectively, because it corresponds to society's self-understanding mediated by mainstream culture. The choice of a
paradigm is not value-free. Weber, it seems to me, did not see this
clearly.

May I add that choosing the appropriate paradigm in sociology is of crucial importance for contemporary theology and the
social teaching of the churches. Contemporary theology has tried
to recover the social meaning of the Christian message. Sin, conversion and new life have a personal as well as a social meaning.
And in order to understand the social evil in which we live and
from which we yearn to be delivered, theology must engage in
dialogue with sociological science. If the Churches want to spell
out the meaning of the Gospel for today's world and offer relevant social teaching, they have to turn to a sociology of evil. Beginning with Paul VI's *Octogesima adveniens*, ecclesiastical
documents urge Christians to engage in "social analysis."[15] Ad
dressing American youth at the Yankee Stadium, John Paul II
said: "Within the framework of your national institutions and in

cooperation with all your compatriots, you will also want to seek out the structural reasons which foster or cause the different form of poverty in the world and in your own country."[16] I have argued elsewhere that in choosing the appropriate paradigm for this analysis Christian theologians are guided by rational-scientific as well as value-theological considerations.[17] In recent years, Christian theologians and the leaders of the churches have chosen to look at their society from the perspective of its victims, the people at the bottom and in the margin. This principle is called "the preferential option for the poor."[18] Church documents have come to look at society through its contradictions.

Earlier in this paper I mentioned that the American bishops could not make up their minds in regard to two different analyses of the present economic decline. They recognized the widening of the gap between rich and poor and the painful human consequences for the whole of society which flowed from this, but they were not ready to designate the causes of this development. The experts who testified before them presented opposing viewpoints, each supported by empirical data and scientific demonstration. Why did the Canadian bishops take sides in this debate? The Canadian bishops argued that the widening of the gap between rich and poor is due to the present crisis and reorientation of capitalism. The Canadian bishops, if I understand their social messages correctly, evaluated the scientific analyses presented to them by the experts not only in terms of empirical verification but also in terms of the paradigm used in the analysis. The bishops were concerned with the ethical dimension operative in social and economic science. They were able to take this step, while the American bishops hesitated, because Canadian political culture covers a wider ideological spectrum.

Weber's understanding of value-free social science became increasingly difficult for me to accept. I realized of course that Weber's emphasis was a corrective. He wanted to protect scholars from government pressure. He also wanted to shield sociology from ideological invasions. Thus he was critical of doctrinaire Marxist sociology which approached scientific research with an antecedently determined concept of infrastructure and superstructure, where the latter was wholly determined by the former. But should it not be possible to protect sociology from ideological distortions without claiming value-neutrality? Why should sociology stay away from evaluative research? Why should sociology not become more explicit about the value-assumptions operative within it?

Science and Commitment

In my studies at the New School it was not Marx but Ernst Troeltsch who made me go beyond Weber. For Troeltsch social science was humanistic and critical. In an essay I wrote while at the New School, later published as an article, I examined Troeltsch's understanding of engaged scholarship.[19] Historical and sociological science cannot be separated from evaluation.

Troeltsch rejected the Kantian distinction between fact and value. He rejected as well the hidden presupposition of this distinction, namely the radical separation of subject and object. For Troeltsch the subject, the researcher, was not a human mind, identical to all other human minds, equipped with a cognitive apparatus ready to encounter the world. The researcher's mind had been constituted by a history, by interaction with culture, by personal experiences and material interests. The researcher belongs to a certain world. He or she is located in an historical context. And, conversely, the social phenomenon under study, the object of research, has also been constituted by an historical development. It too is the result of a social process: it too belongs to a certain world. Troeltsch recognized that in all likelihood a relation exists between the world of the subject and the world of the object. The historical development that has produced the object has had an influence on the shaping of the researcher's mind; and, conversely, the world of the researcher may well have been involved in the formation of the object that is now being studied. The radical separation of subject and object is, therefore, an illusion. Something of the object is in the subject, and something of the subject is in the object. The same history has generated both subject and object. History and social science arrive at reliable knowledge only when the relationship between subject and object has been clarified.

Troeltsch's position is immediately convincing when we illustrate it by the examples that have preoccupied us in this paper, the poor, the unemployed, the native peoples, the victims of society. When a researcher studies social phenomena pertaining to the underclass, then it would appear obvious that the world of the researcher is related to the object under study. The same history has generated subject and object. An attempt to deny this relationship, to approach the research project in an objective, value-free manner, would disguise the historical reality, perpetuate an illusion, and in an unconscious way give social science an ideological twist. In daily life we are well aware that as we walk past a distraught and depressed Canadian Indian on the street, we mourn: we realize that the observer and the observed are interrelated by a common history. They, the observed, are the way they are partly because of the world with which we, the observers, are identified.

For Troeltsch, history and social science research constituted a dynamic process, a back-and-forth, a circle as he himself called it. First the researcher examines the social phenomenon under study by relying on empirical, measurable data (behavior) and on the hermeneutical effort to understand this other world (meaning). Here researchers abandon their cultural presuppositions as much as possible. Here researchers seek "objectivity." But then a second phase begins. By the internal dynamics of the human mind researchers are taken back to their own social world with questions that have arisen from the research. The researchers' own world begins to appear somewhat different to them. They now see certain similarities, certain differences and certain connections between the two worlds. Even the categories in which the researchers have been taught to think become somewhat problematic to them. They discover that their mind-set has undergone a certain change. With this altered mind-set the researchers now return to the social phenomenon under study. There they will make new observations, discover aspects previously overlooked, and gain deeper insight into the world of the object. This back-and-forth will continue. Troeltsch thinks that this process aims at discovering a single perspective in which both worlds, the world of the object and the world of the subject, appear in their historical interrelation. In this process the researchers themselves will have undergone a certain transformation.

Positivistic social scientists regard the researchers' mind-set as non-problematic. When research comes to conclusions that are unreliable and misleading, then positivists suspect that an error occurred in the empirical observations or a mistake was made in the application of logic. They do not suspect that the subject itself could be the source of distortion.

For Troeltsch, on the other hand, the transformation in the researchers' mind deserves the greatest attention. A certain, almost inevitable dynamics forces the mind to compare and bring together the world of the object and its own world, the world of the subject. It is almost impossible to study the prisons of a distant country, the treatment of women in a remote culture or the exercise of authority in a certain period of history, without returning with questions about how our society organizes its prisons, treats women, and exercises authority. Such critical questions can be avoided only if a special effort is made to suppress the mind's inner dynamics.

This dynamics, Troeltsch insists, has an ethical dimension. It is almost impossible for the human mind to interrupt the connection between the "is" and the "ought." When we study what "is" it is almost impossible not to desire immediately what we think "ought" to be. People with different ethical visions will entertain different wishes of what ought to be. But the impulse to relate a given situation to what we think it ought to be is almost universal. Only a special effort of suppression can interrupt this dynamics of the mind. Troeltsch argues that the ethical vision of researchers, their desire for a specific future of their own world, has a research-guiding function. It affects the questions the researchers ask, the slice of historical reality they cut out as "fact," the categories they choose to understand the social phenomenon, and the sensitivity with which they read the empirical data. More than that, the ethical engagement of researchers affects the circle, the back-and-forth, the approach to seeing the two worlds of subject and object together. History and social science, even when faithful to the scientific method, are always an intellectual exercise that promotes a certain cultural vision, a certain kind of society, a certain moral universe.

What is the ethical vision the social scientist ought to adopt? Here Troeltsch remained somewhat vague. He believed that in each society there emerged a rationally discoverable cultural ideal of greater human freedom and greater human depth that remained within the possibilities created by the past and commands social commitment in the present. Troeltsch repudiated absolute values: he thought the task of humanism was to overcome history by history. He was convinced that an appropriate cultural ideal could be worked out for European society after World War I. Troeltsch helped to formulate the problematic that were to preoccupy Max Scheler and Karl Mannheim, even if they came to divergent conclusions. But Troeltsch did not pay much attention to the Marxist insight, later so influential in many currents of political science, social philosophy and liberation theology, that what was needed was a critique of domination and an ethical commitment to human emancipation.

Ernst Troeltsch then differed from his friend and colleague Max Weber. For Troeltsch, social science was not value-free. On the contrary, social science always operated out of a value perspective. Science and commitment went together. There are moments of objectivity when the researcher abandons his or her own world and surrenders totally to the object under study; and there are moments of subjectivity when the researcher returns to his or her own world, undergoes a certain transformation of consciousness, and approaches the object with new questions. The objective dimension, taken with utmost seriousness, protects the research from the influence of wishful thinking or propaganda, and the subjective dimension protects it from becoming an ideology promoting a scientific value-free society.

I found Troeltsch's position that social science always operates out of a value perspective fully convincing. It was validated for me every day as I studied sociological books and articles: the value-perspective of the sociologists always came through to me, even when the authors claimed to be value-free. Sociological studies inevitably have a political impact, if the word "political" is understood in a broad sense. These studies promote an intellectual culture that makes people look at society in a certain way and entertain certain expectations in regard to it. Positivism for instance, despite its claim of total objectivity, is not politically innocent. On the right and on the left, positivism fosters a view of society that is wholly determined by scientifically discoverable laws intrinsic to it. Positivism, on the right and on the left, overlooks creative personal agency: here society is not seen as open to human initiative. A concentration on structures easily makes sociologists neglect the role played by independent human endeavor. Among the classical sociologists, Weber was the one most concerned with protecting human agency and countervailing trends in society. In this Troeltsch did not disagree with his friend. In recent years the work of Anthony Giddens has provided a critical sociology that makes room for, and emphasizes, the ongoing relevance of personal agency.

Since social science inevitably operates out of certain ethical presuppositions, it would be scientifically more appropriate if sociologists laid their cards on the table, revealed their ethical vision of society, and defended their option with rational arguments. A sustained rational investigation of this kind would protect social scientists from prejudice and sentimentality. It would also introduce social science to a sustained ethical discourse. The claim of value-neutrality made by social science has removed ethics from the public debate of social policies. A humanistic, critical social science would give ethical reflection a recognized standing in social and political policy discussions.

This value-oriented understanding of social science was my point of entry into the study of the Frankfurt School. I was greatly impressed by critical theory's critique of domination, by its analysis of the political relevance of culture, and by its insistence on an emancipatory commitment in the social sciences. I was also impressed by the dialectical critique of the Enlightenment. Horkheimer and Adorno persuasively argued that at the beginning the Enlightenment looked upon human reason as the organ by which men and women were meant to free themselves and become the subjects of their own history, but that now, in its present stage, the Enlightenment tradition had become an obstacle to liberation.[20] What has happened? At the beginning Enlightenment reason embraced scientific or instrumental reason as well as ethical or practical reason. Practical reason touched upon the nature and destiny of human being. Practical reason was evaluative. Yet over the last century and a half Enlightenment reason has increasingly collapsed into scientific or instrumental reason. Enlightenment culture has become increasingly concerned with means, no longer with ends. Rationality no longer includes ethical reflection. Ethical reason has disappeared from the social sciences and from the debates over public policy. The scientific world view that emerged leaves no room for rational concern for human values and human destiny.

In response to this dialectic, critical theory does not reject the Enlightenment altogether; it is critical of the romantic option and the conservative strategies that favor a return to a pre-Enlightenment intellectual universe; instead critical theory seeks to overcome the one-sidedness of the Enlightenment tradition by retrieving the ethical dimension of reason. The Frankfurt School advocates a return to practical reason.

Coming to the Frankfurt School from Troeltsch and from my own theological background, I was greatly impressed by their attempt to retrieve practical reason. Many theologians have reacted favorably to critical theory. Yet with many of my colleagues I felt that the Frankfurt School did not take the retrieval of ethical reason seriously enough. They did not ask the question how values are generated, sustained and communicated. They tried to overcome "liberal" reason by a more solitary form of rationality, and hence retained the Enlightenment suspicion of the non-rational elements in community, ethnic heritage and religious tradition. They had few words in which to express their ethical concern and no rites and symbols to celebrate it. A certain insensitivity to the ethical remains a characteristic of the secular left to this day, including sympathetic critics like Jurgen Habermas.

Ernst Troeltsch, possibly because of his theological background, had a much greater sense that ethical convictions were largely mediated through community experiences. This historical understanding of the origin of values was defended against the secular left by another theologian, Paul Tillich, in his interesting book, *The Socialist Decision,* written out of a socialist commitment in 1932.[21] Tillich argued that socialism wanted to overcome the human alienation created by modern individualistic and utilitarian rationality. But because socialism tried to do this simply by applying another form of rationality, a more social form of reason and a more collective form of self-interest, it could never succeed: one cannot overcome the shortcomings of rationality simply by a new application of reason. What was required for socialist reconstruction, Tillich believed, was the rooting of the political effort in value traditions, community experiences, including religious aspirations. By themselves these traditions are dangerous guides in the political order, but if these values are strictly subordinated to justice, to equality, to universal participation, then they could make an essential contribution to the creation of a more just and more human society. Tillich here defended a point of view that has recently been adopted by liberation theology.

Through the impact of liberation theology, this point of view has been taken up in the official teaching of the Catholic Church. The following of Jesus, we are told, calls for a "the preferential option for the poor."[22] This option embodies a double commitment: to look at society from the perspective of the powerless and to witness solidarity with their struggle for justice. The option has a hermeneutic and an activist dimension. Catholics are encouraged to exercise their social responsibility through this option; they are also asked to reread and reassimilate their religious tradition through this option. The preferential option stands against all forms of domination and hence resembles the emancipatory commitment of critical theory, but because of its rootedness in religious experience, tradition and community, the preferential option also differs from this purely secular, emancipatory commitment. In line with Tillich, and following the more recent liberation theology, Catholic social teaching is worried about the social commitment to liberation that is secular in principle.

That social science and ethical commitment must go in tandem is a thesis that is controversial in most sociology departments. For what this thesis means is that sociological research carried on without an emancipatory commitment will arrive at conclusions that in one way or another strengthen the power of the dominative forces. And if sociology is practiced without respect for the spiritual and its historical sources, its conclusions will contribute to the spiritual empoverishment of the present age. Here engagement precedes science, here engagement is the pre-condition of scientific truth. And here the cultural and political impact of sociological research is one of the norms by which its truth is validated.

What are the arguments given in this paper that sociological research understood in this fashion is not propaganda nor an exercise in ideology? I have been critical of positivism and pleaded for a humanistic sociology. At the same time, I have defended the scientific character of sociology. One of the norms of verification remains the scientific method applied to empirical data. This scientific character protects the entire exercise from becoming wishful thinking or propaganda. Secondly I have emphasized the hermeneutical task of sociology. Here the researcher takes seriously the object under investigation, listens to the people whose social action is being studied, abandons pre-conceived notions, and interprets what the social action means to the actors. This process protects the humanistic dimension of sociology. The sociologists refuse to analyze social action by turning at once to causes hidden in social structures, causes that produce their historical effects totally behind the backs of the actors. To prepare themselves for the hermeneutic task researchers want to remain in dialogue with the classical sociological texts. But then there is the third, the critical, evaluative dimension. It is often difficult for researchers to decide when to turn from the hermeneutic to the analytical task. But when the sociologist does search for causes, he or she must choose a particular paradigm around which the data is assembled and in the light of which proposals for possible causes are made. I have argued that the choice of a paradigm has value-implications. It defines an approach to society that is inevitably value-laden. It should be added that the paradigm used in the analysis is simply what Weber calls an ideal type. This means that for each case it is necessary to justify why it is appropriate

to use this ideal type and not another. If the paradigm is abso-
lutized, if it is accorded universal validity, then social science is
in danger of moving into ideology. But critical reflection on the
paradigm can overcome this danger. For all these reasons, therefore, it is no contradiction to affirm the scientific character of sociology and at the same time insist that it is value-based and
value-oriented.

Conclusion

By way of conclusion allow me to summarize my argument. I
have repudiated positivistic social science and called for a humanistic sociology. Yet I did not favor all sociological approaches that called themselves humanistic. I rejected various
attempts to discredit empirical research and the scientific method
in sociology. In my eyes phenomenological sociology does not do
justice to the scientific dimension. I expressed great sympathy for
Max Weber's *verstehende Soziologie* because it embraced both
the scientific and the hermeneutic method in sociology. What
made me uncomfortable was Weber's claim that sociological research tended to be value-free and objective. This claim seemed
to be contradicted by the daily experience of students of sociology who discover a value-orientation in every sociological text
they read. Humanistic sociology, I concluded, has an evaluative
dimension. I favor a sociology that aims at justice, fosters emancipation, and promotes humanity. Sociology should be a critical
intellectual enterprise, critical of the object and critical of the
subject. It should uncover the structures and attitudes of domination in the object and bring to consciousness the subjectivity
of the community of researchers. Sociology is grounded in values
and in turn promotes values. Science and commitment go hand
in hand. While I have great sympathy for critical theory, I feel
that its retrieval of the ethical dimension is too unhistorical, too
rational, too indifferent to the religious sources of the human
quest for value and meaning. I am persuaded therefore that a humanistic sociology that is both scientific and emancipatory remains incomplete as long as the ethical dimension and the

understanding of liberation are not rooted in a religious tradition.

Notes

1. Max Scheler, *Die Wissensformen und die Gesellschaft;* Karl Mannheim, *Ideology and Utopia.*
2. Max Weber, *Basic Concepts in Sociology,* New York, 1969, p. 29.
3. Alfred Schutz, *The Phenomenology of the Social World,* Northwestern University Press, 1967.
4. Peter Berger, Hansfried Kellner, *Sociology Reinterpreted,* New York, 1981, especially pp. 17–55.
5. Jacques Ellul, *The Technological Society,* New York, 1964.
6. John Badertscher, "George Grant and Jacques Ellul on Freedom in Technological Society," in *George Grant in Process,* ed. Larry Schmidt, Toronto, 1978, pp. 79–89, and Douglas Hall, "The Significance of Grant's Cultural Analysis for Christian Theology in North America," in *op. cit.,* pp. 120–129. See also Douglas Hall, *Lighten our Darkness: Towards an Indigenous Theology of the Cross,* Philadelphia, 1976.
7. The Bishops' Pastoral, "Catholic Social Teaching and the U.S. Economy" (first draft), *Origins,* 14 (1984), p. 363. Modified in final version, nos. 178–180, *Origens,* 16 (1986), p. 429.
8. *Ibid.,* p. 342.
9. *Ibid.,* p. 370.
10. G. Baum, "A Canadian Perspective on the U.S. Pastoral," *Christianity and Crisis,* 44 (Jan. 21, 1985), pp. 516–518.
11. Cf. the work of the development economist, Denis Goulet, for instance his "Obstacles to World Development: An Ethical Reflection," *World Development,* vol. 11, n. 7, pp. 609–624, and "Can Values Shape Third World Technological Policy?" *Journal of International Affairs,* vol. 33, Spring 1979, pp. 50–73. Recently Marxist development economists themselves have discovered the crucial significance of the cultural factor. See Peter Worsley, *The Three Worlds: Culture and World Development,* London, 1984.
12. *From Max Weber,* ed. H.H. Gerth and C.W. Mills, New York, 1958, pp. 143–144.
13. G. Baum, "Does the World Remain Disenchanted?" *Social Research,* 37 (1970), pp. 153–202.

14. G. Baum, *Religion and Alienation,* New York, 1975, pp. 58–59.
15. *Octogesima adveniens,* n. 4, in *The Gospel of Peace and Justice,* ed. J. Gremillion, Maryknoll, N.Y., 1976, p. 487.
16. John Paul II's address at Yankee Stadium, n. 4, *Origins* 9 (1979), p. 311.
17. G. Baum, "Three Theses on Contextual Theology," Chap. 10 in this volume.
18. The expression, "preferential option for the poor," is taken from the 1979 Latin American bishops' conference at Puebla, Mexico: see *Puebla and Beyond,* ed. J. Eagleson, Maryknoll, N.Y., 1979, p. 264. For the meaning and the subsequent endorsement of this option see G. Baum, D. Cameron, *Ethics and Economics,* Toronto, 1984, pp. 40–46, and G. Baum, "The Theology of the American Pastoral," *The Ecumenist,* 24 (Jan.–Feb. 1986), pp. 17–22.
19. G. Baum, "Science and Commitment: Historical Truth According to Ernst Troeltsch," *Journal of Philosophy of the Social Sciences,* 1 (1971), pp. 259–277, reprinted in G. Baum, *The Social Imperative,* New York, 1979, pp. 231–254.
20. Max Horkheimer, Theodor Adorno, *Dialectic of Enlightenment,* New York, 1969.
21. Paul Tillich, *The Socialist Decision,* New York, 1977.
22. See note 18 above.

13.
Contradictions in the Catholic Church

It is not easy to interpret the recent changes in the Catholic Church's social teaching. On the one hand there is the claim of liberation theology that the divine promises recorded in the Bible include the liberation of people from economic and political oppression. Christians are called to a radical commitment in the struggle for social justice. This claim has been confirmed by the Latin American Bishops' Conference meeting at Medellin, Colombia, in 1968 and at Puebla, Mexico, in 1979.[1] The technical term for the new commitment is "preferential option for the poor." In his speeches given in Latin America, including the opening address at the Puebla Conference, Pope John Paul II fully endorsed the preferential option for the poor and the commitment to liberation, as long as liberation was not understood in purely economic and political terms. This new orientation, amplified in John Paul II's encyclical *Laborem exercens,* influenced the Canadian and the American bishops in writing their pastoral letters on economic justice. In their own way they, too, adopted the preferential option for the poor.

There are signs, on the other hand, that this new orientation should not be taken too seriously. There is first of all the massive indifference of the majority of Catholics and their priests to the new teaching. Most Catholics in North American parishes have only the vaguest idea of the new movement. The preferential option is supported only by a minority of dedicated Catholics. The Canadian bishops call them "a significant minority," significant because they summon the Church to greater fidelity. There are also public statements of John Paul II which appear to be at odds with the orientation he recommends in *Laborem exercens*. He has been critical of liberation theology. He has demanded that priests not assume leadership positions in political organizations. Sometimes this demand has given the impression that priests should not be involved in politics nor be politically committed. Then there are the actions of the Roman Congregation of the Doctrine of Faith, the former Holy Office, against Gustavo Gutierrez and Leonardo Boff, two influential liberation theologians, even though they have the support of their own bishops' conferences. Finally there is the 1984 Instruction of the Holy Office, signed by its president, Cardinal Ratzinger,[2] which warns Catholics, especially in Latin America, of the dangerous trends in liberation theology, trends that surrender theological reflection to Marxism and thus undermine the Church's unity and the integrity of the Christian faith.

At the same time, the Instruction does not invalidate the new orientation in the Church. In fact, the Instruction specifically confirms that the divine promises revealed in Scripture include the liberation of people from economic and political oppression, and fully endorses the preferential option for the poor of Medellin and Puebla, thereby approving the substance of liberation theology.

Divergent Interpretations

Political analysts and social philosophers who attach importance to the Catholic Church's historical orientation have come to diverging conclusions on what the new movement means. Carl Marzani's "The Vatican as a Left Ally" published in *Monthly Review*[3] offered an optimistic interpretation of the new trend. His analysis of the new movement in the Catholic Church, beginning with Vatican Council II (1962–65), strengthened and sharpened by the Latin American bishops, and climaxing in John Paul's *Laborem exercens,* leads him to conclude that "the Cath-

olic Church is consciously, though slowly and deliberately, dis-
associating itself from capitalism and its institutions as presently
structured."[4] What is John Paul's new teaching? The Pope holds
that workers are entitled, thanks to the dignity of their labor, to
participate in the decisions affecting the goods they produce and
the organization of the productive process itself. According to
John Paul, all ownership of capital, whether private or collective,
is conditional, depending on the use of the capital, on whether or
not it is used in the service of labor, i.e., whether it serves the
people working in the industry, the improvement of the machinery of production, and eventually the entire laboring society.
John Paul II offers a pejorative definition of capitalism. Capitalism is any economic system, by whatever name it may present
itself, in which the priority of labor over capital is reversed.

At the same time, Marzani argues that Pope John Paul is not
a socialist. Why not? Because he has no clear concept of class and
class struggle. Marzani recognizes that John Paul II recommends
a social analysis of economic exploitation. He quotes the words
uttered by the Pope at Yankee Stadium on his 1979 American
visit, calling upon Americans to move beyond conventional charity "to seek out the structural reasons that foster or cause the different forms of poverty in the world and in their own country."
Still, Marzini argues, the Pope opposes class struggle and hence
offers simply an idealistic view of what the world should be like.
Yet in the present historical situation defined by American empire, the cold war, the nuclear arms race, and the threat of world
destruction, socialists should engage in dialogue with Catholics
and look to the Pope as an ally.

A few years later, Joel Kovel's "The Vatican Strikes Back"
in the same *Monthly Review*[5] offered a different interpretation.
Whatever success the new movement in the Church may have
had, Cardinal Ratzinger's Instruction of 1984, published with
the approval of John Paul II, offers clear evidence that the Vatican is determined to define Marxism as enemy number one, to
oppose cooperation between Catholics and Marxists, and to destroy the movement of liberation theology, supposedly tainted
with Marxist ideas.

At the same time Kovel offers a sympathetic interpretation

of liberation theology, a sounder interpretation, in my judgment, than Cardinal Ratzinger's. Kovel recognizes the essentially religious and theological inspiration of liberation theology; he acknowledges that theologians such as Gutierrez and Boff stand substantially in the Catholic tradition and that their use of Marxism is quite "tangential." Liberation theology takes the class struggle seriously at least to the extent that it recognizes that churches are historically located and hence in one way or another take sides in the Latin American liberation struggle. Kovel even acknowledges that liberation theology has a message for Marxists. Liberation theology, in line with the Christian tradition, takes seriously personal consciousness and interpersonal relations. Marxists, Kovel argues, tend to overlook subjectivity. "For Marxism the challenge is to widen the spiritual opening through a deeper appropriation of subjectivity: what is nonrational, aesthetic, tragic, moral, and sacred."[6]

At the same time, Kovel offers a devastating analysis of the 1984 Instruction. He interprets it as the last word of the Vatican, the unambiguous expression of the Vatican's intention to crush liberation theology, and in doing so to undo the new movement in the Church that links Christian faith and commitment to justice. Marxism is to remain the principal enemy. While recognizing various forms of Marxism, the Instruction concludes that all of them, in one way or another, share the essential structure of Marxist thought: a determinist understanding of history, a materialist ontology, and the idea of class struggle as cause of history's forward movement toward ultimate freedom.

Kovel thinks that the Vatican's analysis of Marxism is false. "Unless one adheres to the by now discredited scientism of Althusser, it is impossible to read Marx and Engels as giving credence to the Vatican's image of Marxism."[7] Kovel seems a little too sanguine here. A deterministic version of Marxism, what Germans call "vulgar Marxism," is still strong as the official theory of communism in the Soviet bloc countries. Even in the West a purely scientific Marxism, a minimally qualified economic determinism, a positivism of the left, is still widely accepted among Marxist social scientists. Moreover, the influence of Althusser has by no means been overcome, especially not in Latin America.

Still, Kovel is correct: Ratzinger's Instruction offers a caricature of Marxism. More than that, it presents the wholly unbelievable thesis that those who accept certain aspects of Marxism inevitably assimilate, whether they like it or not, the entire Marxist project.

What Kovel does not notice is that the Instruction avoids setting itself directly against the new movement in the Church. The Instruction endorses the teaching that salvation includes emancipation, and therefore praises the preferential option for the poor. And, abandoning perfect consistency, it refers to the dangerous trend in liberation theology as "the insufficiently critical use" of Marxism, hence acknowledging by implication that a sufficiently critical use of Marxist concepts might be perfectly all right. After all, Pope John Paul's own social thought is strongly influenced by his dialogue with Marxism. The purposeful ambiguity makes the Instruction a mean-spirited and devious ecclesiastical document. Kovel has every right to be angry with it. Where he is wrong, I think, is to interpret this document as the definitive judgment of Vatican and Pope on the liberation movement in the Church.

How can one make sense of the contradictions in the Catholic Church in this area as well as in others? To shed some light on this confusing situation allow me to introduce a useful distinction, drawn from the sociology of organization. What follows is a tentative proposal.

Organizational Logics

Two logics are operative in every organization, the logic of mission and the logic of maintenance. The logic of mission deals with the aim and function of an organization, the purpose for the sake of which it has been established; the logic of maintenance deals with the well-being of the organization itself, its upkeep, security, and perpetuation in the years to come. Both of these logics are essential. Contrary to some people's idealistic impulses, an institution cannot survive if it overlooks the logic of maintenance. At the same time, the two logics are inevitably in some tension. In the discussions how to pursue the institution's purpose, how to allocate resources and plan for the future, the logic of mission finds itself easily restricted by proposals urging the logic of maintenance. Sociologists have argued that there is a trend in every organization, a trend that must be resisted, to put an ever greater weight on the logic of maintenance.

When the concern for the institution's well-being begins to overshadow the commitment to the institution's function, sociologists have argued, a dialectic begins to operate, according to which the excessive concern for maintenance becomes in fact dysfunctional and undermines the institution's well-being. Robert Merton has called this phenomenon "goal displacement."[8] The orientation of the organization is here toward its own perpetuation and support, in disregard of the aim and purpose for which it was established. But when this happens, the organization loses credibility, weakens its hold on reality, and paradoxically fosters its own decline. Robert Merton offers a social psychological theory to explain this phenomenon. He speaks of "professional deformation." He argues that the fidelity of bureaucrats and administrators to the tasks that have been defined for them, their desire to do everything correctly in accordance with the carefully designed plans, and the effort to detach themselves from personal feelings to make the organization more efficient and frictionless in its operation create a mind set among the staff members that becomes increasingly insensitive to the clients, i.e., the group of people whom they are intended to serve. Excessive preoccupation with maintenance makes the staff increasingly unaware of the world in which their organization exists: they lose touch with reality, they undermine the viability of the organization they so desperately serve.

Merton's theory has a *prima facie* credibility. Readers chuckle when they read Merton's famous essay on the topic, because they remember organizations with which they have been associated where professional deformation and subsequent goal displacement have seriously undermined the organizations' effectiveness. Merton proposed his theory as a reply to the thesis of Max Weber that to maximize control, efficiency and predictability, organization must become increasingly autocratic. Weber contrasts "monocratic" with "collegial" bureaucracies.

Merton persuasively argues that Weber overlooked the dysfunctional aspects of monocratic organizations. To overcome professional deformation and goal displacement, Merton proposes, organizations must promote dialogue among the various levels of staff members and between the staff and the people whom they serve. Without the corrective trends of collegiality, institutions become blind.

New Catholic Social Teaching

What happens when we apply this distinction to the understanding of the Catholic Church? I wish to argue that the Church's official teaching, including its social teaching, tends to be formulated in accordance with the logic of mission. Official teaching derives from Church councils, papal encyclicals and national bishops' conferences. Here the Church tries to express the meaning of Jesus Christ and his message of salvation in the social conditions of the times. Here the Church wants to be faithful to its mission in the world. While this official teaching may not be free of all ideological elements, it is produced and communicated at moments of solemnity when Church leaders, in dialogue with their people, try to distance themselves from the obvious levels of institutional self-interest and seek renewed fidelity to the Gospel, which they regard as a transcendent gift to the Church. At these moments popes and bishops have a sense that they do not own the truth, but serve it.

Special moments of distancing and fidelity take place even in secular societies and political parties that define themselves according to principles they regard as universal and depend for their success on the vision and dedication of their members. Even secular institutions are able, at certain special moments, to formulate the ideals they stand for, even if these ideals are inconvenient to the organizers. Moments of this kind are more frequent in religious institutions since they have available a language of conversion, forgiveness and new life which summons the leaders to the required commitment. The Church believes that at such special moments the guidance of the divine Spirit is present to it.

In recent years, the Catholic Church's official social teaching has changed significantly. I have repeatedly interpreted this change as a passage from an "organic" to a "conflictual view" of society.[9] The organic view, expressed from the time of Leo XIII right to the period of Vatican II, supposed that society was a mutually interdependent, hierarchical community, united by common values, in constant need of reform and the enhancement of the common good. This reform was to be promoted by the government, situated above the conflict of the classes, and translated into reality by the moral conversion of all citizens, including owners and workers, to the same values of justice and equity. This was the Catholic version of the widely held Tory social philosophy. From this perspective, Catholic social teaching was able to criticize modern liberal society: its concept of minimal government, its excessive reliance on the market, its individualism and utilitarianism, its indifference to the plight of wage earners and the poor.

When the Latin American bishops met at Medellin (1968) to apply the directives of Vatican II to their own continent, they realized that it would be absurd to look upon their own societies in organic terms. They recognized that their continent was caught in patterns of dependence which pushed the great majority of the people into ever greater poverty. Medellin analyzed the "external" and "internal colonialism" responsible for the economic and social orientation of the Latin American continent.[10] The bishops here opted for a conflictual view of society. Society was divided: there were the masses of the people, the great majority, living at the margin, lacking power and hope; and opposed to them was the network of the mighty, linked to the world capitalist system, which controlled the economic life of the nations. All the relatively small middle class could do here was to choose between the two sides. In this context the bishops no longer used the language of reform and development, proper to a more organic social philosophy; they preferred to speak of "liberation." Social ethics, inspired by the Gospel and seconded by practical reason, demanded a struggle against the forces of oppression.

I have argued elsewhere that this conflictual perception of

society has been adopted by the Church's official social teaching, including John Paul II's *Laborem exercens* and the pastoral messages of the Canadian bishops.[11] In a society marked by grave injustices, Christian love transforms itself into a yearning for justice that the heavy burden be removed from the shoulders of the victims. People are called to struggle for justice. According to this recent social teaching, the people, the great majority including the workers and the poor, are meant to be the subject of their society.

The claim that the people are to be the subject of their history does not transform the Christian message into a Promethean myth, man as the author of his own salvation. Christians hold that people are the subject of their history because God has created them for this and because God is graciously active in their lives, possibly in a hidden and unrecognized way, as the mysterious presence that calls them to enlightenment and empowers them to act responsibly and with courage.

The shift in Catholic social teaching has been considerable. To understand this evolution it would be necessary to analyze the historical period in which it took place. There is no space for this here. It is of interest that John Paul II wrote his encyclical *Laborem exercens* at a time when it appeared that the union movement, Solidarity, was about to transform the Polish system into a more participatory socialism. At the same time, the majority of Catholics have not assimilated this doctrinal development. There is hesitation among Catholics, including bishops, who are still committed to the older, organicist understanding of society and the mildly reformist proposals associated with it. And there is vehement opposition to this new orientation by men committed to the triumph of Western capitalism, whatever the social costs of the world population. In the United States vast sums of corporate money are available to finance opposition to the new teaching of the American bishops.

In search for new conceptual tools in dealing with the preferential option for the poor in a theoretical and practical manner, dialogue with Marxism is a natural step. This has been recognized in ecclesiastical documents. Paul VI argues that Marxism as a total world philosophy and as a political system cannot be reconciled with Christianity. But Marxism as a method of social analysis is a useful partner in dialogue, as long as the Christian partner recognizes the danger of reductionism, that is, the reduction of human consciousness to its economic base without remainder. John Paul II has engaged in an extended, critical dialogue with Marxist social theory.

The Logic of Maintenance

To understand ecclesiastical statements and, above all, ecclesiastical practice, it is important to examine the institutional logic of maintenance. The Church is obliged to be concerned with the requirements of its own institutional life. If Church leadership neglected this aspect, the Church's mission, the proclamation and service of the Gospel, would rapidly decline. At the same time, there is a trend in the Church, as in all organizations, a trend to be wrestled against, to assign priority to the logic of maintenance. If administrators exercise appropriate leadership, the two logics, while sometimes in tension, would for the most part support one another. An institution that pursues its aim and purpose in a competent and spirited manner gains credibility and public support and hence enhances its staying power; conversely, an institution that solves its problems of maintenance gently and efficiently is able to devote more of its energy to its task and mission. Yet in many institutions, including ecclesiastical organizations, the logic of maintenance assumes exaggerated importance. Institutions become defensive; they become hostile to criticism offered by their own members; they feel secure with the old way of doing things, without examining how well the old approach works in the present. Healthy institutions try to resist this regressive trend by bringing their officers into living contact with the people they are meant to serve and with the entire staff. When this does not happen, the concern for institutional maintenance can assume a pathological dimension. Here the institution that so desperately seeks to protect itself, actually initiates its own decline.

I propose that the contradictions in the Catholic Church are due to the as yet unresolved conflicts between the logic of mission and the logic of maintenance. Defensive, narrow and sometimes paranoid institutional concerns make Church leaders speak out and act against principles that in fact belong to the Church's official teaching. This is particularly obvious in *four* areas. The logic of maintenance, which demands that the Church protect its international unity, often prompts the Vatican to disregard the principle of subsidiarity, a constitutive element of Catholic social teaching. Second, the logic of maintenance, which demands that the Church protect its internal cohesion, often prompts the Vatican and regional bishops to condemn class struggle in terms at odds with the new teaching on solidarity of and with the poor. Third, the logic of maintenance, which demands that the Church protect the authority of the ecclesiastical government, often prompts the Vatican and regional bishops to speak out and act in a manner that contradicts the new teaching on human beings as subjects. And finally the logic of maintenance, which demands that the Church protect its economic base, often prompts popes and bishops to manifest their solidarity with the powerful and affluent sector of society, at odds with the newly defined preferential option for the poor.

Whenever the logic of maintenance gives rise to obsessive preoccupation, it not only weakens the logic of mission, it even undermines the maintenance of the institution. Church membership decreases, priesthood and religious life attract fewer candidates, and the Church's public credibility declines. Secular observers might conclude that these contradictions are connatural to the Roman Catholic Church, symptoms of a chronic illness. As a Catholic, a Christian believer in the Catholic tradition, I hold that these contradictions could well be resolved, not once and for all, but in an ongoing process of religious conversion, dialogue and institutional change.

Allow me to pursue these four lines of thought. First, the Church has the right and duty to protect its organizational unity. The Orthodox and the Protestant Churches have chosen to organize themselves on a national basis. Their international fellowship is created by councils and federations. By contrast the Catholic Church has committed itself, in accordance with its reading of the New Testament, to be a world church with a central authority, the papacy. To exist as a vast international organization demands a high price. It needs a central government that has the authority to steer ecclesiastical developments in the different parts of the world. The logic of maintenance demands that the differences between regional churches, between their respective visions, their ethos and their practice, do not become too great. If this happens, or if it is a believed to be happening, Rome intervenes to slow down the development, however valid it may be in itself. Usually these interventions restrict the freedom of regional churches that move ahead and undergo transformation, rather than the churches that cling to the practices and attitudes of the past. Still, the change of the liturgy from Latin to the vernacular demanded that Rome intervene among Catholic groups caught up in the past. Yet, because the shift in Catholic social teaching is so substantial, little effort is made by the Vatican or regional bishops to make Catholic parishes, Catholic schools and colleges, and diocesan Catholic organizations follow the new direction, in particular the preferential option for the poor. The transition must be made voluntarily, through personal conversion. When prominent Catholics, lay people, priests or bishops, utter public criticism of the Church's social teaching, no ecclesiastical pressure is put on them to conform. On the other hand, when bishops or bishops' conferences are seen by the Vatican to be too radical in their dedication to justice or to peace, the Vatican either intervenes directly, as in the case of Raymond Hunthausen, the pacifist archbishop of Seattle, or it shoots at the prominent theologians who help the bishops articulate their social teaching, as in the cases of Leonardo Boff in Brazil and Gustavo Gutierrez in Peru.

Concern for Church unity has often been exaggerated. Confronted by what Popes and bishops interpreted as the nationalist culture of modern Europe, they defended the Latin liturgy as the powerful symbol of the Church's visible unity. Only at Vatican Council II did the Catholic Church opt for a more pluralistic image of itself. The Church presented itself as the Community of communities. At present, the Vatican seems a little unhappy about the Church's pluralistic self-understanding. Vatican Council II also welcomed the worldwide ecumenical movement: Christians are meant to be united in their worship of God and their mission in the world. Yet to this day the Vatican has discouraged liturgical symbols that celebrate and foster this unity among Christians, Catholic and Protestant. An exaggerated logic of maintenance stands here against the free exercise of the Church's mission as defined by Vatican Council II.

Second, the concern for the Church's internal cohesion demands the rejection of a rigid, deterministic concept of class struggle. For if consciousness were wholly determined by one's class location, then the poor Catholics, especially those of the third world, could say to Popes and bishops that they have no teaching authority over them: for then the consciousness of these Church leaders would be wholly shaped by their identification with the powerful and their class interest. The logic of maintenance demands that the Popes and bishops resist the idea that the class struggle passes right through the Church, except in an attenuated form, a form that does not destroy the unit of faith. This point is made very clearly in Cardinal Ratzinger's Instruction.

Does this contradict the Church's social teaching regarding the conflictual nature of society and the need for preferential solidarity? To live up to the exigencies of the two logics, of mission and of maintenance, Catholics want to express themselves on this point in a very nuanced fashion. They want to avoid the Marxist thesis that the class struggle is the key to people's self-understanding and the motor-force of the forward movement of history. In *Laborem exercens*, John Paul II offers a conflictual view of society that is voluntaristic enough to escape the label of Marxism, and yet sufficiently rooted in the material conditions of society to escape the label of idealism. The Pope calls for the solidarity of workers and with workers, and, in the third world, for the solidarity of the poor and with the poor. The solidarity struggle is here not simply generated by the contradictions between the forces and the relations of production; it is a struggle of those who are exploited by the ruling system in various ways, joined by all who love justice belonging to whatever class. This sort of solidarity struggle does not just happen; it has to be created by an effort that is a political and in fact an ethical achievement. This is the voluntaristic element. This solidarity is not produced by simply following the thrust of people's class interest. People's collective self-interest must be accompanied by a new ethical vision of society. In fact, a solidarity movement of this kind becomes powerful only if each group is willing to limit its own collective self-interest to some extent in order to protect and promote the solidarity among all the groups involved.

The solidarity struggle conducted in this sense resembles the class struggle, but it also significantly differs from it. It includes an ethical dimension and hence opens itself to a wider base. It even acknowledges the possibility that the Church itself join in the solidarity struggle. "The Church is fully committed to this cause (the solidarity struggle)," wrote John Paul II, "for it considers it to be its mission, its service, the proof of its fidelity to Christ, so that it can truly be the Church of the poor."[12] The Pope follows here the logic of mission.

But in its concern for internal cohesion and unity, often exaggerated and sometimes pathological, some ecclesiastical documents, among them Cardinal Ratzinger's Instruction, repudiate class struggle in such an unnuanced manner that hardly any room is left for the Church's official teaching of preferential solidarity.

Third, we notice that the logic of maintenance has prevented the Vatican from applying to the Church itself the official Catholic social teaching that human beings are meant to be the subjects of the societies and institutions to which they belong. John Paul II insisted on this teaching. He argued that workers were to be the subjects of the industries in which they labor; they were to be co-owners and co-responsible for decision-making. John Paul II also demanded that the desirable socialization of ownership, which he clearly differentiates from state ownership, must always protect what he calls the "subject character" of society: people must remain free and responsible agents, sharing in decisions that affect their lives.[13] This teaching undoubtedly applies to the Church itself.

The logic of maintenance demands that the Church protect the authority of its ecclesiastical government. Without an appropriate authority demanding obedience, an organization falls apart. But it is an exaggerated, if not pathological expression of the logic of maintenance to refuse the integration of dialogue, consultation, conciliarity and synodal responsibility into the exercise of ecclesiastical government, in greater fidelity to the Church's own social teaching. When the logic of maintenance separates itself from the logic of mission it actually undermines the maintenance of the organization. The Catholic Church is paying an enormous price for the protection of its authoritarian style of government. Catholic teaching counsels greater collegiality and participation. So would a sound sociology of organization.

Finally, the logic of maintenance concerned with the economic base of the organization has led the Church to ally itself with the rich and powerful. Some sociologists have argued that churches by their very nature are identified with the dominant classes. This was Ernst Troeltsch's view, and he was no Marxist. Yet to remain consistent, Troeltsch had to call the *ecclesia* prior to Constantine a sect. While churches in the Constantinian age have undoubtedly been identified with the establishment and the interests of the powerful, there are signs that this age has come to an end and that the churches have attained a new freedom to seek their location in society in accordance with their theological vision.

Carl Marzani correctly points to the emergence of new Catholic orientation that tends to separate the Church from its alliance with the capitalist establishment. He mentions the practice of Catholic groups and movements, often supported by priests and bishops, that reveal this tendency. Just recently, the Catholic bishops of Cuba have, for the first time, asked for dialogue with the Cuban Marxism and for the right of Catholics to participate in the building of a socialist Cuba.[14] In Cuba it may be the logic of maintenance which counsels the bishops. But in most instances the logic of maintenance and its economic concern impede the courageous application of the Church's new social teaching. One must admire the determined fidelity of the Canadian and American bishops to publish pastoral letters that question the existing economic order and arouse the anger and hostility of the political and economic establishment.

Conclusion

What do we conclude from these brief reflections? What direction will the Catholic Church follow in the future? Will the trend observed by Carl Marzani continue? Or is Joel Kovel correct in his view that the Vatican has decided to crush the new liberationist trend in the Church? In my opinion, the Church's commitment to the preferential option for the poor (the logic of mission) is definitive and irreversible. I regard this as an extraordinary happening, possibly of world historical importance. At the same time, one must expect a good deal of opposition to this trend in the Church, inspired by institutional concerns and inherited ideological commitment. Yet this opposition, in my opinion, will not try to undo the theological basis of liberation theology; it will not try to sever the redemption brought by Christ from economic and political liberation nor repudiate the preferential solidarity with workers and with the poor. Instead, the opposition will try to give these commitments a more moderate or more spiritual interpretation. The liberation movements will not be crushed. They will continue their struggle in Church and society, protected by the teaching of Medellin and Puebla and encouraged by papal teaching and many episcopal conferences. Despite occasional setbacks, the movement will gain power. For the religious authority of the preferential option for the poor, ultimately derived from Scripture, is simply overwhelming. It commands the Christian conscience.

In North America, moreover, the presence of the Hispanic Christians, the black church and the native peoples as well as the women's movement and the peace movement in the Christian churches constantly call Church leaders to critical reflection and institutional change. These are historical factors that prevent Catholic bishops from settling into a routine understanding of their ecclesiastical office. It is true that these critical forces do not reach the Vatican in the same way. In fact at this time, there seems to emerge at the Vatican a new interest in promoting the Christian Democratic Parties and presenting Christianity as the protector of a unified and strong Europe.[15] Still, the Vatican has become the center of a world Church. The Latin American church and other third world churches will continue to demand from the Vatican that it live up to the new Catholic social teaching, its own teaching in fact, and allow the Church, at different speeds in different countries and continents, to become identified with the poor and oppressed sector of society, or to use John Paul II's phrase, "to become the Church of the poor."

Notes

1. See D. Dorr, *Option for the Poor: A Hundred Years of Vatican Social Teaching,* Maryknoll: Orbis, 1983, 157–162, 205–212.
2. For text of Instruction see R. Haight, *An Alternative Vision,* New York: Paulist Press, 1985, 269–291. A later Instruction, published in 1986, adopted a more positive view of Liberation Theology. See "Liberation Theology Blessed," in this volume, pp. 104.
3. *Monthly Review,* 34 (July–Aug., 1982) 1–41.
4. Ibid., 27.
5. *Monthly Review,* 36 (April, 1985) 14–27.
6. Ibid., 27.
7. Ibid., 19.
8. Robert Merton, "Bureaucratic Structure and Personality," in *Reader in Bureaucracy,* ed. Robert Merton *et al.* New York: The Free Press, 1952, 361–371.
9. See G. Baum, "Class Struggle and the Magisterium: A New Note," in this volume, pp. 32–47.
10. D. Dorr, op. cit., 159.
11. G. Baum, "Faith and Liberation: Development Since Vatican II," in this volume, pp. 3–31.
12. *Laborem exercens,* n. 8, in G. Baum, *Priority of Labor,* 110–111.
13. Ibid., n. 14, in op. cit., 124.
14. Cf. Latin American Press, February 14, 1985.
15. Ed Grace, "The Churches Behind a United Europe," *Concilium,* no. 141, *Neo-Conservatism,* ed. G. Baum, New York: Seabury Press, 1981, 19–24.

14.
Catholic Foundation
of Human Rights

Since Vatican Council II the Catholic Church has acknowledged and promoted human rights in the society of nations. Pope John Paul has made human rights the center of his mission and the source of the critiques addressed by him to Eastern communism and Western capitalism. Yet in the nineteenth century the Catholic Church repudiated the human rights advocated by modern liberal society. The popes saw themselves as the defenders of the Christian civilization that was being undermined by secular political movements. The Catholic Church, identified with the feudal and later the aristocratic order, repudiated the emergence of the liberal state, condemned liberal political philosophy, and opposed the civil liberties of the French Revolution: freedom, equality, and fraternity.

At Vatican Council II the Catholic Church changed its mind. In the 1940's and 1950's theologians like John Courtney Murray who strongly defended religious liberty still got into trouble with the ecclesiastical magisterium. However, their position was vindicated at Vatican Council II, and John Courtney Murray himself was invited to cooperate in the drafting of the conciliar declaration on religious liberty. Catholics are grateful that they belong to a Church that can change its mind on central moral teaching. In this article, however, I wish to look more closely at the Catholic rejection of civil rights in the nineteenth century. While we no longer endorse the Catholic "no" of the past, there may be a wisdom in it that deserves attention.

The Catholic "No"

Three reasons given by the Catholic Church explained its rejection of liberalism and its denial of civil rights. The popes argued that liberal political philosophy elevated the individual person to such great heights that the social cohesion of traditional society and the sense for the common good were being undermined. Secondly, the popes argued that implicit in the demand for freedom of expression and religious liberty was a relativism in regard to truth. Finally, the popes related political liberalism to economic liberalism and argued that in a free market system the rich and powerful were able to triumph over the poor. Let us look at each of these three arguments.

Traditional Catholic teaching reasoned that the common good of society was more than the sum of the private goods of the individual members. The common good embraces the values, institutions, laws and structures that regulate, in accordance with justice, the interaction of individuals and groups in society and protect them from oppression or exploitation by the powerful. In this perspective, the private good of individuals is subordinated to the good of the whole society. Personal freedoms have their clearly defined limits. The task of government is to enhance the common good, to protect the common values and the inherited moral institutions, and to resist the advance of the new individualism. In this light, the philosophy of liberalism appears as the legitimation of personal egotism, the elevation of private good over common well-being, and the moral endorsement of a competitive, achievement-oriented, free enterprise business civilization. Liberalism appears here as the inversion of the traditional moral order.

Secondly, since the Catholic Church regarded itself as the divinely appointed embodiment of true religion in the world, it repudiated the demand for religious liberty. The idea that each individual is free to decide on matters of religion as if this were a purely private affair implies an indifference to the unity of truth. The notion of religious liberty and of freedom of expression in general was based on a relativism in regard to truth. In liberalism, nothing was true or false, nothing right or wrong: it all depended on the viewpoint of the individual. The Catholic Church believed it had to wrestle against philosophical and political movements that undermined the divine orientation of human being toward truth. Democracy appeared to the Church as a system that negated the truth question and permitted the majority, often to please itself, to decide upon matters of social policy and spiritual orientation.

Finally, the Catholic Church associated the political philosophy of liberalism with economic liberalism. Freedom here meant the freedom of the market. While the defenders of capitalism argued that the free market, operating according to the law of demand and supply, assured the well-being of society as a whole and marvelously transfigured the quest for personal gain on the part of all into a disinterested force that raised the standard of living of the vast majority, the popes argued that the free market enabled the people with resources and cleverness to triumph over the poor, the people with limited possibilities. In a sinful world freedom is of advantage to the strong.

It is curious that the Catholic opposition to civil rights has a certain similarity to the socialist critique of the human rights promulgated by the French Revolution. While Catholics (and Tories in general) rejected liberal society by comparing it with an idealized picture of the old order, socialists repudiated liberal policy by comparing it with an idealized image of future society. The socialist vision was not the old Catholic ideal, the hierarchically-structured organic society based on mutuality, but rather the participatory society, egalitarian in character, in which all men and women participate in the social processes that define their common existence. Socialists argued that the very limited political participation available in liberal democracy (voting for members of parliament every few years) disguised the cruel fact that people were excluded from participation in the economic life and hence remained deprived of social power. Karl Marx even argued that just as in the past Christians told people that they were all brothers and sisters in the Lord and thus disguised the cruel reality of exploitation and unbrotherliness in Christian society, so now the liberals tell people that they have identical political rights, thereby making invisible the economic inequalities in liberal society and the radical impotence of the poor.

Still, the arguments raised by socialists against liberal society were similar to the Catholic arguments. Socialists argued that liberalism undermined social solidarity and pushed people into individualism and competitiveness. Marx thought that capitalism inevitably produced "egotistic man", i.e., persons who define themselves in terms of their own enterprise, their own careers, and their own economic future. The socialists believed that this universal egotism could not be overcome by the moral seriousness of a few high-minded individuals; egotism could only be transcended through the creation of a new economic system based on joint ownership and participation in decision-making. Secondly, socialists argued that liberalism promoted relativism in regard to truth and hence undermined the society-guiding power of reason. Liberalism, they thought, encouraged a pluralistic view of society; it looked upon society as a compromise (in favor of the rich) of competing interest groups. The socialists argued that reason is capable of discerning the contradictions in society, the contradictions that damage sections of the people in the present and that prepare the eventual dissolution of the system in the future. The liberal emphasis on pluralism, they argued, belittles the power of reason, interprets social contradictions as tensions in balance, and reconciles people to the presence of the poor and destitute. Finally, socialists argued with the Catholics that the defense of personal freedoms in society made it easier for the powerful and resourceful to be victorious over ordinary working people. To announce the rule of freedom in the jungle gives free reign to the predators.

The socialists then, with reasons similar to those offered by Catholics, argued against the human rights of the French Revolution as part and parcel of liberal ideology. The human rights the socialists did proclaim, which today are often called "socioeconomic rights", were the right to life, to health, to food and shelter, the right to work, the right to education, and the right to participate in the building of society. These were precisely the rights which liberalism overlooked.

Political and Socio-Economic Rights

We note that these socio-economic rights were closer to the Catholic tradition than were the civil liberties. Traditional Church teaching, reformulated and applied in papal social doctrine, defended people's right to life and health, to sustenance and work, and to "a living wage", even though it did not include the specifically socialist right of people to participate in the essential social processes. Catholic conservatism argued that in an organic society decision-making and responsibility for the common good must be in the hands of the highest authority. The Catholic defense of socio-economic rights were not anti-hierarchical and egalitarian, even though in more recent times the Catholic defense of the right to co-determination has radical social implications.

The evolution of Western society has led to the tragic split between the two sets of human rights, the civil liberties that guarantee people's political rights and freedoms, and the socio-economic rights that guarantee people's participation in the making of society and the production and distribution of wealth. Liberal democratic societies pride themselves of enjoying civil liberties; they neglect the socio-economic rights since these seem to contradict the nature of capitalism. Communist societies claim to protect people's socio-economic rights while for all practical purposes denying their civil liberties. This split is the source of much non-communication between Western capitalist and Eastern communist societies. The defense of civil rights is understood by the Eastern communist countries as an ideological defense of liberalism and a disguise of the refusal on the part of capitalism to honor the rights to life and health, the right to food and work, etc.

In the declarations made by the United Nations the two sets of human rights, civil liberties and socio-economic rights, are affirmed simultaneously. This double affirmation is today endorsed by the Christian Churches, including the Catholic Church. Pope John Paul II has given this wide concept of human rights a properly theological foundation. It is based, he argues, on God's presence to human beings and history as revealed in Jesus Christ. In his speech to the United Nations the Pope even argued that this recognition of human rights was generated by the present generation as a response to Auschwitz. For this reason Auschwitz must never be forgotten. Pope John Paul has given human rights great centrality in his teaching. He makes them the source of social criticism addressed to East and West alike. The Pope accuses the communist countries of the East of violating the civil liberties of people, including religious freedom and political dissent, while he accuses the capitalist countries of the West of neglecting the socio-economic rights. In support of a major current in contemporary Christian social teaching, Pope John Paul argues that capitalism widens the gap between the rich and the poor and systematically excludes workers and wage-earners of any kind from ownership and participation. Capitalist societies do not guarantee the inclusion of people in the wealth of society but, on the contrary, push ever greater numbers into the margin.

It is curious indeed that the Catholic Church has come to defend human rights, including civil liberties. Have Catholics become converted to liberalism? Have theologians sought a theological foundation for liberal political philosophy? A prolonged reflection on the Catholic "no" to political freedoms has shown that it contains insights that must not too easily be abandoned. I do not favor a conversion to liberalism. What is necessary, I wish to argue, is that Catholic thinkers must find a non-liberal theoretical foundation for the defense of human rights, i.e., a theoretical basis that does not promote individualism and undermine social solidarity, does not relativize truth and trivialize the truth question, and does not act as legitimation of the free market economy. Even though we regret the Catholic "no" to civil rights of the past and deplore the suffering which this opposition to freedom has caused—indeed we are called to repentance in this regard—Catholics may well want to defend the progressive component of this Catholic "no" in contemporary society.

Non-Liberal Basis of Human Rights

The theoretical foundation of civil liberties, I wish to argue, is not simply the dignity of the human person which as *imago Dei* has an infinite value. Such a theory would legitimate liberal political philosophy. I wish to argue, on the contrary, that the theoretical basis for civil liberties and all human rights is the common good of society, i.e., the values, institutions, laws and structures that mediate relations between persons and groups in accordance with their high dignity. Thus the rights to dissent, to religious worship, and to form associations and organize opposition are not granted simply because the subjective demands of persons must not be violated, but rather because the objective order, the common good, the structures that mediate communication between people, would be damaged whenever these rights are missing. Violation of civil rights not only harms the people who experience repression; it also damages the common good, the quality of life in society, and hence all sections of the population. If the structures that mediate the interaction of persons and groups in society are unjust or distorted, then not only is each member of society in potential danger but the defects in the objective order will affect public consciousness and create a perverted moral sense in the whole of the population. Without these freedoms society as a whole communicates a false and distorted self-understanding to its members. The violation of political freedoms and in fact of all human rights creates a false and potentially dangerous perception of the social reality, a social illness as it were, with damaging effects on all levels of society.

Understood in this manner, I wish to argue, human rights (political as well as socio-economic) do not nourish individualism or undermine social solidarity, but on the contrary enhance the common good. If the right to life, health, food, work and shelter are denied to some sections of society, then the structures that determine the interrelations of persons and groups in society are damaged by grave injustice, and the harm done will not only cause great suffering among those physically affected but also vitiate the perception of human life on the part of the privileged section of society. Such unjust structures create hearts at odds with human justice and deaf to the Christian message. Similarly I would argue that the demand for political freedom and egalitarianism protects and promotes the common good. We demand these freedoms not only for the sake of men and women who suffer discrimination; we demand it as an essential dimension of the common good, without which the quality of life in society would be damaged, without which injustice would incarnate itself in social institutions, pervert human consciousness and erect obstacles to a true understanding of the Gospel.

Institutional racism, and this includes racist language, harms not only the race that is disfavored; it harms the whole of society because to the extent that these institutions and this language shape human consciousness they create damaged personalities among the privileged, men and women in whom the *imago Dei* is distorted and who see the world falsely. The same arguments hold for the women's movement. This movement demands equal rights for women not simply because of women's dignity as persons but more especially for the sake of society as a whole and the quality of social life. The subjugation of women creates a distorted self-understanding in the male population and casts a social illness on the whole of society. This argument shows that sexist language is not a matter of negligible import. Language belongs to the objective order; it has effects beyond the intention of the speaker. A language that marginalizes women or makes them invisible cannot be made harmless by the love and generosity which the speaker bears in his heart. The preacher, for instance, who addresses his congregation as "brethren" may have no intention of excluding the women, and may not in fact offend the women present at the service, but his manner of speaking damages the common good, the structures that mediate social communication, and hence protects and promotes a social illness.

To argue on a non-liberal basis for the civil rights of homosexuals, for their freedom of expression, of assembly and association, it is necessary to show that the denial of these rights not only damages the minority—homosexual men and women—but at the same time distorts the common good and lowers the quality of life in society. If my argument is correct, the rights of homosexuals cannot be defended simply with reference to the dignity of persons. In his *The Church and the Homosexual,* John McNeil, intuitively following the Catholic tradition, tries to establish that the repression of homosexuals and the promotion of homophobic attitudes damage society as a whole and that the freedom of homosexual men and women in society will have a clarifying and elevating effect on all human relations.

What about the second Catholic argument that liberalism implies indifference to truth and fosters relativism? To find a non-liberal basis for human rights, I wish to argue, it is necessary to show that the modern freedoms are no threat to the quest for truth, but that they in fact enhance the joint search for truth in all areas of human knowledge. In this argument let me follow the ideas of Cardinal Karol Wojtyla, the present Pope John Paul II, set forth in the last chapter of his book *The Acting Person.* The cardinal here demonstrates that for the sake of the common good and the common quest for truth, the operative attitude in a just society must be solidarity. All are involved in building social life together. All recognize that the common project transcends their own private goods. But since society contains some contradictions and imbalances and since it finds itself in varying historical circumstances, it is necessary, for the sake of the common good and the discovery of truth that there be room for dissenting voices. The cardinal distinguishes between "inauthentic opposition" which is based on the pursuit of purely private concerns and "authentic opposition" which proceeds from solidarity and concern for the whole. Authentic opposition leads to dialogue, a dialogue indispensable for the quest of truth. Without the structural guarantee of political freedoms a society is gravely damaged in its constitution and hindered in the on-going search for truth. In other words, political freedoms are not concessions made in favor of the dissenting voices on the basis of their personal dignity, but they are upheld for the sake of the common good, the structural integrity of society and the creation of consciousness. These freedoms, then, far from encouraging indifference to truth and value relativism, are actually societal prerequisites for the discernment of truth.

Finally, if we pay critical attention to the nineteenth-century Catholic "no", we want a theory of human rights that does not act as a legitimation of the free enterprise economy. In the Catholic perspective with its emphasis on the common good, the market is acceptable only in the context of an economic policy devised by government for the protection of public well-being. The arguments we have given for the political freedoms do not apply for free enterprise. Because of the scarcity of resources, the freedom of the rich implies the increasing disinheritance of the poor. We note that the public ownership of the means of production advanced by socialism is not the only economic model that promises to facilitate a cooperative, rational order of production and distribution. It is quite conceivable that free enterprise thrives within limits clearly defined by a government responsible to the people. Because of the growing inequality in the world and the widening gap between the developed and the underdeveloped world, Catholic teaching with its stress on the common good has become more emphatic in its demand for a planned economy.

A Catholic theory of human rights based on non-liberal political theory creates a closer link between political and socio-economic human rights and lends itself to a new conversation about civil liberties with the communist countries of Eastern Europe. While the prevailing theories of human rights may sound to them like ideological defenses of liberal society, a theory based on the common good may appeal to them and make them see that the denial of civil liberties which they practice does not in fact protect the collective well-being but undermines and distorts it. Through Pope John Paul II, a Christian witness from the second world, the Catholic Church is in conversation as never before with two distinct political societies, and it may be necessary to find a language, a new language, that can be understood by both.

Collective Rights

From the Catholic perspective with its accent on the common good, it is not enough to speak about the political and socio-economic rights of the members of society. We also must affirm the collective right of people to define their place in history. The liberal tradition has neglected this. Thanks to the political struggle of colonized peoples for self-determination, justice and development, the international community of nations has come to recognize the right of peoples or "nations"—entities that need careful definition—to define their own political future. The right of collective self-determination, recognized by the United Nations, is in keeping with the Catholic understanding of human rights.

When the people of Quebec in Canada generated a national self-consciousness and demanded the democratic right to self-determination, English-speaking Canadians, for the most part heirs of the liberal tradition of democratic rights, found it difficult if not impossible to recognize a collective right, the right of a people. When the provincial government of Quebec legislated that parents who move to Quebec must educate their children in French, the public language, English-speaking Canadians, heirs of the liberal tradition, tended to find this offensive and unjust. They argued that parents have the right to choose the language of education for their children. Against this Quebeckers argued, even while they disagreed on the precise formulation of the law, that the collective right of a French-speaking people to defend their survival on the vast English-speaking North American continent prevailed over the private right of parents. We note in passing that the provincial government guaranteed the right of English-speaking Quebeckers to an English-speaking school system.

In a recent pastoral letter the Catholic bishops of Quebec upheld Quebec's collective right to self-determination. The bishops made it clear that they had no recommendation in regard to the coming referendum in which Quebeckers were about to decide their future. This choice, the bishops argued, was up to the people of Quebec. What the pastoral letter does defend is the principle of collective self-determination. Quebec's future within the present confederation, or in a modified Canadian union, or in some form of independence will have to be decided first of all by the Quebeckers themselves. This is their collective right. While this right seems rational and well-grounded to the Catholic bishops, it is difficult to grasp for English-speaking Canadians who think about human rights in personal, not in collective terms. In a political philosophy that stresses the common good, it is clear that a collective right transcends the rights of individuals, even though—if our reasoning on the preceding pages is correct—the good of the collectivity can only be protected if the civil liberties of minorities and of individuals are upheld. We note that the Quebec bishops insist that a nationalist quest for self-determination is just only if it envisages the protection of the civil liberties of minorities.

Human rights are a complex set of laws protecting various aspects of human life in society. We have mentioned civil liberties, socio-economic rights, and the collective right to self-determination. Is it possible to determine rational priorities among these various rights? If a new nation is formed in some part of the world and unable to guarantee all human rights at the beginning, which are the more important rights that such a nation must respect at once? Can a hierarchy of rights be rationally established? This sort of question is congenial to the tradition of Catholic social thought, though until now very little attention has been paid to it. Christian Bay, a (secular) political philosopher at the University of Toronto, has written extensively on the priorities among human rights and produced a set of arguments that are congenial to the Catholic natural law tradition. He argues that the fundamental human right is the right to life itself and hence the right to be protected from violence, torture and bodily harm. Appended to this right is the right to nourishment and health. The second level of human rights has to do with the collectivity. It includes the right of a people to define themselves, to affirm their culture, their language, their religion, and their political identity, and this includes more remotely the right to be educated and become an active participant in the social project. Finally the third level refers to civil liberties. Bay provides persuasive arguments to solve very difficult questions. It is not easy to establish a priority between bread and freedom or between health and religious liberty. Still, it seems to me that it is an indispensable task of political philosophy to clarify the relation among the various human rights and to establish a set of criteria by which priorities can be determined.

We have discussed the Catholic tradition of social thought. It would be mistaken to suppose that Protestant social thought has always been a defense of liberalism and capitalism. It would be possible to show how some Protestant Churches have moved from the defense of individual freedoms, including the free market economy, to a criticism of liberalism, an emphasis on public well-being, and even an endorsement of a cooperative, rationally planned economy.

Rights in the Church

Is the Catholic Church morally obliged to protect the human rights of its own member churches and individual Catholic believers? Have regional churches, such as the Dutch church or the church of Brazil, certain rights to define themselves in accordance with their historical aspirations or must they be coerced to follow the universal legislation of the central authority of the Vatican? Can the Church systematically exclude from some levels of ministry certain sections of society, for instance black people or women? Under what circumstances must the Catholic Church recognize for its own members the right of dissent, of assembly and association? Do believers in the Church have the right of due process, and can they appeal to ecclesiastical courts if they think that the decision of the authorities has not followed the norms of justice? If the Catholic Church were a voluntary organization, the question of human rights within it could not be raised. It is perfectly licit to establish an association of like-minded people that is governed by rules of their particular preference. If people do not like these rules, they need not join the association; and if members become impatient with them, they could leave. Conflicts within such an association are never civil rights issues.

The Catholic Church, however, presents itself to the world as the sacrament of the unity of the human race; it looks upon itself as the community of salvation which embodies God's justice in the world and which symbolizes and anticipates the future of humankind as the reconciled community. The Catholic

Church regards itself as the revelation of God's will for the world, and for this reason, I wish to argue, it must recognize human rights within its own organizational structure. The Church is not a voluntary association. It regards itself as created by God in Jesus Christ. The traditional argument that the Church must protect a supernatural treasure, a divinely established common good, is of course quite valid, but if there is any cogency in the arguments on the preceding pages this treasure, this common good, must be defended precisely through the active, faithful cooperation of all the communities and members of the Church. The Spirit works through all. While the ecclesiastical government has supreme authority, it can exercise this authority in fidelity to the Spirit only in a context in which human rights are guaranteed. The denial of human rights in the Church, if the arguments given above are correct, distorts the communication of the *depositum fidei*. The denial of these rights, be this for regional churches and for individual Catholics, not only harms those whose freedom has been curtailed, but damages the structures that mediate communication in the Church and thus distorts the consciousness of all. If these freedoms are not observed, I wish to argue, then popes and bishops, the decision-makers, are the ones whose consciousness is falsified the most, and their witness to Jesus Christ assumes an ambiguous quality. Is the Church's defense of human rights authentic and credible if it fails to recognize human rights in its own organizational life?

15.
The Retrieval of Subjectivity

Christian theology in dialogue with Critical Theory has discovered that religious statements and religious attitudes have political meaning. They contribute in one way or another to the building of society (*polis*). The first effort of this 'political theology' has been to overcome the individualism implicit in much of modern Christian life and thought. This first phase consists of the 'deprivatizing' of the recent Christian tradition[1]. Political theologians try to recover the social dimension of the Christian message. Yet after the negation of individualism and the recovery of the social, the issue of subjectivity remains. People still ask questions about the meaning of personal life, people still have to cope psychologically with their existence, people still yearn for inwardness and prayer. Political theology must, therefore, enter into a second phase, the negation of the negation, that is to say the politically responsible retrieval of subjectivity. This intellectual endeavour is of interest to the secular left as well. In this article I wish to give a brief account of the two phases, de-privatization and retrieval, and then elaborate on what this retrieval may mean for psychotherapy.

Critique of Christian Individualism

In this section I wish to show, at least in outline, how existentialism, psychotherapy and pietism have made Christian thinkers

focus on the human person in abstraction of his or her social condition.

1. Existentialists, be they religious or secular, make personal
anxiety the stepping stone for the true understanding of human
life[2]. Anxiety reveals to people the inauthenticity of their lives.
To be truly human, to live authentically, means to affirm oneself
in freedom, to assume responsibility for one's life. But since society has such a powerful hold on us we easily succumb to the
temptation of living inauthentically: we let ourselves be determined by external causes, we forget ourselves in the tasks of
everyday living, we follow the drift of society without making
responsible personal choices. We live in the world not as persons
but as things, as objects, carried forward by the cultural stream.
The inauthentic mode of existence is troubled and anxious. We
are challenged by the possibility of authentic existence. We are
not left alone by the summons of the truly human. What does a
person do in this state of anxiety? The temptation is to escape
this anxiety by hiding more deeply in inauthentic existence; we
turn to compulsions, to power, to sensuality. Yet another choice
is available to us. We may recognize the true nature of human
being, the need for decision, the call to affirm ourselves in freedom. As we assume responsibility for our life, and commit ourselves to live as free subjects, we overcome anxiety and enter
upon the authentic mode of human existence. While secular existentialists believe that this passage from anxiety to freedom is
wholly self-induced, religious existentialists hold that the Christian message, or, more widely, God's gracious call, is operative
in this transition.

The existentialist analysis has greatly influenced Christian
theology. The analysis of anxiety as outlined above has been used
to clarify the human situation by theologians as different as Rudolf Bultmann and Karl Rahner. Paul Tillich (in his American
phase) and Reinhold Niebuhr had their own existentialist analysis of anxiety and liberation; they differ among themselves and
differed from the Heideggerian approach utilized by Bultmann
and Rahner. All existentialist theologians, however, analysed abstract human being, a person as such in history as such. The trou-

bled and searching subject was defined without reference to the historical conditions of his or her concrete situation.

While political theologians admire existentialists for the discovery that the human subject is not a substance but must be constituted through commitment and affirmation, they regard the existentialist analysis of anxiety as false, illusory and politically irresponsible. It is wholly misguided to understand people's anxiety in abstraction from the concrete conditions of their lives and move directly to the elevated plane of subjectivity. If a man, the sole bread winner of his family, holds a job without security, unsafe in times of unemployment and economic decline, he suffers from anxiety because he does not know how he will feed his family if he loses his job. When a Pakistani woman brings up her children in Canada, she is filled with anxiety because her sons and daughters will have to face the racism of contemporary society. It is ultimately irresponsible to argue that the anxiety of the colonizer and the colonized is in essence identical, that their human predicament must be analysed in the same fashion and that the overcoming of this predicament follows the same spiritual path. The situation becomes absurd when we regard as in principle identical the anxiety experienced by the inmates of a concentration camp and the anxiety of the commandant. It is not possible to speak of the common human need for salvation, shared by the executioner and his innocent victims.

It could be argued that the existentialists address themselves to the class to which they belong, to the middle class, to people whose social location does not damage their basic humanity and who for this reason firmly believe that they can define themselves as subjects and free agents by an act of interiority. Existentialists might admit that in situations where humanization demands the transformation of society, people need a more collective self-understanding and can become subjects of their own history only as they act together in solidarity. Is it possible to defend the existentialist analysis as appropriate for the middle class? I think not. For the bracketing of the concrete conditions of human existence only confirms the indifference of the middle class in regard to the oppressive conditions inflicted upon the lower levels of society: the impact of unemployment and inflation on the workers and their families, the harmful effects of racist and sexist discrimination, especially among the poor, and the conditions of exploitation in the Third World upheld by Western capitalist society. It is irrational to admit that the existentialist analysis is not useful for struggling peoples in situations of oppression and at the same time to recommend its usefulness for the middle class.

A freedom for which others must pay with their subjugation, is not true freedom at all. Human freedom is indivisible. A person is ultimately able to affirm himself (herself) in true freedom before God and society only when there are no more slaves and captives left in the world. Political theology, therefore, regards existentialism as an influence that threatens to transform Christian theology into an ideology of the middle class and an expression of mainstream culture.

The psychotherapeutic approach to the human person differs considerably from existentialism. It is less abstract, it takes into account the psychological history of the individual, it focuses on the interpersonal relationship through which, from infancy on, the person has constituted himself or herself. Still psychotherapy in its effort to overcome the brokenness in people's lives abstracts from the wider social context and the historical conditions which shaped the family and affected interpersonal relations. Psychotherapy regards people as individuals who bear an illness, or at least who have been wounded by their inability to deal with interpersonal relations, especially at an early age. Psychotherapy holds that people can be liberated from the compulsions or the paralysis produced by their past experiences only through the resolution of the old conflicts, the release of repressed energy, and the entry into creative responses. Psychotherapy looks very closely at the history of a person's relationship with others and at the psychic powers that inhibit and release human action; in this sense, psychotherapy is less abstract than existentialism. Yet psychotherapy is still caught in contemporary individualism, still abstracts the person from his (her) place in society, still perpetuates the idea that it is possible to understand people's suffering by focusing on their personal biography, abstracted from the history of their social class.

Psychotherapy 'privatizes' the perception of human life[3]. By locating the source of anxiety in the unresolved conflicts of infancy, it makes invisible the contradictions of society that tear at people's lives.

When people perceive the relationship to their social environment as neutral (and the middle class are taught to think of themselves in that way) then the significant story of their lives begins with birth. The factors that shape their personal experiences and affect their consciousness appear to be all in the family. But when a person belongs to an oppressed class or a colonized people, then the factors that shape personal life are recognized as antecedent to the family, as conditions of oppression that color every aspect of family life and influence every stage of personal development. Such persons realize very well that it is impossible for them to come to self-knowledge, to deal with their brokenness and reach out for personal freedom, by concentrating on their personal biography abstracted from the concrete conditions of their oppression. Such persons recognize that authentic self-understanding demands a critical analysis of the social reality and a clear understanding of the conditions of inferiorizations.

Middle class people think that their relation to society is neutral, and that they are able to define themselves and become free subjects independently of all political considerations. It is only after they have become true selves, only after they have matured in their personhood, that such persons may decide to turn to the political order, concern themselves with justice in society and play an active part in public life. Their relationship to the political order is perceived as optional. But is this true? In fact, the experience of middle class children and the relation to their parents are shaped by the structure of middle class society. Mother and father have socially defined roles, the family exercises an economic function in society, childhood experiences prepare boys and girls for their roles in the social order. Conventional psychotherapy easily disguises how much people are shaped by their class and its function in society. The neutral relationship of the middle class person to society is an illusion. Even middle class people cannot come to realistic self-knowledge without an analysis of the concrete conditions of their existence.

Psychotherapy has been as influential in Christian theology as existentialism. Liberal theologians, both Catholic and Protestant, have made use of paradigms drawn from psychotherapy, such as illness and health, resistance and growth, compulsion and freedom, to articulate the passage from sin to new life promised in the Christian message. Christ is healer; salvation includes personal transformation, the overcoming of self-destructive drives and entry into greater freedom. The encounter with Christ leads to self-knowledge. Because Christ affirms the faithful, they are able to face the truth about their destructiveness and, at the same time, recover the power of earlier affirmations extended to them in infancy and childhood, affirmations since forgotten or repressed, which now become the source of vital energies. The encounter with Christ leads people to a new, more healthful and creative relationship to their own drives. And yet, while this sounds attractive, the psychotherapeutic model becomes a spiritual instrument of privatization and generates a theology that legitimates the individualism of contemporary culture.

A third 'privatizing' influence on Christian theology is pietism. Originally pietism was an imaginative, creative response to highly formalized religion, in which subjectivity received little attention. Pietism was a spiritual movement based on the soul's private encounter with God. Its anti-hierarchical, democratic spirit often made it into a progressive force in society. And yet the emphasis on the soul had cultural consequences in the long run that were not intended. In pietism the person experiences himself (herself) as separate from the body and its concreteness, separated from other people and the political community, separated even from the divinity, who is conceived as the invisible Other drawing near at times of prayer. Prayer is the meeting of the alone with the Alone. The soul is here perceived as a spiritual monad, constituted by factors wholly intrinsic to it, to which other people are external and incidental. The soul is most itself when it shakes off its bodily insertion into the historical community. The self gains access to its deepest meaning to the extent that it brackets the human history to which it belongs. Only the soul that has successfully detached itself from world and worldly care, is made ready to welcome the merciful Godhead, itself living beyond history.

Political theology must ask to what extent the experience of oneself as separated soul is grounded in particular historical conditions. At one time it may have reflected a political movement for greater personal autonomy against the collectivism of traditional society; at a later time, when this struggle had been won, it became the reflection of modern, economically-based individualism. From the perspective of political theology, pietism falsifies the self's relation to the community and to history. Since other people and in fact the community are in very concrete ways constitutive elements of a person's historical self-making, one does not see how they can be discarded at a moment of heightened self-awareness. Such an artificial purging of one's self-experience breaks the links with the historical matrix of personal existence and fails to recognize the triune God present in history as the ground of life, as the love that binds people together, and as the word of faith communicated among them.

The first task of political theology is to recover the social dimension of the Christian message and explore the social implications of personal experience, religious and secular. This task is by no means completed when the Christian message has been 'deprivatized'; this negation is only the first phase. The second phase is to retrieve the meaning and power of subjectivity, beyond individualism, in a politically responsible way. We must proceed to the negation of the negation. Even after existentialism has been found wanting and people have come to experience themselves as part of a societal project, they will still ask questions about personal meaning, still wrestle with personal failure, still deal with sickness and death. What should they be told? After anxiety and neuroses have been understood largely in social and political terms and people are engaged in the struggle to change society, they may still suffer from depression, they still may be prevented by psychological barriers from living freely and acting wholeheartedly. What should they be told? Is there a psychotherapeutic wisdom that is politically responsible? After pietism and its influence on theology have been overcome and people acknowledge the divine presence in their common struggle for justice and peace, the question of personal spirituality remains. What is a private prayer after the rejection of pietism? Political theology, in fidelity to its intellectual project, must deal in its own way with the quest for personal meaning, the struggle for psychological well-being, and the inner journey toward spirituality.

The Retrieval of Subjectivity

The literature of the political left is on the whole quite insensitive to the personal dimension of human existence. This has had devastating political consequences. We must insist that the joint struggle for a more human society does not relativize the worth and dignity of the person. Even during and after whole-hearted political engagement, reformist or revolutionary, the personal factor remains. It seems to me that Christian thinkers of the left are well qualified to recover, from a politically engaged position, the personal dimension of human existence. Christians cannot overlook the personal factor because the Gospel with its social message is addressed to personal consciousness. Listening to God's word, believers discover themselves as subjects, as responsible agents called and empowered to act on behalf of themselves and of society. Overcoming individualism in the Church's message does not make less important the subjectivity of each individual. From the perspective of political theology, then, the quest for personal meaning, the struggle for mental well-being, and the journey toward interiority are meant to be exercises, not of individualism, but of social praxis.

It would be appropriate, if, in this paper, I dealt with the retrieval of the existentialist question, psychotherapeutic wisdom, and the search for spirituality. Yet there is no space for this here. What I will do instead is to make a few remarks about the social recovery of existentialism and spirituality, and then explore in greater detail how psychotherapy can be part of a responsible social praxis.

1. Even after the entry of people into a common historical project, even after the passage from the privatistic search for authenticity to the joint struggle for justice in solidarity with the oppressed, there do remain personal failures and frustrations, the experience of defeat, and the encounter with illness and death: there is, moreover, the realization that however successful the collective project may be, it still remains vulnerable to distortions produced by selfishness and corruption. Human anxiety cannot be totally accounted for by an analysis of the contradictions of society. Even in, through and beyond the historical project to rebuild society, people remain, time and again, threatened by the loss of personal meaning.

There are many ways in which an existentialist analysis of personal life could be fitted into a politically responsible perception of society[4]. A persuasive way of doing this as a theologian, i.e., as a reflective Christian believer, is to account for the restlessness and the yearning experienced by politically alive men and women in terms of a summons (possibly with a capital S) ever present in their experience, a summons to care for other people, a summons to social justice for all, especially the poor, outsiders and marginals. This call is never silent in personal life. It prompts criticism of the prevailing order; and it is operative in the struggle to replace the present order by a more human one. This call demands that the end as well as the means of the struggle for justice respect the dignity of people, collectively as communities and individually as persons. This call makes people restless and alive; it inspires protest not only against the oppression experienced personally but also against the oppression inflicted upon others. This call prompts the mind to critical activity and prevents the heart from resting in happiness as long as injustice reigns in the lives of others. This call, moreover, is experienced not as an echo of one's own mental activity but as a challenge to one's mind and heart. It is a call that addresses us, to which we must listen, and without which we cannot fully define ourselves. This call reveals itself, at least for the Christian believer, as the divine Summons, the Word of God, operative in the raising of consciousness, made known in the scriptures, incarnate in Jesus Christ, and interpreted through the Church's experience, especially through its present experience.

Fidelity to this call becomes a matter of authenticity and constitutes the meaning of personal life. This fidelity involves both action and interiority. The neglect of this call or willed infidelity to it, either by uncritical conformity to the existing order or by identification with a revolutionary movement not open to self-criticism, introduces inauthenticity and falseness into personal life. The flight from this summons, moreover, has political consequences; it will make people cling to the present order despite its injustices or make them fanatical supporters of radical movements. Fidelity to the summons, on the other hand, activates political participation and produces a sense of personal meaning that remains intact even if the common project should suffer defeat for a time or if, through accident or illness, active participation is prohibited. Fidelity to this call nourishes a spiritual life that is not weakened as personal strength ebbs and death approaches. Why? Because the divine Summons in personal consciousness is identical with the call extended to all people, operative in history, empowering men and women to struggle against oppression and build a truly human society. God's personal call links us to others and to the whole of history. And since the efficacy of this call has been revealed in Christ's death and resurrection, the believer experiences consolation even in the face of failure and death. The divine call is unto life, in this world and beyond. In this perspective, the existentialist drama of authenticity and self-making has social meaning. The quest to become truly human is social praxis.

2. The preceding remarks also shed light on the search for a spirituality beyond pietism. The language of "God and the soul" has become of doubtful authenticity. At one time, soul language recorded the emergence of the autonomous self from a collectivist existence defined by tribal or feudal loyalties. Yet in modern times, the church's soul language reveals the isolation of the self from others and the breakdown of solidarity and participation. The divinity who addresses this isolated soul has itself been ex-

cluded from the world: it is no longer the God of the Bible, alive in the historical self-making of the human race.

The spiritual testimony coming from Christians involved in costly struggle for justice, reveals that religious experience explodes the illusion of the separated soul. Religious experience discloses the embeddedness of the self in the community and the dependency of the self on others in the struggle for personal freedom. Religious experience destroys the illusion of private life and assigns people their place in salvation history. In prayer and spiritual 'highs' God does not appear as the invisible Other, speaking from outside of history but as the One who grounds the interconnectedness with others, illumines the meaning of the historical struggle and appoints the believers to participate in it. Even Christians who live in less endangered situations, middle class Christians who have become politicized, report that religious experience discloses to them their embeddedness in the historical community. Their encounter with God explodes the walls of the self. The others, especially the oppressed, become lodged in their heart and modify their personal self-experience: 'the others' are present especially in moments of spiritual encounter and contemplation. If prayer were simply the soul's encounter with God, the concern for others, even for the oppressed, would become a distraction. But in the emerging spirituality, the presence of 'the others' in personal consciousness mediates an abiding call to responsibility and casts a shadow of sadness, willingly received, over every aspect of personal life, even over the moments of joy. Contemporary religious experience will not allow that people create for themselves, through gifts of consolation, islands of happiness from which the memory of the afflicted has been banned. Contemporary spirituality has acquired a special note of seriousness. Even ecstasies of personal bliss and spiritual elevation take place under the shadow of the Cross: religious experience assures that 'the others' are never excluded from personal consciousness. Prayer assigns the believer his or her concrete place in the drama of the world's redemption. Prayer thus reveals itself as social praxis.

After these all too brief remarks on existentialism and prayer, we turn to the subject to be given special attention in this paper, namely the exercise of a politically responsible psycho-therapy. Is there a therapeutic approach that refuses to promote the privatization of life and legitimate the obsessive individual-ism of contemporary culture? Is there a psychotherapy from the left?

3. The question is not a new one. Wilhelm Reich, student, col-laborator and eventually antagonist of Freud, raised this ques-tion at the outset of the psychoanalytic movement[5]. He clearly saw that the structure of the family, which according to psy-choanalytic theory significantly affects the infant's unconscious, is not a given, not defined by human biology or natural law, but a product of the social order and the system of production. Psychic life reflects social structure. And in turn, the transfor-mation of psychic life may challenge social structure and hence have political meaning. Between the two world wars, the social thinkers of the Frankfurt School tried to use psychoanalytic the-ory to gain a better understanding of the oppression operative in society and the increasing success of the fascist movement[6]. Their research produced such divergent readings of Freud as those of Erich Fromm and Herbert Marcuse. In a recent study, Gad Ho-rowitz has carefully re-read the Freudian corpus to gain a deeper understanding of the social and political meaning implicit in the great psychoanalytic discoveries.[7]

My own concern in this article is not so much theoretical as practical. People committed to social movements occasionally do have anxieties and emotional disturbances that disable them. What should they do? To whom can they turn? Conventional psychiatry and psychology operate out of highly privatized pre-suppositions. Mainstream psychotherapy threatens to undo the patient's political commitment. Is there a psychotherapy of the left?

A. The first remark I wish to make is that people, men and women, who struggle for social justice and resist institutional oppression of one kind or another usually belong to various groups and networks. They do not struggle alone. Sometimes the members of these groups live together; at other times they simply meet at regular intervals. Even if the politically committed belong only to loosely defined networks, they still rely on one another, they clarify their ideas in discussion, they arrive at their strategy in joint sessions, they find themselves bound to one another in solidarity. The raising of consciousness takes place in community. In third world countries, the struggle for justice is based on small groups or teams. In these countries committed Christians belong to grassroots communities, defined by common worship and common action. In one way or another, the struggle for justice takes place in community. The group, the team, the network are indispensible.

The common struggle in these groups or networks, I wish to argue, has been experienced by the participants as therapeutic. While there exists no systematic research to demonstrate such a claim, it is my impression, based on conversations with men and women from various parts of the world, that people experience psychological transformation through their participation in a joint struggle for justice. I have met missionaries who after years spent in Latin America or the Philippines return to their home in North America as liberated persons; their ministry in grassroots communities transformed them into warm, dedicated, expansive human beings, with flowing energies and a clear sense of themselves. Many people have told me that their involvement in groups and networks has led to personal growth beyond the self-doubts and inhibitions previously felt. Despite the abiding awareness of the structures of evil, people committed to the struggle for justice usually appear self-possessed, cheerful and energetic, free to respond to others and ready to extend their friendship.

It should be possible, it seems to me, to clarify the healing impact of these groups and networks with the help of psychotherapeutic theory. I wish to mention in particular three factors, the affirmation by the comrades, the struggle against super-ego and the entry into self-transcendence.

First, let us look at the affirmation by the comrades. Since people who have been oppressed or marginalized tend to become prisoners of their own imagination, and passively accept their lowly position, the struggle for justice must begin with self-affir-

mation. It is generally recognized today that the structures of exclusion and inferiorization under which people live are
internalized by them: they come to think of themselves as lacking
in worth, as deserving contempt. They easily derive their self-image from the view the dominant society has of them. This phenomenon has been called 'self-hatred'. A recent study of
oppression inflicted on Jews, blacks and homosexuals has described various psychic mechanisms of distortion, produced by
the structures of oppression, which inflict uncertainty, anxiety,
and inner conflicts on these groups, even as they seek to respond
to their oppression[8]. The same study examines the efforts of these
groups to break out of the distorted imagination, acquire a new
self-understanding, and fight for a society in which they can live
at peace. For most people subject to oppression, the entry into a
new self-understanding takes place in groups and networks. The
affirmation of the comrades mediates new power.

    To be affirmed, in the face of negations uttered by society,
has profound psychological consequences. If this affirmation is
offered not only by one or two persons but by a community, the
impact on one's self-perception is enormous. "Black is beautiful"
was the slogan of the black movement that broke the false self-
image created by centuries of oppression. We are told who we
are by others, by parents, by culture, and by the social structure.
For this reason the escape from self-defeating self-images demands the support of groups or networks. The affirmation of the
comrades produces a rupture in one's self-experience.

    Even middle class men and women who identify themselves
with struggling groups experience the liberating effect of their
comrades' affirmation. If these men and women have been un-
committed before, involved in pursuits of purely personal interests, then the affirmation of the comrades lifts them out of their
isolation, inserts them into a stream of energy, and expands their
horizon in unanticipated ways. From reports of priests and sisters
who have joined the struggling people of Latin America or the
Philippines, it appears that the affirmation by the comrades
broke the uncertain self-image they had of themselves and healed
the ruptured relation to their own vital energies. Returning to

their communities in North America, they appeared like new persons.

It has been argued that the early Methodist movement in 18th century England communicated a sense of dignity and self-confidence to the workers, the new class created by the industrial revolution.[9] While these workers were negated by the class structure of society, the organization of factory life and even the customs of the established church, they were now affirmed by the Spirit of God. This affirmation was mediated through the Methodist prayer groups. Affirmed by the Spirit, the workers carried their heads high, encountered the powerful as equals, and created organizations to transform society. Contemporary liberation theology in Latin America follows the same theological perspective. While the wicked world negates the poor and destitute, God affirms them. God is on their side. God speaks to them through the solidarity of their comrades.

This leads us to the *second* therapeutic factor, the struggle against super-ego. Since the groups and networks of which we speak struggle against the established order and oppose traditional authority, they also wrestle, possibly unbeknownst to themselves, against their own super-ego. According to Freudian theory, super-ego refers to the psychic mechanism by which people insert into their psychic life, usually below the level of consciousness, the norms and precepts of society, mediated in infancy through the authority of the parents. Thanks to the infant's ability to pick up signals and directives from the family, he (she) enters into consciousness, learns the basic social skills, and becomes a member of society. While super-ego is an indispensible mechanism, it demands a very high price. For even as we grow up and begin to make our own preferences, super-ego continues to be operative. It reminds us of the taboos of childhood and picks up present precepts from society, in accordance with early childhood experience. Super-ego tells us what to do, intimidates us, prevents us from following our deep desires and from realizing our highest aspirations. Super-ego makes us conformists, subservient to all forms of authority, repressed, cut off from our vital energies and from our imagination. Super-ego, in the Freudian perspective, is not only the law-giver operative in our psychic life, it is also the accuser, the judge and the punisher. While essential to man's entry into consciousness, super ego is at the same time the organ of repression. Super-ego creates feelings of guilt in us so that we willingly submit to the punishment. To become well, to discover one's own powers and talents, to get in touch with one's energies, to recover the hidden sides of one's personality, it is necessary to struggle against super-ego as the inner tyrant.

People who wrestle against external authorities often discover that another struggle has gone on in them, the struggle against super-ego. To their own surprise their personality changes: they overcome feelings of anxiety and guilt, gain access to libidinal energies, and experience new inner freedom.

There are groups and networks of people, united by the same spirit or the same commitment, yet not at odds with the *status quo*. Such people experience the affirmation of their comrades but do not find themselves wrestling against super-ego. They remain conformists. Religious congregations that approve of the existing social order or even wish to give it greater stability are likely to advocate life styles that are highly conventional. The attitude toward sexuality is here highly significant. Movements that do not challenge the existing order tend to stress sexual conformity, while men and women involved in liberation movements often find themselves in sexual partnerships that contradict the moral code in which they have been raised. The struggle against super-ego seems to release sexual powers. It is not surprising that men and women who struggle against the conditions of their oppression perceive the ambiguity of the family, i.e. they become aware that certain aspects of family life legitimate oppressive structures in society, and hence they often seek new partnership relations that reflect their radical notion of social justice. Throughout Western history radicals and heretics have been accused by their enemies of practising 'sexual license.' On the other hand the great defenders of 'law and order' have desired strict control over the 'restless masses' as well as over their restless instincts. People's relation to their own sexuality becomes the metaphor of their politics.[10]

This leads us to the *third* therapeutic factor operative in groups and networks, namely the entry into self-transcendence. Already the affirmation by the comrades and the struggle against super-ego enable people to transcend the limitations of their personality. In a deeper way, in a manner not recognized by Freudian psychology, people emprisoned in self-preoccupation experience self-transcendence when their principal concern reaches beyond themselves to include other people or an historical cause. In capitalist society we are all turned into individualists. We are taught to promote ourselves, to look after our own affairs, to put ourselves (and possibly our family) first. For some people this means dedication to financial success; for the greater number it simply means dedication to private life, to the enhancement of personal existence. Capitalist society steers us into such high expectations of success or personal fulfillment, that we find ourselves constantly frustrated. We become our own principal pre-occupation, forever disappointed. The passage out of this prison through identification with a cause or solidarity with other people, in other words through self-transcendence, is experienced as liberating.

Identification and solidarity enable us to live for others, to serve a cause that transcends us, to see our personal problems in a new light, and to participate in new emotions, in sorrow, fears, hopes and joys, that connect us to society. Here life transcends middle class existence, be it scattered or frantic. The anxiety induced by the struggle for achievement, success or recognition gives way to care and openness to a more embracing reality.

The healing power of self-transcendence is not without its ambiguities. People have joined strange cults and irrational movements because they desired to experience personal liberation through identification and solidarity. Freud himself recognized this when he remarked that some people are able to transcend their personal neuroses by joining a religious tradition. He argued that through religion, which was for him a collective neurosis, individuals may well be delivered from the symptoms of their own emotional disorders. The entry into a great illness heals the little illnesses. While Freud's positivistic interpretation of religion is not convincing, his observation is nonetheless im-

portant. Self-transcendence is politically and personally dangerous, at least in the long run, when it takes place through
identification with irrational and destructive powers. At the same
time if it is in keeping with rationality—and movements for social justice and the struggle against oppression certainly are—
then self-transcendence leads to freedom and personal well-
being.

Self-transcendence is related to the old biblical word 'sacrifice'. Since this word has been used by those in authority to make
people submissive, uncritical, and long-suffering under the burden of an unjust system, it is no longer acceptable to many Christians. Women rightly claim that the biblical concept of 'sacrifice'
has been employed to undermine their own powers of self-affir-
mation, make them feel guilty whenever they follow their own
interests, and train them to become persons too prone to sacrifice
themselves for others. Is it possible, we must ask, to de-ideologize
the word 'sacrifice'?

Useful in this context are Hegel's reflections on the two
meanings of the word 'alienation'.[11] There is an alienation, he
argued, that is inflicted upon people against their will. The structures of society rob them of the space in which they may exercise
their freedom and live a life in accordance with their gifts and
aspirations. Society is here experienced as the enemy. But as the
historical struggles for freedom change society, overcome the
structures that inflict alienation and lead people toward greater
self-possesion, a point will be reached when, out of a solidarity
with those who are still oppressed, the liberated shall voluntarily
renounce some of the opportunities they now enjoy. The liberated will recognize that their liberation is partial as long as a single slave is left. Liberty here issues forth in sacrifice. Hegel calls
this alienation. It is, however, an alienation that is not inflicted
by society, but one that is freely endorsed out of inner richness
and solidarity with others. Hegel believed that there can be no
rational transformation of society without this sort of self-alien-
ation out of love. By using the same term 'alienation' he indicated
the double task a) to wrestle against sacrifices that are imposed
and b) to gain the freedom where sacrifices do not undermine
personal affirmation but in fact constitute it. At this level, then,

self-transcendence does not break persons but makes them. The biblical language of 'bearing the cross' and 'following Christ' may therefore be de-ideologized. Sacrifice produces life.

This brief discussion of three factors offers psychological reasons why political commitment in groups or networks has therapeutic consequences. People are made well as they join the struggle for justice.

B. What happens if this therapeutic impact is not enough? What happens when engaged people experience anxiety and feel their energies fading? What if they 'burn out'? Such men and women are indeed in need of psychotherapy. But if they go to practitioners trained in conventional psychiatry or psychology, will they find adequate comprehension? Will not the 'privatizing' trend built into psychotherapy render people's political commitment suspect in the eyes of the practitioner? Will their struggle be interpreted as a symptom of masochism, or as immature rebellion, or as an extended anal phase, or as some form of paranoia? What is needed is a psychotherapeutic wisdom from the left. The primary therapeutic experience, I repeat, is participation in a movement: there people find transformation, growth, energy, hope. If during certain periods in people's lives participation is not enough, then it is necessary to turn to an appropriate therapy, at least for a time. Is there a therapy from the left?

It is possible to argue that traditional psychotherapy operates out of one of two models relating the person to society. One may speak here of models of 'social adjustment' and of 'personal integration'. Following the first model, the therapist tries to help the patient to come to terms with the demands made on him (her) by society. The patient learns to understand that his (her) profound desires are founded in childhood experiences and make no realistic claim on the present. If the origin of these feelings is recognized, if the patient relives some of the as yet unacknowledged pain, he may well leave behind his desires or fears. Having become more modest and more rational, it is now possible for him to live in society and assume responsibility for his life choices. Freud himself, by calling the demands of society 'reality principle' and the personal wishes and desires 'pleasure principle' promoted a therapeutic practice that aimed at adjustment and adaptation. The therapist helps the patient to abandon infantile dreams and illusions and accept the social reality as it is.

Yet it is also possible to read Freud differently. What the therapist tries to do, it may be argued, is to help the patient recover aspects of his (her) life that have been repressed, to re-assimilate the hidden wishes and desires, and to integrate them into his (her) personality. Here therapy intends to be liberating. What the patient has to learn is that the accuser and judge is not the parent nor even society but his (her) own super-ego, and that it is possible to wrestle against super-ego, lay hold of the repressed energies and become a bigger person, more rooted, more vital, more integrated. While the therapeutic model of 'social adjustment' corresponds to a conservative political outlook, the 'personal integration' model reveals a liberal political attitude to society. Here the therapeutic effort is not to adapt to society as it is, but to bracket society, to concentrate on one's personal journey, to grow into a rich and versatile personality, and to regard society as a remote framework, with which one may or may not be concerned, depending on personal taste. The quest for personal integration betrays middle class preoccupation.

The people who suffer from structural oppression, especially the poor, are so deeply hurt and distorted by their experience of society that a purely private project of personal integration does not make sense to them. They simply cannot afford to bracket society; their primary task, on which depends their very survival, is to wrestle with society. Is it possible that the wounds the oppressed have received could become for them a vital source of social passion? Such a passion may make them one-sided and partial, but it would empower them to organize among themselves and change the existing order.

Is there a psychotherapy from the left? Is it possible to approach personal healing in a manner that does not remove from consciousness the societal structures of oppression and hence foster a political indifferentism that serves the worst forces in society, and that at the same time respects the great mystery of personal life, the rootedness of one's personal journey in a web of life, made up largely by interpersonal relations, especially those of early childhood, and inscribed, in part at least, in the unconscious? The theological task of recovering subjectivity in a politically responsible context includes such an inquiry.

What I propose is a psychotherapeutic approach that is willing, following the analytical methods of the great masters, to uncover the wounds received, mainly in the family, and the repressions and overcompensations associated with them, and then proceed to a socio-political analysis to locate the origin of these wounds in the social order. Why did parents treat their child in this manner? Why were they constantly fighting? Why did they encourage rivalry among the children? Socio-political analysis should be able to show that the roles played by father and mother were largely defined by the social order distorted by various patterns of oppression and exclusion. What was the parents' experience of poverty, of insecurity, of failure? If they belonged to the middle class, how much were they caught in competitiveness, in the search for private enjoyment and the superficial life defined by commodity fetishism? Even the personal malice of the people who have hurt us in the past cannot be understood unless a socio-political analysis helps us to locate their malice in the historical predicament. What I wish to argue, then, is that a politically responsible therapeutic approach must include two analytical phases, the personal-familiar and the socio-political.

The struggle to be well, then, not only demands that we face and respond creatively to the wounds received in the process of growing up but also that we analyze and resist the structures of oppression, with which these wounds were connected. Personal wounds have social roots; and we do not overcome the effect of these wounds in a responsible manner unless we are willing to confront their social causes. A therapeutic approach of this kind reveals to the patient that the oppressive structures of society are not external to him (her) but internal: they are part of his (her) personal history. To struggle for justice, then, becomes an existential necessity. A therapeutic approach of this kind is a social praxis.

Of crucial importance in a politically responsible psychotherapeutic process is the distinction, made with the help of an experienced therapist, between one's personal problems and one's opposition to the unjust social order. I wish to call this 'the therapeutic distinction'. Without the ability to make this distinction, patients would be led into total confusion. They would project their personal problems on their social environment, and use the struggle against this environment as a way of escaping from self-discovery. They would bring to the political struggle a false passion that must have destructive consequences. Any failure in the political project would make these people vulnerable to renewed depression and breakdown. Sometimes people speaking at political meetings make everyone feel uncomfortable. Their tone of voice, their gestures and their choice of vocabulary create the impression that these people are wrestling with profound personal difficulties. Because they have not been helped to make 'the therapeutic distinction' they create confusion for themselves and disturbances in the public arena. If they find such help, if they learn through therapy to see more clearly and sort out their feelings, then they may well reach a point where their struggle against oppression becomes their entry into personal freedom.

The model of psychotherapy that is politically responsible, then, is not 'social adjustment' nor 'personal integration' but what I wish to call 'social praxis'. This approach to personal healing has been worked out first of all by groups that have experienced social and cultural oppression. They have made the discovery that conventional psychotherapy was in fact a bearer of symbols that contributed to their oppression. Women, black people, Hispanic Americans, homosexual men and women, each in their own way, have objected to mainstream psychiatry and psychology. They have pointed to the unacknowledged ideological elements in these theories. In their search for greater personal health, these people learnt to relate their psychic wounds to the structural oppression inflicted on them. The struggle to be well for these groups demanded critical resistance to the dominant culture. Sometimes they angrily rejected the whole of the psychotherapeutic tradition. Yet when they realized that in order to be well and remain rational in the passionate wrestling for social change, it was of crucial importance to distinguish clearly between personal problems and public endeavours, they appreciated again, after the negation, the psycho-analytic approach with its emphasis on the unconscious and the years of infancy. What is important is that psycho-analysis be joined in tandem with socio-political analysis.

From the considerations offered in this article it is clear that the social connectedness of personal illness applies not only to the oppressed groups but also to the successful middle class. It is precisely the illusion of the middle class that a person's journey is only incidentally related to society, that a person is related to the political order only if he or she chooses to do so, and that it is possible for people to transcend politics by delving into the search for their soul, be it by therapy or religion. For the middle class, too, I wish to argue, psychotherapy must become social praxis.

Psychotherapy as social praxis abandons the ideal 'social adjustment' and 'personal integration.' There can be no integrated personality in a wicked and unjust world. In a society such as ours persons can be rounded, balanced, in harmonious possessions of all powers, only if they are willing to close their eyes to the existing oppression and their heart to the people pushed to the margin. Contemporary church teaching demands that we permit ourselves to be touched or even wounded by the misery in the world and then analyse its historical causes. Personal integration is an illusory ideal. We are all profoundly hurt by the ever expanding power of economic exploitation, political domination, racist exclusion, and sexual discrimination. The answer to this is not the quest for a balanced personality but social passion. The effort to be well in a distorted world and to live with a sense of political responsibility may well turn us into one-sided personalities, into people who lean against the storm, and renounce the exploration of some of their talents. The symbol of health in a sinful world may well be Jacob who limped after wrestling all night with the angel. Or Jesus carrying his cross. The measure of health then is not the successful adaptation to the environment, nor the achievement of personal integration, but the freeing of libidinal energy for social praxis.

Notes

1. For the new meaning of political theology and its de-privatizing task, see especially J. B. Metz, *Theology of the World*, Seabury, New York, 1973, and *Faith in History and Society*, Seabury, New York, 1979. For political theology in an American context see M. Lamb, "The Challenge of Critical Theory," *Sociology and Human Destiny*, ed. G. Baum, Seabury, 1980, pp 183–213.
2. Cf. John Macquarrie, *An Existentialist Theology: A Comparison of Heidegger and Bultmann*, Harper and Row, New York, 1965.
3. This problem is dealt with by many authors. Cf. B. Brown, *Marx, Freud, and the Critique of Everyday Life*, Monthly Review Press, New York, 1973, P. A. Robinson; *The Freudian Left*, Harper and Row, New York, 1969; M. Schneider, *Neurosis and Civilization*, Seabury, New York, 1975.
4. See, for instance, D. Soelle, *The Repression of the Existential Element or Why So Many People Become Conservative*, in *Concilium* Volume 141: *Neo-Conservatism: Social and Religious Phenomenon*, edited by G. Baum, New York: The Seabury Press, 1981.
5. *The Sexual Revolution*, New York, 1969.
6. M. Jay, *The Dialectical Imagination*, Little Brown, Boston, 1973, pp 86–112.
7. G. Horowitz, *Repression*, University of Toronto Press, Toronto 1977.
8. B. Adam, *The Survival of Domination*, Elsevier, New York, 1978.
9. B. Semmel, *The Methodist Revolution*, Basic Books, New York, 1973.
10. G. Baum, "Sexuality and Critical Enlightenment, Dimensions of Human Sexuality," ed. D. Doherty, Doubleday, New York, 1979, pp. 89–94.
11. R. Schacht, *Alienation*, Doubleday, New York, 1971.

16.
Neo-Conservative Critics of the Churches

This is a preliminary essay on a topic that has not been carefully researched. In recent years Christian individuals and groups have reacted very strongly against 'the shift to the left' that has taken place in the social teaching of the Christian Churches and Church Councils. In North America in particular, Christians who sometimes call themselves 'neo-conservatives' have raised theological difficulties, proposed new political ideals and recommended new pastoral policies to the churches.[1]

The New Social Gospel

What is meant by 'the shift to the left' in ecclesiastical teaching? In the social doctrine formulated by the highest authorities of Church bodies, Anglican, Protestant and Catholic, as well as by Church Councils, we find an essentially identical analysis of the structures of sin characteristic of today's society. We are told that something is wrong with contemporary capitalism. Capitalism widens the gap between the rich and the poor, especially between rich and poor nations; it permits the power over resources and production to pass into the hands of an ever smaller élite; it not only produces exploitation in many parts of the world, including regions of poverty in the industrialised countries, but it also creates a materialistic culture, an achievement- and pleasure-oriented business civilisation that estranges people from the substance of their humanity. What these Church documents advocate is a more rationally planned economy, greater sharing of wealth and more participation in decision-making, the extension of democratic processes to economic life, and the examination of local and national problems in the light of the needs of the entire global community.

The Catholic Church in North America has followed this new approach. By way of illustration I wish to refer to two ecclesiastical documents. The first is the Labour Day Statement of 1976, written by the Canadian Catholic bishops, entitled 'From Words to Action', which focuses on the injustices in Canadian society, defines social sin in terms of institutional oppression, and outlines various steps in the struggle for justice in Canada. These steps include the re-reading of the Scriptures from the viewpoint of the poor, a willingness to listen to the marginalised and disadvantaged peoples of Canada, a careful analysis of the socio-economic causes of injustice and oppression, and political action to remove these causes from society. The bishops acknowledge that this new discipleship of Jesus has been embraced only by a small minority of Catholics, but they call it 'a significant minority' because it summons the entire Church to greater fidelity.

The second document I wish to mention is the pastoral letter, 'This Land is Home to Me', signed by twenty-five American bishops of the region of Appalachia, a poor region of the United States. The pastoral letter analyses what social sin means in that part of the country and what steps should be taken leading towards social salvation. The structural evil that has led to perpetual exploitation of the Appalachians is an economic system characterised by two principles, 'technological rationality' and 'maximisation of profit'. Technological rationality assures that the decisions regarding the land and its people are made in terms of perfecting the technological functioning of the extractive industries and the production connected with them. Decisions affecting people's lives are here made as if workers were tools in the process of production. The maximisation of profit, the essential principle of capitalism in its early and in later phases, assures that decisions regarding production aim at increasing the profit of owners or investors and hence at drawing from the workers the maximum labour power at the lowest price that is legally possible. Both of these principles, the Catholic bishops tell us, are at odds with the Church's social teaching. As remedy the pastoral letter advocates the co-operation of various centres of power in the country such as federal and state governments, labour unions and citizens' organisations, in restricting the power of the large corporations and forcing them to make decisions in consultation with the Appalachians concerned with protecting their land and its inhabitants.

We note in passing that these two documents, as well as other ecclesiastical statements on social justice, have adopted elements of liberation theology without being wholly committed to its theoretical basis. In particular, this ecclesiastical teaching accepts the notion of social sin, recognises that the redemption which Jesus brought includes the liberation of people from the structures of oppression, and affirms that the demand for social justice is an essential element of the Christian message. These ecclesiastical documents do not go as far as liberation theology inasmuch as they do not analyse to what extent the Church itself as part of the dominant culture has become a symbol of legitimation for the conditions of oppression. The ecclesiastical documents, therefore, do not try to formulate Christian message and Christian prayer in a more politically responsible manner.

The Old Social Gospel

Some of the neo-conservative critics of the Churches have argued that the new Social Gospel is simply a revival of the discredited old Social Gospel, which had its beginnings in the last decades of the nineteenth century, reached a high point in the years prior to World War I, and continued, albeit in weakened form, into the Twenties. These critics believe that Reinhold Neibuhr's refutation of the Social Gospel in the Thirties and early Forties retains its validity in regard to the present movement. Niebuhr criticised the Social Gospel for two reasons.[2] First, he argued that the advocates of the Social Gospel were liberals, inspired by ideas of social evolution, insensitive to the reality of sin and ignorant of the vast power held by the classes that defend the existing order. Whether this criticism is valid for the best theologians of the Social Gospel is questionable: Niebuhr's arguments aimed more directly at a certain widely-spread mood, moralistic and optimistic, created by the Social Gospel. Niebuhr formulated his criticism in the Thirties when he himself was strongly influenced by Marxist thought. Marx's sense of class struggle and what Niebuhr called 'his catastrophism' appealed to the American theologian who then understood the biblical doctrine of sin as the conclusive repudiation of social evolution and trust in progressivism. Secondly, Niebuhr opposed the Social Gospel because it seemed to him that its social policies were based on unrealistic expectations in regard to the future, on what he called a 'utopian' vision of history, and on a false interpretation of the divine promises. God's promises, Niebuhr argued, cannot be fulfilled in history. To expect the coming of the kingdom in historical time is not only an expression of naïvete, it represents even more a loss of the sense of divine transcendence.

Do these arguments retain their validity *vis-à-vis* the new Social Gospel of contemporary Church documents and liberation theology? They do not. In the first place, the new Social Gospel is critical of liberalism, overwhelmed by a sense of social evil, keenly aware of the powers that oppose justice and peace, and is in fact affected by Marxist thought, the social theory that influenced Niebuhr to reject the old Social Gospel. In the second place, neither Church documents nor liberation theology expect the coming of God's kingdom into history. The theological rationale of the Christian political commitment is not taken principally from eschatology. Contemporary theologians have learnt from the mistakes of the old Social Gospel. The utopia for tomorrow is clearly distinguished from the kingdom of God ever pressing upon us and yet ever unrealised. The theological reason for the Christian commitment to social justice is the so-called 'the option for the poor'. This means that when confronted by social struggles and the conflict of power, the Christian, following the call of Christ, opts for solidarity with 'the poor', the oppressed, the marginalised, the peoples and classes that suffer dehumanisation by existing social, economic and political structures. It is not a naïve expectation of God's kingdom that makes Christians critics of contemporary capitalism; it is rather faith in Jesus Christ as the one who judges the structures of sin, who reveals that the human world can be changed, whose grace empowers people to act, and whose message is a vector moving history toward the overcoming of dehumanising social systems.

We note that in this new Social Gospel we have the identification of social radicalism and religious orthodoxy. The transcendent Trinitarian mystery of God is seen as present in history and operative in the lives of men and women and their societies. This theory is sometimes called 'panentheism'. Here the Infinite does not stand over and against the finite; here the Infinite is in and through the finite—as matrix, as judgment, as summons, as power, as creativity, as horizon. According to Christian dogma this theory is in keeping with orthodoxy as long as the union of the Infinite and the finite is seen not as a product of necessity or natural law, but as based on grace, on divine initiative, on personal gift, on God's free self-communication.

Theological Objections

The attack on the new Social Gospel (usually formulated by social thinkers who are not theologians) often presents itself as a defense of divine transcendence, although not in the Niebuhrian sense of that word. Because the new Social Gospel understands the Christian message as revealing the divine involvement in the transformation of the world, it is accused of overlooking divine transcendence. What the accusations mean by divine transcendence, however, is the reference to a superior divine world, elevated above human history, towards which Christians are destined by their faith and/or the existence of the sacred radically distinct from the profane, the *tremendum et fascinosum*, the divine self-manifestation in historical moments of worship and ecstacy. The neo conservative 'Hartford Theses', originally planned by Richard Neuhaus and Peter Berger, were intended to be a public warning against trends in modern Church life that overlook divine transcendence.[3] What was being criticised was

the view that Christian revelation is the entry of God into humanity's self-realization, into the redemption of history, into the
process of humanisation, emancipation and pacification of the
entire human race. In the perspective of the Hartford Theses,
such an understanding of Christian revelation is too 'secular' and
too this-worldly: it tends to weaken people's sense of the supernatural, make them neglect the heavenly world in their hearts
and engender indifference to their own death and the life that
awaits beyond it.

Yet the neo-conservative defenders of 'transcendence' have
failed to offer appropriate theological arguments. For them the
'transcendent' is honored either by acknowledging a heavenly
world or by accepting the division of life into the sacred and the
profane. For reasons of their own, they want to defend this perception of transcendence at all costs. But in the Scriptures the
most extraordinary manifestation of divine reality is in the human passage from sin to grace, in the Spirit-created conversion
of the heart, in the Passover from oppression to freedom and
from death to life. To believe in a divinity in heaven is not Christian faith unless that divinity be seen as gracious towards men
and women, redemptively involved in their lives, and present to
them as a source of new life: and to experience the *tremendum
et fascinosum* is not Christian unless it initiates the worshippers
to personal transformation and empowers them to responsible
action in the world. Neither the affirmation of a heavenly world
nor the encounter of the sacred implies divine transcendence in
properly Christian terms. The encounter with God in faith is always redemptive. Ecstasies and elevations are not moments of
transcendence in the Christian sense if they do not transform the
worshippers as they return to earth and face their fellow human
beings. Classical Christianity, in its traditional dualistic and its
modern panentheistic form, acknowledges that God's self-revelation and self-communication are salvational, *propter nostram
salutem,* aimed at the transformation of human life.

In *Christianity and the World Order,* an attack on the new
Social Gospel, the English historian Edward Norman argues that
the social teaching the Churches have adopted over the last decade, undermines Christian faith because it does not express

man's relationship to eternity and because it does not reflect religious experience. Let us look at these arguments separately. Norman claims that the Christian message is 'by nature concerned primarily with the relationship of the soul to eternity.' This pietistic interpretation of Christianity can hardly claim the support of the New Testament and the ancient creeds. Jesus has always been understood as the savior of the world. God has always been proclaimed as creator, redeemer and sanctifier of humankind. The advent of Christ was clearly recognised as an event of world historical meaning and consequence. It is true, of course, that this world historical dimension was not usually understood in terms of socio-political transformation: such a reading of the gospel had to wait for the emergence of a critical political imagination in Western history. But at no time in the Church's history has the redemption brought by Jesus Christ been summed up as access of human souls to eternity. Even from the beginning, the Church saw itself as God's people with a mission and destiny in history.

How is the new Social Gospel related to religious experience? When we read the literature produced by writers identified with political or liberation theology we learn that the inherited piety has indeed become problematic. The religious experience into which Christians were initiated usually encouraged a dualistic perception of Christian faith. Piety often reflected an understanding of the God/man relationship that today no longer fits the socio-critical stance adopted by many Christians, especially in Third World churches. In the light of the new Social Gospel, the self-enclosed soul or self has become problematic. Is a person's isolated existence *vis-à-vis* the rest of society and *vis-à-vis* God divinely planned? Or does it rather express an alienated state, induced by a competitive economic system and an individualistic spiritual culture? I wish to argue that the Church's new social teaching is based on, and accompanied by new religious experiences, at odds with pietism, which explode the walls of self, reveal to people that they are embedded in classes or movements and generate a new sense of solidarity with others. This transcendence of soul-centredness is experienced as divinely grounded, as a gift, as something to be grateful for, as God's presence. The only way a person lives authentically is to let 'the others' become part of his or her own self-destination.

Some Latin American Christian poets have been overwhelmed by the liberationist perspective implicit in their religious experiences. Their encounters with divinity do not elevate them above history and detach them from the miseries of this world. Such experience would be regarded as politically dangerous by them. Religious experience for them is a gracious entry into a consciousness that discerns God not as the invisible other whose presence dims the world, as the Alone with the alone, but on the contrary as ground, vector and horizon that unite them with their brothers and sisters struggling for justice. Religious experience here makes people recognise, with fear, trembling and ecstasy, the place assigned to them in salvation history. God is the link to others, solidarity, the forward movement uniting those who yearn for redemption.

For many Christians committed to social justice, religious language has become suspect because the meaning assigned to this language by the dominant culture legitimates the existing order despite its injustices. For this reason these Christians often refuse to speak about inwardness and religious experience. They search for a secular vocabulary. Sometimes they create the impression that they have little interest in the openness of faith to the divine voice and the divine presence. Catholic activists, I am prepared to argue, do not see a conflict between political radicalism and the mystical tradition. The ancient Catholic teaching of the *via negativa,* the dialectical negation of all God-language, has a special affinity to the new spiritual direction of the contemporary Social Gospel.

The New Class

The neo-conservative authors, we repeat, do not only oppose liberation theology and political theology; they also criticise the social teaching of the Churches which, as we have seen, has been influenced by liberation theology but does not follow its method in a consistent manner. The neo-conservative authors believe that the churches have been seduced into error. Peter Berger argues that the Churches lost their nerve in the Sixties when they permitted themselves to be influenced by youth culture and protest movements and integrated some of their aspirations into the Christian understanding of freedom.[4] The neo-conservative writers suggest that the Churches and Church Councils have been misguided by radical men and women on their staff. Edward Norman makes explicit use of a neo-conservative theory to explain the Church's shift to the left. He argues that the ecclesiastical staff workers responsible for the new policies belong to the so-called 'new class', the group of intellectual and cultural agents that produce science and the works of culture and that, for reasons of their own, have made Marxism the fashionable philosophy.

The theory of the new class is used by the neo-conservative thinkers to explain the widespread unrest and discontent in the relatively affluent countries of the West. Why are the young people so unhappy? Why do the various minorities lose their patience? Why do women aspire to new power in society? Why do people criticise the capitalist system that has enriched them? The reason for this unrest, we are told, is not found in the contradictions and injustices built into the institutions of modern society, that inflict alienation and oppression upon various sections of the population; the reason is rather to be found in the influence of the growing class of disgruntled intellectual and social workers who spread discontent and criticism through their cultural creativity. We notice that while neo-conservatives are usually 'liberals' in their political philosophy, here they adopt a classical conservative theory, first elaborated by Edmund Burke, who assigned the cause of the French Revolution not to the oppression of the *ancien régime* but to the destructive influence of French philosophers and political thinkers. Contemporary neo-conservatives offer several reasons why today's intellectuals spread contempt for capitalist society.

The members of the new class are usually employed by government in schools and other agencies. They are envious of scientists and engineers who work for private enterprise and receive higher remuneration. The new class is envious of the salaries paid by industry. The intellectuals despise business skills and entrepreneurship. The men and women of the new class have become hyper-critical of society because they do not have access to power. For this reason they concentrate on the negative aspects of present society, they belittle the achievements of the present system and overlook the manner in which they themselves have profited from it. They focus on the inequalities in capitalist society, some of which are simply connatural to any social order. Through their writings they make people impatient with their lot and engender in them wholly unrealistic expectations in regard to the future. What the new class wants is more power. They involve themselves with minorities and offer their help to the underprivileged because this disguises their own selfish aims and grants them a moral victory over the rest of society. They want to gain power through the backing of these minorities. The new class favors the public over the private sector, and for this reason has become critical of capitalism. The extension of government spending on education, social service and poverty programs creates jobs for members of their own class. They promote a social theory that protects their own economic interests. And they turn to Marxism as the intellectual weapon against the present system because it suits their anger. Today Marxist theory in the capitalist countries has become an ideology of the new class in its quest for greater social power. The neo-conservative critics of the Churches argue that members of this new class have gained influence in ecclesiastical agencies and are responsible for the Churchs' shift to the left.

This theory of the new class is unconvincing. It is in fact outrageous to suggest that people protest against economic exploitation, racial discrimination and other forms of inferiorisation only because they have become victims of subversive propaganda.

Still, the question does remain why the Churches at this time have opted for a left-wing perspective. What are the social forces that have moved ecclesiastical organisations to this new approach? The great majority of Christians has certainly remained indifferent to the question of social justice. The Canadian bishops, in their pastoral declaration, openly admitted that only a minority of Catholics follow the new approach. They added that this minority is often under attack in the congregations, especially 'by the more affluent and powerful sector' of the Catholic community. It would not be difficult to demonstrate that the shift to the left in the Churches' teaching is to a large extent due to the impact of Third World Christians on the consciousness of First World Churches. This process began at the Geneva Conference of Church and Society in 1966. For the Roman Catholic Church, the significant turning point was the Synod of Bishops held at Rome in 1971 where the Latin American perspective worked out at the Medellin Conference (1968) was taken up in the social teaching of the world episcopate. At the level of the highest leadership the Churches have recognised that the basic conflict in present society is between North and South, between the industrialised countries of the capitalist West and the socialist East on the one hand and on the other the underdeveloped countries of the other continents that are moving into greater dependency, destitution, and related forms of human misery. It is here, in the encounter with the Third World, that the Christian Churches have discovered that the issue of private ownership of resources and productive machinery has become a moral and even a spiritual problem.

While we reject the theory of the new class in the form outlined above, it is possible to argue that salaried persons with a modest income, whose work is interesting and demands dedication, such as church workers, social workers, teachers and other persons employed in cultural tasks, often display great sympathy for a socialist system in which all work in society is remunerated on precisely these terms. Why could not everyone work and live that way? These people realise that the wealthy would find it difficult to lower their standard of living, but they often forget that the great majority of workers have such burdensome and uninteresting jobs that dedication is not an adequate recompense. Moreover, to people who work for church organisations and pastoral programmes simplicity or 'the simple life' has a special spiritual meaning, and hence they easily think that their own life style is an answer to the grave problems of the present.

Defence of Capitalism and Pastoral Policy

The neo-conservative critics consider it their special responsibility to defend the present capitalist system. Michael Novak has made this the major effort of his intellectual career.[5] Capitalism is the indispensable basis of social pluralism and personal freedom. In particular, the critics offer an alternative theory of contemporary alienation, one which accounts for the malaise of modernity in terms of the growing influence of technology and bureaucratic administration. Following Max Weber they argue that technocratic society with mega-structures dominating every sphere of human life, is gradually undermining personal freedom and personal creativity. Modern society, moreover, defined by increasing rationalisation, dissolves traditional values, secularises social bonds and religious symbols, and destroys the non-rational aspects of life that give meaning and joy to human living. The neo-conservative critics use this theory to show that the socialist analysis of alienation is wrong. It is not the division of society into rich and poor, masters and servants, owners and workers, that is the principal cause of present unhappiness; it is rather the growing rationalisation of life that causes dehumanisation and affects people in the wealthy suburbs as well as the poor neighbourhoods. Alienation transcends class division. The view that socialism would significantly transform human life is an illusion, a dangerous myth, which makes people dream of an impossible future, sends them into utopian politics that are bound to fail, and weakens their will to reform present society.

The neo-conservative writers even criticise the shift to the left in the Church's social teaching, even though this teaching does not go as far as recommending a socialist economy. The reason why capitalist society is so chaotic at this time, neo-conservatives argue, is that people are no longer dedicated to it. What has taken place is a crisis of culture. People have become soft; they shy away from hard work; they seek personal fulfilment and pleasure; they have abandoned what Max Weber called 'the Protestant ethic'. Contemporary permissive culture, we are repeatedly told, is at odds with requirements of the economic system. Neo-conservative writers ask the Churches to return to a

more authoritarian form of religion and make normative again
the old virtues of industry, dedication, sacrifice and asceticism.
In today's world the Christian religion must become the guardian
of public virtues and the symbol system that promotes consensus
in society. Religion must live up to its essential nature of being
the sacred canopy sheltering the social order. (We notice here the
inner connection between the neo-conservatives' stress on transcendence and their defence of the present order.)

In the writings of Peter Berger, the neo-conservative position
is elaborated with great sophistication.[6] Berger is more sensitive
to the malaise of modernity than other neo-conservatives, but he
agrees with them that in the developed countries of the West socialism offers a wholly illusory solution. Capitalism is here to
stay. Even the mega-structures that dominate all aspects of public
life and induce a sense of impotence and meaninglessness, cannot
be overcome: they are demanded by the giant proportions in-
dustrialisation has achieved. What men and women have to learn
is to survive in capitalist society and save their humanity. What
is needed in this predicament is the creation of 'mediating structures', small organisations in which members still know one another, make joint decisions and mediate life to one another in a
personal way. Mediating structures can be religious congregations, ethnic organisations, urban neighbourhoods and other
voluntary associations. We must create islands of authentic humanity in the midst of the technocratic society that supplies us
with material goods but leads to spiritual despair. The important
pastoral task of the Churches, therefore, is the creation of tightly
woven parishes and communities, in which people can experience themselves as creative human beings. Local churches must
become oases of human well-being. Berger suggests that the
Churches should drop their critical approach to capitalism and
the promotion of radical social change: they should turn to a
wholly different pastoral task, the formation of mediating structures, in which people can find God and their humanity.

Berger's emphasis on mediating structures is important. Em-
ile Durkheim was the first sociologist who recognised the need
for such institutions in modern society. Yet from a Christian
point of view it is important to distinguish between mediating

structures that isolate people in their own circle of contentment and those that bring people together in supportive communities to make them strong in the struggle for justice. The first kind, the islands of happiness, detach people from the societal project and hence strengthen the existing order, while the second kind, the supportive communities with wider outreach, are dynamic agents of social change. If the churches want to learn from the sociology of mediating structures and at the same time remain faithful to their social teaching, they should conceive their parishes and congregations as missionary communities, as communities where vital, personal interchange nourishes authentic humanity and at the same time generates urgent concern for justice in society.

How strong will this neo-conservative trend become in the Churches? On the highest level of authority at least, the Churches will remain committed to a spirituality that includes concern for the hungry sector of humankind and thus continues to promote radical social criticism.

Notes

1. The best known authors in the USA are Peter Berger, Richard Neuhaus and Michael Novak. Their views are endorsed by other writers and editors of Church publications. In England Edward Norman has begun to write in the same vein.
2. See the articles by John Bennett and Arthur Schlesinger in *Reinhold Niebuhr: His Religious, Social and Political Thought,* edited by C. W. Kegley and R. W. Bretall (New York 1961).
3. The so-called Hartford Appeal denounced thirteen erroneous theses that allegedly pervaded American theology. See *Against the World for the World,* ed. P. Berger and R. Neuhaus (New York 1976).
4. P. Berger *Facing Up to Modernity* (New York 1977) p. 194.
5. See J. L. Walsh 'Making the Case for Capitalism' *Commonweal* (22 June 1979) 366–369.
6. See P. Berger *The Homeless Mind* (New York 1974).